Marlborough

Marlborough

HERO OF BLENHEIM

John Hussey

WEIDENFELD & NICOLSON

First published in Great Britain in 2004
by Weidenfeld & Nicolson

A CIP catalogue record for this book is available from the British
Library.

ISBN 0-297-84686-8

Printed in Great Britain by Butler and Tanner

Weidenfeld & Nicolson
The Orion Publishing Group Ltd
Orion House, 5 Upper Saint Martin's Lane, London, WC2H 9EA

www.orionbooks.co.uk

List of Contents

List of Maps *8*

Foreword *9*

Preface *15*

Notes on dates *18*

PART ONE

The path to power, 1650–1701

CHAPTER 1   A Servant and His Master:
John Churchill and Royal James, 1650–88 *21*

CHAPTER 2   Discontents and Distrust:
Marlborough and William III, 1689–1701 *32*

PART TWO

The causes of the War of the Spanish Succession, how governments conducted it, and the tools they used

CHAPTER 3   The Spanish Succession:
France and the Grand Alliance *45*

CHAPTER 4   Opposing Strengths, Opposing Systems
and the Constraints of War *53*

CHAPTER 5   Queen Anne's Army *62*

PART THREE

The first two years of war

CHAPTER 6   The First Campaigns, 1702–3 *75*

PART FOUR

*'To secure the liberties of Europe':
the Blenheim campaign, 1704*

CHAPTER 7   'The Affairs of Germany Require a Farther Help',
Winter 1703 into Spring 1704 *83*

CHAPTER 8   'Over the Hills and Far Away',
May and June *91*

CHAPTER 9   'The Watch on the Rhine',
May and June *103*

CHAPTER 10   The Schellenberg,
2 July 1704 *112*

CHAPTER 11   Tallard Advances:
Marlborough Burns Bavaria, July *122*

CHAPTER 12   French Advantages Thrown Away:
Allied Unity Restored, Early August *132*

CHAPTER 13   'Within the Memory of Man There Has Been No
Victory so Great as This':
John to Sarah, 14 August 1704 *140*

CHAPTER 14   The Aftermath of Blenheim *153*

PART FIVE

High tide and the turn, 1705–10

CHAPTER 15   War Policy and the Campaigns of 1705–9 *161*

CHAPTER 16   The Campaign of 1710:
The Ruin of Marlborough's Domestic Position *167*

PART SIX

The supreme manoeuvre:
'Ne Plus Ultra' *and Bouchain, 1711*

CHAPTER 17   The Complications of Deceit, Disorganization and
Smallpox, Spring 1711 *175*

CHAPTER 18   Marlborough Probes the Great French Defensive Lines,
May 1711 *180*

CHAPTER 19   Villars Frustrates Marlborough,
June and July 1711 *190*

CHAPTER 20   The Tables Turned: Marlborough Passes the Lines,
4–5 August 1711 *203*

CHAPTER 21   'The Best Conducted Siege We Have Made in This War':
Bouchain, August and September 1711 *212*

CHAPTER 22   How It All Ended *220*

APPENDIX

The Loss of Arleux , 23 July 1711 *227*

Acknowledgements *233*

Sources consulted *235*

Notes *245*

Index *247*

List of maps

Europe in the reign of Queen Anne *14*

'My last territorial demand' –
the menace of Louis XIV's expansion *46*

The march to the Danube *96*

The Schellenberg, 2 July 1704 *114*

The Battle of Blenheim, 13 August 1704 *141*

The campaign of 1711 *181*

Foreword
by Major General Julian Thompson

MARLBOROUGH WAS WITHOUT DOUBT one of the greatest military commanders in Anglo-American history; pre-eminent perhaps. Even the Duke of Wellington, the nearest British contender, was not called upon to operate at such a high politico-military strategic level. Eisenhower, with whom one might be tempted to compare Marlborough's breadth and span of command, nowhere near approaches his skill as a field commander or his wide-ranging political responsibilities. On the accession of Queen Anne, Marlborough, who was already the English commander-in-chief in the Low Countries, was appointed captain general of land forces in England and Wales. In late twentieth-century terms this was the equivalent of combining the posts of c.-in-c. British Army of the Rhine and c.-in-c. United Kingdom Land Forces. In addition, Marlborough was entitled to give strategic advice to the Cabinet when English troops went to other war theatres, which today is the prerogative of the Chief of the Defence Staff. In addition to his other appointments, within weeks of becoming captain general Marlborough also secured the post of Master General of the Ordnance.

As John Hussey explains, to cover the ten great campaigns in which Marlborough served demands more space than he was given. For this masterly account he has chosen Marlborough's 1704 campaign – the brilliant march from the North Sea to the Danube, culminating in the stunning victory of Blenheim – and his last campaign, which John Hussey characterizes as a masterpiece of manoeuvre.

We also get a vivid portrait of Marlborough's development, including his early and formative years in the latter half of the seventeenth century, in which he lived two-thirds of his life. It was a century characterized by religious fear, hysteria, plots and betrayals – dangers through which Marlborough trod a 'winding path' with great skill. Although, as the author laments, there is no space for Marlborough's personal life, we do get an insight into his abiding love for his wife, Sarah, illuminated by short extracts from his love letters.

The European political and grand strategic scene in which Marlborough operated is skilfully covered, as are the constraints of war practised at the time – an era of much change both tactically and operationally. The author draws attention to the flaw in Clausewitz's analysis of warfare of the period: by hardly mentioning Marlborough, he overplays the conservatism of commanders at the tactical and operational level of war in the period between Gustavus Adolphus and Frederick the Great. By this oversight Clausewitz shows himself to be bounded by his own introverted Prussian experience.

John Hussey also provides an excellent résumé of the contemporary government machinery for administering the Army and managing the war. As he explains, Queen Anne's army until 1707 consisted of three armies: English, Scottish and Irish. Up to that time Scottish and Irish regiments were transferred to the English establishment to serve abroad. Only in 1707, at the Union of Parliaments, did the British Army emerge from the combination of the Scottish and English establishments; the Irish being left separate. So, as he points out, in the first years of Anne's reign it is correct to call the army overseas 'English', a distinction 'the French maintained until the twentieth century', and one which is used in this book.

We also get a very informative section on tactics, and how Marlborough surprised the French by his unorthodox deployments on the field of battle. By the early eighteenth century French military practice, as so often happens in successful armies, had ossified. Their commanders had failed to modify their tactics to meet the challenges brought about by new technology in weaponry; for example, improvements in the design of muskets.

John Hussey also challenges the view of eighteenth century warfare being frozen into total immobility by fortification and logistics, a perception partly fostered by Clausewitz, through his examination of Marlborough's method of command and logistical skill. By caring for his men on the long march from the Low Countries to the Danube, the furthest the English had marched from a base since the Black Prince's Spanish expedition over three centuries earlier, Marlborough showed that an eighteenth-century army could cover great distances and still arrive on the battlefield fit to fight.

We are reminded of the limitations of contemporary maps, and hence the careful and painstaking reconnaissance necessary to establish what routes existed, and even in which direction streams and minor rivers flowed. The staff work needed was all the more remarkable when one bears in mind how much of it was done by Marlborough himself. A staff system as we understand it did not exist.

This was an age when a successful commander had to spend an inordinate amount of time immersed in minor details, to a degree that a Montgomery, or a Patton, or most modern generals would not countenance. By the twentieth century highly trained and efficient staffs in most armies had relieved the commander of much of this time-consuming effort, allowing him to stand back and view the big picture. In Marlborough's day a commander often stood or fell by the quality of his own staff work, and in this as in so many other respects Marlborough was a master.

He was truly a great commander.

L'homme le plus fatal à la grandeur de la
France qu'on eût vu depuis plusieurs siècles …
Il avait, par-dessus tous les généraux de son
temps, cette tranquillité de courage au milieu du
tumulte, et cette sérénité d'âme dans le péril
que les Anglais appellent *cold head*, tête froide.

VOLTAIRE *Siècle de Louis XIV*, Chapter 18

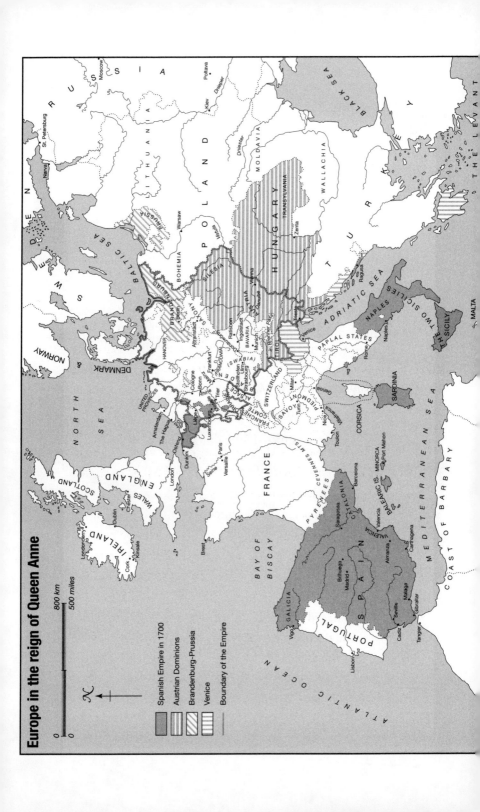

Europe in the reign of Queen Anne

Spanish Empire in 1700
Austrian Dominions
Brandenburg-Prussia
Venice
Boundary of the Empire

800 km
500 miles

RUSSIA
Moscow
St Petersburg
Narva
Poltava
Kiev
Dnieper
Dniester

SWEDEN
NORWAY
DENMARK
BALTIC SEA
NORTH SEA

LITHUANIA
PRUSSIA
Warsaw
POLAND
Vistula

HANOVER
BRANDENBURG
Berlin
Altranstädt
BOHEMIA
SILESIA
SAXONY
Regensburg
Ingolstadt
BAVARIA
Munich
Blenheim
TIROL

MORAVIA
Vienna
Danube
HUNGARY
TRANSYLVANIA
Zenta

MOLDAVIA
WALLACHIA

TURKEY
BLACK SEA
THE LEVANT

UNITED PROVINCES
Amsterdam
The Hague
Ostend
Dunkirk
Cologne
Bonn
Trier
Frankfurt
Mainz
Rhine
Strasbourg
ALSACE
FRANCHE COMTE
Luxembourg
Liège

SWITZERLAND
SWABIA
Ulm
Höchstädt
Brenner Pass

SAVOY
PIEDMONT
Turin
Nice
Villafranca
Toulon
Milan
Genoa
Venice
ADRIATIC SEA
Ragusa
PAPAL STATES
Rome
Naples
NAPLES
THE TWO SICILIES
SICILY
MALTA

IRELAND
Londonderry
Dublin
Cork
Kinsale
SCOTLAND
WALES
Chester
ENGLAND
London
Brest
Seine
Versailles
Paris
FRANCE
CEVENNES MTS
PYRENEES

BAY OF BISCAY

ATLANTIC OCEAN

PORTUGAL
Lisbon
Vigo
GALICIA
Madrid
Brihuega
SPAIN
CATALONIA
Saragossa
Barcelona
BALEARIC IS.
MINORCA
Port Mahon
VALENCIA
Valencia
Almanza
Cartagena
Seville
Malaga
Cadiz
Gibraltar
Tangier
COAST OF BARBARY
MEDITERRANEAN SEA
CORSICA
SARDINIA

Preface

TO WRITE AN ACCOUNT of Marlborough the commander as he
served through ten great campaigns would require far more space
than this volume can offer. I have chosen, therefore, to concentrate
on two campaigns: an expedition, and then a masterpiece of blood-
less manoeuvre.

It was natural to choose Marlborough's 1704 campaign, that
remarkable project to save the Habsburg Emperor in Vienna and thus
the whole Alliance from collapse, the first fruit of which was the capture
of the Schellenberg, which culminated in the great victory of Blenheim.
Other Marlburian campaigns such as Ramillies may be more fasci-
nating to a military specialist, but 1704 demands inclusion not only
for its place of honour as the first in the sequence of his greatest campaigns, but because of the intrepidity with which Marlborough undertook to carry his army from the North Sea to the Danube, the skill
with which he did it, and the gamble he was prepared to take in return
for the prayers and the (poorly fulfilled) promises of his stricken ally.

I present also the duke's last campaign, technically his masterpiece as a 'manoeuvre' general: bloodlessly crossing the strong *Ne
Plus Ultra* Lines, followed by a most audacious siege successfully
accomplished against considerable odds. My reading of the affair at

Arleux which preceded the passage of the Lines (Chapter 19) differs from almost all previous studies of the campaign. In order not to encumber the text with argument I have placed the detailed reasons for my conclusion in an Appendix.

Histories of campaigns require a context. Because Marlborough's role as a commander-in-chief in a great coalition war embraced international policy, strategy and diplomacy – as well as military administration and operations – I have prefaced my accounts of 1704 and 1711 with summaries explaining why the war came about, how governments coped with its problems, how armies were constituted, as well as outline sketches of the military operations in the campaigns of 1702–3 and 1705–10. I have to confess that I have used only one Dutch source to any great extent, van 't Hoff's *The Marlborough–Heinsius Correspondence*; Colonel Wijn's military history has never been translated into English, though how a Dutch interpretation can affect purely English accounts of events was shown long ago by Professor Veenendaal's analysis of the 1708 campaign and his later chapter on the war in the *New Cambridge Modern History*.

Marlborough was comparatively old before he secured the power and opportunities which he craved. His strangely insecure personality, formed by the difficulties of his childhood, drove him onwards and sometimes into dark and troubling conspiracies. The later seventeenth century was a time of religious fear and even hysteria, of plots and betrayals, through which Marlborough trod a very winding path. At the height of mid-Victorian certainty Macaulay in his *History* and Thackeray in *Henry Esmond* attacked Marlborough's character, principally on this score; eighty years later Winston Churchill went to the other extreme. I hope to have set down the salient points without bias. Regrettably there is no space for his personal life, his love letters to Sarah, his joy in his garden and his delight listening to the nightingales as he lay in his camp bed, which would redeem the austerity of campaign history.

There is no extended 'summing up', no comparison of Marlborough against Alexander, Hannibal, Napoleon, Wellington, Lee, Moltke, Haig, Eisenhower or Alanbrooke. How can you compare or rank Lister against McIndoe, the Oxford crew of 1928 against the Cambridge eight of 1956, or Fred Archer against Lester Piggott, let alone Princess Diana against Charles Darwin (as BBC viewers think they can)? Even for Marlborough's great comrade Eugene of Savoy, it is with considerable hesitation that I set down a very brief and tentaive assessment. But there is one comparison implicit throughout: that with John Churchill's exact contemporary William of Orange, who was for thirty years of his life Louis XIV's greatest opponent, and whose policies extended beyond his death in 1702.

In the calm of later life Henry St John, Lord Bolingbroke, wrote not only the finest short account of Marlborough's campaigns, which is inscribed on the Column of Victory at Blenheim Palace, but also an assessment of William III and Marlborough in Letter VIII of *The Study and the Use of History*. The passage I now quote leaves out matters which concern the Partition Treaties and Utrecht, but the words illuminate the circumstances and personal qualities which the Column of Victory does not mention: 'By [William III's] death, the Duke of Marlborough was raised to the head of the army, and indeed of the confederacy: where he, a new, a private man, a subject, acquired by merit and by management a more deciding influence, than high birth, confirmed authority, and even the Crown of Great Britain had given to King William.' Those words 'new', 'subject', 'merit' had a particular resonance in the hierarchical society of the eighteenth century and would at that epoch have sharpened the contrast between the two men. More recently Correlli Barnett has identified Marlborough's special quality as 'enduring such strains and grappling with such a weight and variety of responsibility as have befallen no other English soldier in history'. Those assessments of 1736 and 1974 go to the heart of the matter. They *place* Marlborough in military history.

Note on Dates

IN 1582 POPE GREGORY XIII reformed the calendar to correct inaccuracies in the old Julian one. The Gregorian or New Style (NS) calendar, which was adopted by most Continental states, was ten days ahead of the Julian or Old Style (OS) calendar from 1582 to February 1700, and eleven days ahead thereafter. Thus 2 August 1654 (OS) was 12 August 1654 (NS) and 2 August 1704 (OS) was 13 August 1704 (NS).

Until England adopted the Gregorian calendar in 1752 people in England who corresponded with the Continent often identified dates with the addition of OS or NS or used both dates, such as 2/13 August 1704.

Confusingly, for some purposes the year started on Lady Day, 25 March. In this book all dates are Gregorian or New Style, unless specifically marked OS, and the years run from 1 January.

PART ONE

The path to power,

1650–1701

CHAPTER 1

A Servant and His Master:

John Churchill and Royal James, 1650–88

JOHN CHURCHILL – WHO EVENTUALLY BECAME among the richest and was certainly the greatest of his sovereign's subjects, the most uniformly successful general of his time with a dukedom, a palace and a principality as rewards – was born in a half-wrecked wing of a Devonshire house in May 1650 to a defeated Cavalier captain of horse, in a household which had been ravaged and rendered almost destitute by the English Civil War.

The Churchills had risen through the law to the minor squirearchy, helped by marriages to more prominent families, the Winstons in one generation and the Drakes in the next. Captain Winston Churchill was an ardent Royalist, but his widowed mother-in-law, Lady Drake, held for the Parliament in the Civil War: her house was sacked by the Cavaliers and she herself ejected, but with the collapse of Charles I's cause she returned to one wing of her house, giving shelter to her daughter and son-in-law and their babies. The Churchills endured fines and sequestrations, and, if they drew upon Lady Drake's charity for the first ten years of John's life, Winston must silently have smarted under his benefactress's unwelcome political opinions within doors, and feared eavesdroppers, informers and malicious neighbours without.

The Churchill children likewise learned very early to speak and act with caution.

We know little of John's childhood; no boyhood friend recorded anything and he himself never referred to these years of refuge and poverty, but they are the probable source of his lifelong insecurity, his frugality and craving for money, his habit of insuring with both sides, of conciliating, and of keeping his own counsel. Winston sired twelve children of whom five died in infancy, John being the third-born and second surviving child; John would prove a good son and a faithful brother, finding military appointments for the boys and later ensuring that his beloved elder sister Arabella's second family obtained places at Queen Anne's court.[1]

For Winston himself could do little for them, even when Charles II's Restoration in 1660 enabled him to enter Parliament and gain minor office – and a knighthood in lieu of financial compensation for his sufferings. John at least scrambled through several terms at St Paul's School, while Arabella became a maid of honour to the first wife (d. 1671) of James, Duke of York, the heir to the throne and Lord High Admiral. Imbued since childhood with the Cavalier doctrine that the royal Stuarts' virtues and defects enjoyed divine sanction and their demands required unquestioning obedience, the Churchills were complaisant when Arabella became James's mistress and delighted when John consequently obtained a page's post in the duke's household, aged 16.[2]

This page proved so pleasing and able that in 1667 Duke James procured him a free commission in the King's Guards. The puny Army of John Churchill's youth numbered under 6,000 men (Cromwell's had been over 40,000), whereas in France the finest army in the world, led by Condé and Turenne, had a peacetime establishment of 150,000 men. The English Army was employed mainly as guards, or in garrison at home or in the new colony of Tangier. It knew little of Continental warfare, for war with the principal enemy, Holland, was usually fought at sea – with soldiers as marines. Although John did not go to Tangier, where colonial warfare was continuous, he served as a marine with Allin's naval expedition to the western Mediterranean in 1670 and saw Lisbon, Gibraltar, the Mediterranean ports of France, Italy, Spain and the Balearics, memories that he drew upon in his years of power.

In 1671, bronzed and dashing, this penniless subaltern became the ardent lover of the spendthrift, promiscuous Duchess of Cleveland, one of the King's most active bedfellows. Even then his obliging charm averted all retribution other than Charles's sneer that Churchill did it for wages – and certainly when the duchess did give him £4,500 he promptly invested it in an annuity.

Churchill served aboard Duke James's flagship in the 1672 war with the Dutch, where his bravery earned him a captaincy; by 1673 he was advanced to the privileged post of one of James's gentlemen of the bedchamber. When Charles II sent troops under his bastard son Monmouth to act as land auxiliaries with the French against the Dutch and Germans, Churchill went likewise; he saw action under the great Turenne in operations near Heidelberg and in Alsace in 1674, invariably winning praise for his intrepidity and skill, although he clearly disliked French methods and their treatment of civilians. His cool ability, his charm, his invariable luck brought him the recognition of the great, including Louis XIV. His contemporaries were more divided: some began to form a 'Churchill ring' – others disliked him for his luck, greed for money and stinginess, and his reputation for 'carrying tales' to the great.

At 25, after eight years in the army and with plentiful experience of fighting by sea and land, Lieutenant Colonel Churchill returned to the court and met the love of his life. Sarah Jennings, a 15-year-old maid of honour to James's second wife, was virtuous, pretty, imperious, highly ambitious – and penniless.[3] She enslaved Churchill so absolutely that to overcome his needy father's opposition to the match John resigned to him his reversion to £1,000. They were married when she was 17. He always loved her to distraction and she – whose influence was so greatly to help and then ruin his career – adored him despite all her tantrums. What he meant to her blazes from her message when she was 32 and he was incarcerated and in great danger: 'wherever you are, whilst I have life my soul shall follow you, my ever dear Ld Marl, and wherever I am I shall only kill the time, wish for night that I may sleep, and hope the next day to hear from you'.

JOHN WAS A MODERATE ANGLICAN and Sarah 'low church'. They were the intimate servants of the heir to the throne and his wife, and yet the Duke and Duchess of York were proudly Catholic in a country that had for over a century feared, hated and harassed Catholicism. That English Catholics were few in number made no difference: the threat always loomed. The Civil War had been between Protestants, and the Restoration represented a compromise between Anglicans and the 'sects', though once back in Parliament the Anglicans again monopolized power and suppressed residual Cromwellianism. But soon the growing power of France, its threats to Protestant Holland and its worsening persecution of Huguenots at home revived anti-Catholic fears. In 1670 James, heir to the throne, had announced his conversion to Rome and there was a well-founded suspicion that the ostensibly Protestant Charles II would like to turn over England to Catholicism. In 1673 taking Anglican communion became an obligatory 'test' for public office and rather than conform, James resigned his posts. Remarrying, he chose a foreign Catholic. Thus Anglicans began sensing a dilemma: how to protect their creed if the 'divinely appointed' Stuart dynasty promoted Catholicism, how to remain 'passively obedient' to a monarch if he menaced the established church. Matters worsened when Protestant hysteria in 1678 over a 'Popish Plot' threatened James's reversion to the succession and forced him into exile in Brussels and then Edinburgh.

Churchill did not immediately or willingly face the dilemma. He remained his master's trusted servant in secret missions to secure the help of Louis XIV and Charles II in defence of James's rights. Yet he was too observant not to realize how James's personality was deteriorating from that of an energetic if imperceptive man to that of an obstinate, blinkered bigot who was indecisive in a crisis. In Scotland James proved himself a harsh viceroy; when he and his suite were wrecked aboard the *Gloucester* his obstructiveness, interference and last-minute departure by the ship's only boat (loaded with his luggage, and guarded by Churchill) led directly to 150 deaths, to which he seemed quite indifferent. By 1682 Churchill and the other few Protestant servants were clearly disillusioned, but they remained in his employ.

Once the 'Popish Plot' madness had subsided, James returned home, even to loyal rejoicings. Churchill's faithfulness was rewarded with a Scottish barony. When in 1683 James's Anglican younger daughter, Anne, married a Lutheran Dane, Prince George, Churchill, now colonel of the Royal Dragoons, was chosen to escort the bridegroom to England. Upon Anne's marriage Sarah left the Yorks' household to become her servant: given Sarah's character, the Yorks' Romish observances must have been anathema. Anne was quickly dazzled by Sarah's brilliance, but she and George cannot have been blind to the husband's sagacity – and Churchill soon found that he had at least as much influence with the young Protestant 'Denmarks' as he had with his own master, Catholic James. The balance of interest was shifting.

JAMES SUCCEEDED CHARLES II in February 1685, promising to respect the laws and institutions, the Anglican church and the Protestant religion; and a reassured and delighted Parliament rashly granted him substantial revenues for life. Churchill was advanced to an English barony and succeeded James as governor of the lucrative Hudson's Bay Company. When in June Charles's bastard son Monmouth claimed the crown as the Protestant and 'legitimate' heir, landed in Dorset and was joined by remnants of 'the Good Old [Cromwellian] Cause',

Anglicanism rallied to the king. Brigadier Lord Churchill instantly raced west with 300 cavalry and, though outnumbered, ceaselessly harassed the several thousand armed rebels.

Though Churchill had been promised reinforcements and the overall command against Monmouth (his leader in 1673), after twenty-four hours James appointed instead Lieutenant General the Earl of Feversham. In all but capacity the choice of this Huguenot of high birth and of senior social and military rank to Churchill may have been justified, but he was known as 'weak to a degree not easy to be conceived'. Churchill resented the snub (and the possible implications): 'I see plainly that I am to have the trouble, and that the honour will be another's.'

Feversham advanced ponderously with his large army, pushing the rebels west to Sedgemoor, where Monmouth was defeated by the regulars' discipline, artillery, and Churchill's energy. The month-long rebellion collapsed. The lacklustre Feversham received the Garter and command of the 1st troop of Horse Guards, but at least Churchill was promoted Major General and succeeded Feversham with the 3rd troop, relinquishing the Royal Dragoons. Churchill took no part in the cruel aftermath of Sedgemoor and his comment that 'this marble fireplace is not harder than the King's heart' says much about his dislike of the royal inhumanity that applauded 'the bloody assizes'.

There is an illuminating characterization of Churchill in his thirties, penned by Bishop Burnet:

> He was a man of a noble and graceful appearance, bred up in the court with no literature [i.e. a deficient education]: but he had a solid and clear understanding, with a constant presence of mind. He knew the arts of living in a court beyond any man in it. He caressed all people with a soft and obliging deportment, and was always ready to do good offices. He had no fortune to set up on: this put him on all the methods of acquiring one.

Burnet's original draft had said that 'money had as much power over him as he over the King' , but that begs the question: 'did Churchill really have "power" over James?' The evidence suggests rather that Churchill was most influential when compliant, and that in large matters James took no heed of his views.

Monmouth's rebellion had obliged James vastly to increase his standing army. None disagreed. But next the king breached statute law by 'dispensing' officers from taking the obligatory Anglican sacrament: soon Catholics (under 2 per cent of the population) held 10 per cent of all commissions in an army now nearly 20,000 strong. In Ireland James was purging its Protestant army and making it Catholic. Abroad, James's cousin Louis XIV was forcibly extirpating French Protestantism and threatening the security of Protestant states. When Parliament showed disquiet it was prorogued and was never summoned again in this reign. The Admiralty was directly under the king and the command of the fleet was given to a Catholic. Places in the Privy Council and the Treasury were being taken by Catholics. Anglican laws against Catholics and Dissenters were lifted; the universities' Anglican rights were threatened. Twenty-one shires found their Lord Lieutenants replaced; charters of local municipalities were 'remodelled', altering electoral rights.

By 1687 observers foresaw crisis in England, which in turn would affect the position of the Protestant states in Europe. The foremost European Protestant, William of Orange, grandson of Charles I and husband of James's elder daughter, Mary, sent his confidant Dykevelt to advise moderation: James ignored him. Leading Englishmen told Dykevelt that William should intervene and Princess Anne sent Churchill ('one that I can trust, and I am sure is a very honest man and a good Protestant') to tell the emissary her own fears. There are several reports of Churchill's opinions in these months: in 1685 he had told the Huguenot Lord Galway 'that if the King was ever prevailed upon to alter our religion he would serve him no longer, but would withdraw from him'. Now he wrote to William *in clear*: 'my places and the King's favour I set at nought, in comparison of being true to my religion. In all things but this the King may command me.' He even spoke – in vain – to the king of the perception that he was 'paving the way for the introduction of Popery', which might have 'consequences which I dare not so much as name, and which it creates in me a horror to think of': James merely turned away. Churchill requested a military posting overseas, but was refused. Yet he did *not* 'withdraw' from his place: perhaps, like many others, he hoped for the best while fearing the worst. He also had a degree of reinsurance, a second 'place' reliant upon the future inheritance of James's younger daughter, Anne.

In 1688 further royal measures provoked a petition from Anglican bishops. For this seven of them were charged with seditious libel and imprisoned in the Tower. There was consternation. Then James's queen gave birth to a son, thus ending Protestant hopes that Princesses Mary and Anne would inherit the crown and restore the Anglican position. The bishops were tried and immediately acquitted, even James's troops camped near London cheering the verdict. Seven magnates ('the immortal seven') sent a cipher letter to William promising to join him if he should come with sufficient force to establish 'a free Parliament'.

In August Churchill wrote to William, *again in clear*. For the sake of his religion and his country, he said, he placed himself in William's hands: 'if there is anything else that I ought to do, you have but to command me, and I shall pay an entire obedience to it'. It is the strongest proof of Churchill's conviction that his master's policies had to be opposed, for the letter placed him entirely at William's mercy: disclosure meant a traitor's death. He knew the risk to which he was now irrevocably committed; Sarah recorded that he 'made [legal] settlements to secure his family in case of misfortune'.

In the autumn James suddenly awoke to reality: he began reversing all his policies: ejected officials would be restored; Parliament would be recalled. But the imminence of Williamite invasion made him halt the reversal. By now Navy and Army were rife with conspiracy. When the invasion fleet sailed, adverse winds and disaffection hampered the Royal Navy, and William landed with 15,000 foreign soldiers at Torbay on 5 November 1688.[4] Proclaiming he had come to safeguard Protestantism and a free Parliament, William stayed at Exeter awaiting the promised support. Few joined. James and Feversham marched from London on 17 November with 29,000 troops, but by 19 November some senior officers were disappearing though few of the rank and file defected.

Churchill, newly promoted lieutenant general but without specific command duties, stayed close to James on the march west. Anne's husband, George, had also come. From the 19th onwards James dithered at Salisbury and suffered repeated nosebleeds, Feversham vacillated, Churchill was for advancing west. Morale sank. On the 23rd James opted for retreat, in itself an indication of how little Churchill's opinions really swayed James in important matters, and that same night Churchill, some colleagues and 400 horse went over to William. A stream of senior desertions followed, including Prince George's. Princess Anne fled Whitehall with Sarah.

Churchill's defection, and its timing, was decisive in averting a battle, but switching sides is an ugly matter and it received little praise: William was even displeased that more troops had not deserted with him. Churchill's desertion paralysed the royal army and broke James's nerve. Having persistently ignored the probable consequences of his own actions, James burst out: 'my daughter hath deserted me, my army also, and him that I raised from nothing the same, on whom I heaped all favours; and if such betrays me, what can I expect from those I have done so little for?' The pathos was unfeigned yet self-deluding. The countrymen 'he had done so little for' owed him nothing. Had coronation oaths been kept and the majority's tenets respected none of this would have occurred. However, Churchill had served for so long, had benefited so much, and stayed at James's side so late that his 'betrayal' was never forgotten or entirely condoned; when finally abandoning his place with James he was sure of a place in the new dispensation. Much later, when he and the Tories parted over policy in Anne's reign it added an edge to their hostility.

Churchill had left a final letter warning that false counsellors were subverting Protestantism and planning the imposition of Catholicism: if James rejected them and returned to his 'true interest' then Churchill, who owed the greatest personal obligations to the king, would hazard life and fortune 'to preserve your Majesty's person and lawful rights'. Significantly, when James was proving untrustworthy in subsequent negotiations and some Whigs were for putting him under arrest, Churchill was recorded as among those against it. Churchill's advice in his letter was what many Anglicans would have given, for neither the 'immortal seven's' letter nor William's manifesto called for a change of monarch: if stronger safeguards could have been secured by William's intervention and guaranteed by a free Parliament many Anglicans and Tories would probably still have preferred a repentant James as king. (In fact this was wishful thinking, for James was at heart unrepentant, and as impossible in negotiation as his father.) But William soon saw that he might win the crown by outmanoeuvring his father-in-law, who continually wavered and hedged till he had lost all but his blindest adherents and, increasingly fearful, fled the country after dissolving the armed forces and judicial authority.

Even then Churchill and others advocated a regency, which implied either a wish to retain the old regime in some form, or alternatively an intention to secure some official role for Anne. A Dutch king was clearly not envisaged or desired. But William was a Protestant with his army holding London, and finally Churchill joined the majority in accepting that there was no alternative to William and Mary as monarchs. Anne's claims were a complication resolved only by her making what she termed 'her abdication', letting William take precedence over her for his lifetime. In this delicate matter Churchill proved a masterly conciliator, but both Mary and William distrusted and even disliked him and, when told that Churchill 'might perhaps prevail' upon Anne to waive her claim, William sharply declared that 'Lord Churchill could not govern him' as he did Anne. It was not a good augury.

CHAPTER 2

Discontents and Distrust:
Marlborough and William III, 1689–1700

WILLIAM PRIZED ENGLAND for the enhanced prestige its crown bestowed and the resources it could bring to the international coalition against Louis XIV. He spent much of the year 1689 strengthening his grip upon England, remodelling the Army and launching the European war against France.

William did not prize the English, preferring wherever possible to use Dutchmen; and the English, not a few of whom had not wanted him as king and remembered the old commercial rivalry with Holland, accepted him and the Dutch with mixed feelings. Those who had assisted William had necessarily to be rewarded, Churchill being reconfirmed in his army rank and colonelcy of the 3rd troop of Horse Guards, promoted privy councillor, and raised to Earl of Marlborough, an extinct title to which the Drakes had been very remotely connected by marriage. But William had never liked Churchill, and his abilities, ambition and influence were seen as potentially dangerous, so that Marlborough was placed under better-trusted servants or eased from the centre of events. Clearly he was the soldier most competent to superintend the remodelling of the English Army, but though he drew up the plans it was William's follower, Marshal

Schomberg, who checked and sanctioned the proposals. When war started Marlborough was sent to Flanders with a major contingent, 11,000 Englishmen, but he was to serve under William's kinsman Waldeck.

For much of the 1689 campaign Waldeck did little, and Marlborough devoted time to improving training (regarded by contemporaries as his fetish); but in late August the French attacked at Walcourt only to be defeated by outflanking attacks from each wing, Marlborough with his English leading the left. The French lost 2,000 men and six guns; Allied losses (mainly English) were about 600. It was not a 'great' victory, but this first Anglo-French encounter in the Nine Years' War showed English fighting grit, for which Marlborough and his men received somewhat lavish praise. William rewarded him with the colonelcy of the Royal Fusiliers, an ordnance unit.

However, Jacobite uprisings in Ireland and more briefly in Scotland had more than offset any advantage in Flanders. In March 1689 King James had landed at Kinsale in southern Ireland, and with an army of 36,000 Irish Catholics, plus French officers, arms and money, had conquered all Ireland save a few towns in the north. For a general with such experience of strategy and administration William's ineptitude was unpardonable: not till August did he dispatch Schomberg with a proper force; even then he let maladministration and winter almost destroy it, while 6,000 French reinforcements landed at Kinsale to join James. Had the French fleet been deployed in the Irish Sea William could have lost Ireland permanently and the threat at England's back must have hobbled his European strategy. But instead the French cruised off Sussex, and so in June 1690 William landed in Ireland with troops from England and Flanders, and smashed James at the Boyne in July. James fled to France and William soon returned to England, leaving the campaign unfinished. Ominously, large Jacobite forces were still active in western Ireland.

In William's absence Marlborough commanded the troops left in

England. Many, like Queen Mary, now feared invasion, for the French had defeated Waldeck in Belgium and the Allied fleets off Beachy Head; moreover the Irish war was but half decided and might still be lost if William had to withdraw troops. It was then that Marlborough first showed his grasp of combined sea- and land-power, of balancing defensive and offensive: if the Allied fleets remained 'in being' (as they did), invasion was unlikely; meanwhile, a conjoint naval–military offensive against the two principal southern entry ports of Ireland could cut the vital French supply line into Ireland and isolate and starve Jacobite armies. Queen and council opposed Marlborough's plan as too risky in itself, doubly so with autumn coming on – until William (still in Dublin) overruled them.

Within four weeks Marlborough had assembled eight battalions (6,000 men), collected eighty-two transports and obtained a naval escort, and had – despite adverse September winds – completed the voyage and broken into Cork harbour. Cavalry and artillery came from forces William had left in Ireland (precedence problems arose with a German duke commanding the cavalry, giving Marlborough a testing foretaste of coalition diplomacy). Cork, though defended by forts, walls and marshes, was taken after five days. Marlborough hastened to Kinsale, finding the town abandoned but the garrison holding two forts dominating the estuary. He captured one fort by assault, but found the other required a regular siege. His cannon were delayed by atrocious roads and the siege was undertaken without them in a wet October. Nevertheless, within two weeks the defenders surrendered. Marlborough made his brother Charles commandant, and returned to England just two months after first orders had been issued.

In the long if not invariably happy history of British conjoint expeditions Marlborough's first independent command merits a high place for strategic vision, co-ordination, use of (limited) time, and success. Fortescue's verdict is right: 'in the matter of skill the quiet and unostentatious captures of Cork and Kinsale in 1690 were far the most brilliant achievements of the [Irish] war'.

But that brilliance contrasted too clearly with the ill-managed, half-finished campaigns of Schomberg and William. Marlborough hoped in 1691 to complete the work in Ireland; a Dutchman was appointed. Sent instead to Flanders he was not employed in any major operation. The Master Generalship of the Ordnance had been vacant since Schomberg's death at the Boyne; when Marlborough requested the post it went instead to Schomberg's son. Distrusted by the queen, disliked by the king, he was perhaps unwise to press his cause through the Denmarks, who were themselves at cross purposes with the sovereigns. When a Garter vacancy had lasted for nearly a year Anne and George both wrote to William asking for it for their friend: they were ignored.

Marlborough, already seen by William as 'governing' Anne's 'court in waiting', unwisely played upon English hostility to William's 'parcel of Dutch footmen'. Continental soldiers trained in Dutch drill and discipline were being preferred to British 'amateurs' so that even those not cold-shouldered – Mackay, Lanier, Talmash – were disgruntled. Yet Marlborough had been rewarded, even if not to his own satisfaction. As David Hume was to write two generations later, his desertion of James in 1688 'required ever after the most upright, disinterested and public spirited behaviour to render it justifiable'; it was wrong and foolish to foment discontent among his army 'ring' and engineer anti-Dutch motions in Parliament. Burnet noted that it was 'certain he was doing all he could to set on a faction in the army and nation against the Dutch and to lessen the King', and also recorded the king's remark that 'he had very good reason to believe that he [Marlborough] had made his peace with King James and was engaged in a correspondence with France'. This was true: Anne and Marlborough had both sent submissive, hypocritical letters to James.[5]

This decade was remarkable for the number of ministers and

commanders of James's reign who took (and often retained) office under William – Shrewsbury, Godolphin and Admiral Russell – but who then conducted a servile, insincere correspondence with their former master. Dislike of the Dutch, setbacks in the field and rumours of invasion encouraged reinsurance with the exiled James. William despised but condoned this correspondence – when Secretary of State Shrewsbury admitted it to him William refused his resignation. But in Marlborough's case his record, his army network and a leakage of William's secret plan for an attack on Dunkirk put matters on a different footing: when questioned about the leak Marlborough somewhat lamely replied that he had told nobody 'except his wife' – an excuse which scarcely satisfied the king.[6]

The joint monarchs' distrust of Marlborough combined with their determination to break Sarah's growing hold over the princess, for the famous correspondence between Sarah and Anne as equals – 'Mrs Freeman' and 'Mrs Morley' – had begun in 1691.

In January 1692 Queen Mary demanded that her sister, Anne, dismiss Sarah. Anne refused. The next day Marlborough was dismissed from the Privy Council and lost all his posts and colonelcies, valued at up to £11,000 per annum, and his place with the Hudson's Bay Company. An observer heard from senior statesmen 'and Lord Marlborough himself; and all agreed in this, that the King, besides other things of high misdemeanour, said he had held correspondence with King James'. William told courtiers that Marlborough had spoken and behaved so infamously that, had he not been king, a duel would have been necessary. Anne was expelled from court and denied all royal courtesies. The sisters never met again. The princess in adversity saw her favourites as victims of her now hated brother-in-law 'Mr Caliban', and she promised a 'sunshine day' whenever she should ascend the throne. Meanwhile Marlborough felt the full weight of royal hostility. When a forged 'treason plot' implicated the Archbishop of Canterbury, Marlborough and others (May 1692), he alone went to the Tower, and when after long delay he was released on £6,000 bail his friends Halifax and Shrewsbury were dismissed from the Privy Council for standing surety.

By spring 1694 Shrewsbury, now restored to office, was working on William to employ Marlborough again; the exiled James even thought that William had 'offered' something. Given Marlborough's desire for William's favour and for re-employment, one might expect him to have avoided dealings with the Jacobites at this time, yet deep suspicions remain to this day that he (though certainly not he alone) sent to King James Allied plans for an attack on Brest.

The French Brest squadron had destroyed a great Allied merchant convoy in 1693, and the Allies determined to destroy the squadron in its home dockyards. The secret was soon out: in April 1694 London newsletters published full details and on 28 April (OS) even gave a forecast sailing date of 4 May (14 May NS). Jacobite agents reported conversations with William's senior ministers. One agent, Floyd (or Lloyd), having seen Marlborough, visited Admiral Russell, the incoming First Lord of the Admiralty, and then Godolphin, First Lord of the Treasury. The latter apparently said that an English force would 'infallibly appear before Brest'. Floyd's information reached Versailles on 21 April (OS)/1 May (NS).

As far back as 14 April (NS) Louis XIV had ordered his greatest engineer, Vauban, to improve Brest's defences; now on 1 May he wrote to him that news 'from several quarters' made defensive preparations even more urgent. On 27 April (OS)/7 May (NS) the squadron slipped away to the Mediterranean, thus vitiating the primary Allied objective. The escape was soon known in London and throughout May news came of military reinforcements going to Brest. Shrewsbury was now averse to the scheme; so was Godolphin – who had always disliked putting ships into the constricted Brest inlet; typically Russell blew hot and cold. On going to the Continent in mid May William ordered priority for Mediterranean operations, yet nobody cancelled the Brest project. Indecision and inefficiency delayed preparations into June – a stark contrast to the 1690 Cork and Kinsale expedition. When the doomed expedition eventually arrived off Brest the inlet bristled with fortifications. Against professional advice General Talmash (England's leading soldier since Marlborough's disgrace) attempted a landing in Camaret Bay, was repulsed, and died of wounds.

Much of this tale of delay, muddle and ineptitude in persisting with a discovered plan after its objective had sailed away has nothing to do with Marlborough. Floyd recorded no information from him. But there is a Jacobite document which does implicate him. The senior agent Major General Sackville allegedly sent an 'express' cipher letter to James in France on 3 May (no Style given). Sackville reported that 'Lord Churchill' had told him this day that he had just learnt that the forces at Portsmouth, which he specified, were destined for Brest, one part sailing 'tomorrow' (4 May), the rest with the troops in ten days. Undoubtedly the true value of this information was much reduced by its having already appeared in the public newsletter of 28 April (OS), and Marlborough may have guessed (or gathered from his allies Russell and Godolphin) what Floyd was likely to have reported two weeks earlier. We now know – but of course Marlborough could not be certain – that Louis already had full information 'from several quarters' by 1 May (NS). Thus, whether Sackville's information was sent on 3 May NS or 3 May OS (which was 13 May NS) it cannot have affected the king's decision.

But that much having been said in mitigation, can Marlborough really be exonerated from sending military information to the enemy, from increasing the risk to the lives of English soldiers and sailors for merely personal ends? Was the document perhaps a forgery? If not, did Sackville transcribe a message from Marlborough or did he concoct it from the newsletters? Why should Marlborough do it? If he did, was it with government connivance? What of his military oath?

Apologists have maintained that the document is a Jacobite forgery, being merely a deciphered copy in the hand of the decipherer. The various arguments for forgery were advanced by Colonel Parnell in 1897 and adopted wholesale by Sir Winston Churchill in 1933, but many of them were convincingly demolished by the historian Godfrey Davies in 1920 (though Sir Winston virtually ignored him), who made a reasonable case for the authenticity of the key document. Davies also inclined to the view that Sackville did not invent the message. He concluded that Marlborough probably sought to reinsure himself against a Jacobite restoration 'by the most harmless acts of disloyalty which would achieve the end in view', namely, by sending public information. That undoubtedly fits much of his correspondence with the *exiled* court in these years, but on this occasion that would be folly just when he was hoping to regain a place in the *ruling* court.[7] Nobody knows whether he thought on 3 May that the plan would be abandoned or reduced to a mere feint to distract French forces. Did he perhaps act with official consent? When Marlborough offered his services to ministers after the expedition's failure, William's icy reply: 'I do not think it for the good of my service to entrust him with the command of my troops', makes that theory unlikely, and certainly shows suspicion of treacherous intent.

And so the question abides concerning this blackest accusation in Marlborough's entire career. If any commissioned officer, though unemployed and out of favour, sends genuine military plans (albeit from the newspapers) to the enemy, potentially embarrassing the efforts of his brother soldiers and sailors, is that not essentially playing the double agent – and treason?

FOLLOWING THE CHILDLESS QUEEN MARY'S death in December 1694, Anne's position as heiress strengthened and William accepted this. Marlborough's position, perhaps understandably, did not. However, when Fenwick's assassination plot against William was uncovered in 1696 and Fenwick implicated the ministers Godolphin and

Shrewsbury, Admiral Russell and the out-of-favour Marlborough, William dismissed the allegation. Fenwick damaged his case by continually changing his story; he was eventually executed. They all denied the allegation, Marlborough the most boldly – and indeed assassination seems against his whole known character. Reinsurance through correspondence with James is not the same as plotting murder.[8]

By 1696 the war had exhausted all Europe – though the financial reforms it forced on England created there a stronger foundation for any future war. There had been so few military successes that given Marlborough's later career it may seem unfortunate that after 1691 his talent was not used. Such an opinion is probably mistaken. William was a poor commander in battle, he distrusted Marlborough and did not appreciate advice: a brilliant subordinate would have been in an impossible position, either accepting possibly disastrous decisions or becoming insubordinate by ignoring them. Either way he might have been broken or destroyed. His unemployment in this war may have been to England's long-term advantage.

By the peace treaty of 1697 Louis XIV recognized William's title as king and Anne's reversionary rights. William decided that her sole surviving child, the Duke of Gloucester, should be educated for his future role as king, and, upon Shrewsbury's declining the boy's governorship, William relented so far as to restore Marlborough to the Privy Council and give him the governorship worth £2,000 p.a., a post he held until the sickly child died in 1700. With the peacetime Army greatly reduced in importance, William also restored Marlborough to his Army rank but denied him control of units by not giving him any colonelcies. The Marlboroughs, after some years of near penury, were at last prospering again.

During these years of Mrs Anne Morley's and Mrs Sarah Freeman's friendship, Mr Freeman's influence with the Morleys had continued to grow. Sidney, Lord Godolphin now joined Anne's circle as 'Mr Montgomery'. Five years older than John, he had become a page at court in 1662 and had risen through skill and tact ('never in the way, and never out of it', said Charles II) to become one of the most useful crown servants and expert financiers. He was a Privy Counsellor of long standing, a Treasury minister almost continuously from 1679 to 1690 and First Lord of the Treasury 1684–5 and 1690–96. He had worked conscientiously for James, stayed with him till his fall, and then worked conscientiously (though not entirely loyally) for William. He and Churchill had always been close companions and in 1698 his son married the Churchills' eldest daughter. The great alliance of the next reign, the Morleys, the Freemans and Mr Montgomery, was forming for the 'sunshine day'.

While William's health steadily declined, he spent the summers of peace in his beloved Holland, and Marlborough on each occasion was one of the Lords Justices ruling in his absence, but relations remained frigid and Marlborough complained to Shrewsbury in May 1700, 'The King's coldness to me still continues.' This changed only when the international crisis about who should inherit the enormous possessions of the dying king of Spain came to dominate all men's minds.

PART TWO

The causes of the War of the Spanish Succession, how governments conducted it, and the tools they used

CHAPTER 3

The Spanish Succession:
France and the Grand Alliance

A PRESENT THREAT and a looming crisis confronted western Europe at the end of the 1690s, and they were interlinked: 'the exorbitant power of France' would certainly complicate the succession in Spain and its possessions in the Netherlands and Burgundy, Italy, Sardinia, Sicily, the New World and the Pacific whenever the childless King Carlos II of Spain should die. Henceforth these two great themes dominated Marlborough's career. He understood what French hegemony would mean for Europe and beyond; he feared that Louis would inflict Catholicism on England; he knew the French Army and had observed its treatment of subjugated provinces. For his entire time in authority in the next reign he was absorbed in reducing French power and seeking a solution to the Spanish succession.

Once Louis XIV had consolidated power inside France he began aggressive war abroad. Between 1667 and 1697 he fought two major and two minor wars interspersed with diplomatic offensives. Constantly interfering in the domestic politics of his neighbours, resurrecting old claims and inventing new ones so as to push his frontiers ever outwards, Louis sought to reduce Spanish power, destroy the 'Godless' Dutch Republic and displace the Habsburgs from the elective

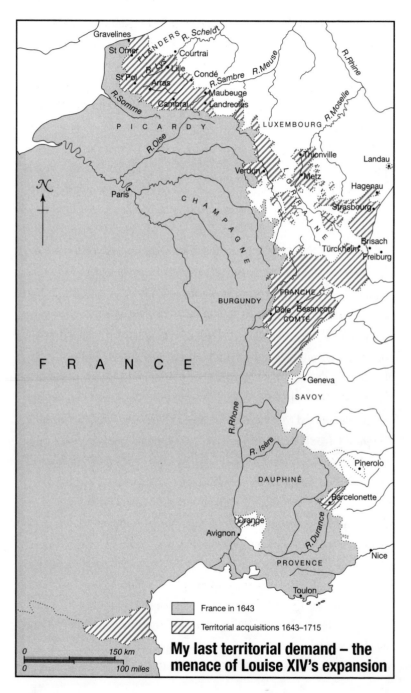

Gravelines
St Omer
FLANDERS
R. Scheldt
Courtrai
B.Lys
St Pol
Lille
Condé
R.Sambre
R.Meuse
R.Rhine
Arras
Cambrai
Maubeuge
Landreoles
R.Somme
PICARDY
R.Oise
LUXEMBOURG
R.Moselle
Thionville
Landau
Verdun
Metz
Hagenau
Paris
CHAMPAGNE
LORRAINE
Strasbourg
Brisach
Türckheim
Freiburg
BURGUNDY
FRANCHE
Dôle
Besançon
COMTÉ

F R A N C E

Geneva
SAVOY

R.Rhone
R. Isère
Pinerolo
DAUPHINÉ
Barcelonette
Orange
R.Durance
Avignon
Nice
PROVENCE
Toulon

| | France in 1643 |
| | Territorial acquisitions 1643–1715 |

My last territorial demand – the menace of Louise XIV's expansion

0 ———— 150 km
0 ———— 100 miles

German Imperial throne to which he felt he himself had claims. He offered help to the Stuarts so that Catholicism might be restored in England. His fourth war (1688–97), provoked largely by these initiatives, held off a great European coalition for nine years until mutual exhaustion brought peace. Even then, all feared further French aggression, for whatever assurances Louis's diplomats gave his victims, no demand had ever proved to be his last. Treaties and solemn truces could not be relied upon to outlast his mood. Louis, 'the Most Christian King', browbeat the Pope and claimed independence from papal jurisdiction. He gave a new twist to the traditional French policy of being 'Catholic at home, Protestant abroad'. He sought to extirpate heresy within his frontiers by persecution, and beyond them by military might, yet when Muslim Turkey laid siege to Catholic Vienna in 1683 Louis was conspicuous among Christian sovereigns in his lack of concern and his refusal to aid the Habsburgs.

Ominously, the hereditary rivals, Bourbon and Habsburg, both had valid claims of blood and marriage to succeed the childless Carlos II. It was the supreme achievement of William III to induce Louis to sign a Partition Treaty (1698) whereby a compromise candidate, a Wittelsbach baby prince, a blood relation in a minor state, should inherit the greater part of Carlos's dominions, but with France and the Habsburg Emperor Leopold receiving substantial territorial compensation. The treaty gave each claimant an increase in power without surrendering any land they actually possessed, and represented the best chance for avoiding war. Within weeks of that signature the baby died mysteriously. Through immense patience William eventually persuaded Louis to sign a new Partition Treaty with England and Holland (March 1700) whereby the dauphin would receive substantial lands in Italy, Sicily and elsewhere, while the emperor's younger son, Archduke Charles, would inherit Spain and the other territories. This the Habsburgs rejected.

Then in November 1700 Carlos died, and his will wrecked

William's efforts. The will bequeathed the entire inheritance to the dauphin's younger sons, Anjou and then Berri (the eldest, Burgundy, was destined for the French throne). Should they refuse, the whole inheritance would be offered to the Habsburg Archduke Charles, and after him to the Duke of Savoy (a more distant relative). By rejecting partition and insisting on an undivided inheritance Carlos also bequeathed European war. The Habsburgs had rejected William's half loaf; they would never accept the virtual nothing offered by third place in the will. The will thus limited Louis's choice to all or nothing, for he knew that war-weary Holland and England would not support him if he rejected its terms but sought to impose partition by war. With foreboding he accepted the will. His grandson Philip of Anjou became Felipe V, *el Borbon*.

Emperor Leopold began to resurrect the anti-French Grand Alliance which had fought the last war. Though demanding help to gain the entire inheritance, he was slow to recognize his helpers' needs. He coveted most the Spanish lands in Italy and thought the Spanish Netherlands (Belgium) a distant nuisance, yet Belgium, the Channel and the narrow seas – areas of constant French activity – were vital to Holland and England. Moreover, the Dutch and English feared that trade with 'the Spanish Indies' would be totally lost to France if the Bourbons and not the Viennese Habsburgs acquired them; Vienna was relatively indifferent to their worries. To secure a Habsburg commitment over Belgium and trade, William III (with the principal Dutch statesman, Anthonie Heinsius) accepted Leopold's demands for Spanish possessions in Italy, and especially Milan. This Italian dimension in Austrian policy would repeatedly complicate the strategy of the new Alliance.

There was to be another complication. Recently the Habsburgs had been successful in their wars with the Turks, liberating the old kingdom of Hungary. The leading Imperial general Margrave Lewis of Baden was joined in the late 1690s by a new and brighter star,

Prince Eugene of Savoy, whose great victory at Zenta (1697) led to peace on the Balkan front for nearly twenty years. But Emperor Leopold treated Hungary as a conquest, abolished its old constitution and forcibly imposed Catholicism on its largely Protestant people. Almost inevitably rebellion flared in 1703 when it seemed that French troops might reach Vienna; thereafter Hungary dangerously weakened Austria's war capacity.

Had Louis not ignored English and Dutch concerns, general war might have been delayed. For both countries the last war had been almost ruinously expensive, with few victories to show for it; merchants wanted time to recover and a chance to rebuild trade; many were instinctively hostile to involvement in Vienna's problems; and there was initially little public concern over Felipe V. But in 1701 Louis's declaration that Philip of Anjou (Felipe V) retained a reversionary right to the French throne if Louis's eldest grandson should die childless was interpreted as plotting the absorption of Spain by France. French troops entered the Spanish Netherlands in Felipe's name, occupied Spanish fortresses, and forced the Dutch garrisons from their vital 'barrier forts' (such as Nieuport, Oudenarde, Ath, Mons, Charleroi, Namur and Luxembourg) till only an isolated Maastricht remained in Dutch control. Louis embargoed English imports to France and announced that Spain would follow him. When the exiled James II died in France in September 1701, Louis recognized his Catholic son as 'James III, King of England', challenging 'the Glorious Revolution' and breaching the Ryswick treaty of 1697 signed with William which guaranteed Anne's rights of succession, rights which Parliamentary statute had confirmed for her and her Protestant cousins in Hanover as recently as June 1701. Louis's actions proclaimed supremacy of his whim over international and English law.

The whole experience of the past thirty-five years was thus confirmed. Louis could not be trusted; only force could confine France's ambitions. And Louis was to find his reputation made sensible compromise impossible, for when the War of the Spanish Succession brought France ever closer to disaster, Louis's increasingly desperate attempts to negotiate a settlement with Allied leaders failed in no small measure because, even when he was genuinely prepared to concede satisfactory terms, men with long memories like Marlborough were convinced that he would prove false.

WILLIAM'S HEALTH WAS FAILING at a time when his life's work was at risk. In Holland he could rely on Heinsius; but who in violently partisan and unpredictable England would maintain his policies? William conquered personal aversion. He chose Marlborough, whose diplomatic skills had not been used since 1685; whose only independent command had been in 1690, with 8,000 men; who had been excluded militarily for ten years; who had been anti-Dutch and politically malcontent – or worse. But Marlborough's links to Anne were such that he must be loyal to her, and if his mind and abilities were engaged in creating the new Grand Alliance England's next monarch would sustain it.

By a treaty of 1678 the Dutch claimed English military assistance and in June 1701 William appointed Marlborough to command this twelve-battalion contingent, later increased by five cavalry regiments and six more battalions, and all in need of Marlborough's skills as a trainer. In August he was also appointed ambassador extraordinary and plenipotentiary to the Dutch, with instructions to negotiate a 'perpetual alliance' with them, and then to secure the agreement of the Emperor Leopold's envoys, while keeping in play the French envoys at The Hague. Negotiations were complicated by the emperor's quite independently sending Prince Eugene of Savoy with an army to take Milan from the Bourbons. Nor were Austrian aristocratic foibles helpful: in 1688 their ambassador in London had complained that Churchill had come 'from nothing'; now Sinzendorff at the Hague irritated Marlborough with 'his Vienna breeding' and remained one of

Marlborough's most unforgiving critics throughout the war.

On 7 September 1701 Marlborough and representatives of the Dutch and the Empire signed at The Hague the Treaty of the Grand Alliance. Ostensibly to preserve peace, it meant war. The separation of France from Spain was essential. Although the future of the Spanish mainland kingdom remained unclear, 'partition' was agreed, with certain specific land acquisitions, trading rights and 'the Dutch barrier' (though not its final sovereignty) all stipulated. The Allies committed themselves to a 'joint' approach to any peace negotiation – a condition which would hamper attempts at peacemaking in the years after 1706 – and to maximum mutual 'succour and assistance' in case of 'invasion'.

Marlborough had been assiduous in promoting William's views but he remembered that those who had negotiated the Partition Treaties on the king's behalf had been impeached by a discontented Parliament, and so he prudently informed leading members of both Houses of each step taken. Ratification of the Hague treaty was thus assured, pleasing England's allies by this firm and rapid commitment; in return some months later Marlborough induced the Allies to sign an additional clause binding the Alliance to fight until Louis should recognize England's Protestant succession.

Haggling over troop quotas continued all winter at The Hague, demanding all Marlborough's reserves of patience and determination. The quotas were eventually fixed for England at 40,000 soldiers (18,000 native born) in seven cavalry regiments and thirty-three battalions, and 40,000 sailors. The partners promised 82,000 Imperial troops for the French war (out of 108,000 total for the Empire), and 100,000 Dutch ('besides what they send to sea'). Meanwhile, he had brought in minor states like the Palatinate, Hesse, Holstein, valuable for the troops they could hire out; he had studied the Baltic war of Sweden against Denmark, Russia and Saxony-Poland for its effect on the west, and ensured through some intricate diplomacy that the francophile warrior king of Sweden remained neutral. In a few months at The Hague, from being a new, unfamiliar and untested diplomat Marlborough had become a central figure in European affairs, known to all and possessing a remarkable grasp of the issues. Few men about to command in war have been so perfectly instructed in its aims and familiar with its leaders.

Anticipating war, King Louis moved to encircle the Dutch Republic. Through the connivance of two brothers hostile to the Habsburgs, the governor of the Spanish Netherlands and the Elector of Cologne (who was also bishop of Liège), he advanced through their territories to the Meuse/Maas and the Cologne Rhineland, a march completed by the year end.

And then in March 1702 William III was thrown from his horse, broke a collarbone and died. The Dutch were shaken, fearing that the unifying force within the Grand Alliance had gone. So thought Louis, and his confidence was understandable, though mistaken.

CHAPTER 4

Opposing Strengths, Opposing Systems and the Constraints of War

THREE DAYS AFTER WILLIAM'S DEATH the new queen, attended only by the Marlboroughs, charmed both Houses with a declaration of her intentions. The concepts may have been those of her Dutch predecessor but they were expressed in a satisfactorily English way, and also reassured an apprehensive Alliance alarmed at Louis's strength.

The Bourbons held the central position, a compact land bloc with the advantages of interior lines and a unified, autocratic French supreme command at Versailles. France was ready, powerful and well defended, and though Spanish strength and organization fell far short of France's, Louis had steadily reinforced Spain's outlying territories with French troops and generals. Whereas in the previous war Spain had been part of William III's alliance, now its ports in Europe and elsewhere were closed to English and Dutch trade, and Spanish bullion would assist Louis's war effort. Gone was the tight ring around an isolated France which had characterized the last war.

The Bourbons also held a slight advantage in manpower. France's population stood at 19 million souls and Spain's perhaps 5 or 6 million, whereas on the Allied side the basic statistics were some 5 million in

England and just under 2 million in Holland, while the Austrian crown lands had about 4.6 million. How many lived in the German states is unknown; the Thirty Years' War had taken its toll, and not until the opening of the nineteenth century would the level of 1618 (20 million) be reached once more. Militarily the same situation held. France's fine standing army was now some 270,000 strong and money had been lavished on it; the Spaniards had 60,000 men, brave but less trained. Holland, Austria and England respectively furnished an initial 100,000, 82,000 and 40,000 soldiers for Flanders, Germany and Italy.

At sea the situation was different; and since navies cannot feature prominently in a short account of what was predominantly a land war, a slight digression is necessary. The apogee of the French navy's power and efficiency had been reached in 1690; thereafter, though it still outbuilt England (though not Holland) in ships of the line, it was progressively starved of finance and the effects were gradually seen. (Spain's fleet was a negligible factor throughout.) Tiny Holland not only had kept a sizeable army, but had also maintained a battle fleet of nearly a hundred ships; but by 1702 the strain was telling and of the two Allied fleets it was the English which was emerging as the more powerful. England's quota for the joint Anglo-Dutch naval effort became 'five out of eight' and in fact came to much more, since by 1712 the effective Dutch battle fleet was no more than thirty ships, while England's was around a hundred. England's shipbuilding continued unhampered and unconstrained throughout Anne's war, during which the Royal Navy took 35 per cent of all expenditure. By contrast in France the navy was granted only 7 per cent of expenditure and after 1707 all French construction stopped. The French decline meant that sea battle was almost never sought by the Bourbons, who gradually turned to commerce raiding as an efficient and cheap form of war, using privateers from bases like St Malo and Dunkirk. Protecting Allied convoys required different construction programmes (cruisers) and a changed emphasis in operations, but Allied battlefleets continued to threaten enemy ports and stations, check enemy sea movement and exert diplomatic pressure on neutral coastal states throughout the War of the Spanish Succession.

Initially, however, the western Mediterranean was a French lake, with the Balearics, Sardinia, Sicily and the toe of Italy in their hands: French squadrons could protect sea movement of troops between Spain and Italy and penetrate the Adriatic to check Austrian sea movements out of Trieste towards northern Italy or Naples. Bourbon pressure on Savoy-Piedmont and Portugal increased Allied worries. Savoy astride the Alps between France and Italy had been forced to give passage to French armies, and once France held Milan, the small Italian duchies further east let her advance to the borders of Venice, so that the Brenner Pass into Austria came in sight. Franco-Spanish pressure forced Portugal to sign a treaty of friendship in 1701, denying the Allies her Brazilian bullion and closing her harbours and markets to them. This left the Allied fleets without bases south of Land's End and limited their stay in the Mediterranean to four summer months.

On land, French armies stood poised to invade a barrierless Holland from Belgium and the Cologne Electorate. In Alsace a French army faced Margrave Lewis of Baden, whose Imperialist force at Stollhofen covered the Rhine and the Black Forest. Hanover, Prussia and many minor German states supported the emperor, but the 'neutral', well-armed Elector Max Emmanuel of Bavaria was suspected of favouring the Bourbons and plotting to enlarge his possessions and acquire a crown. With Iberia safe and the Po valley and southern Italy gripped, western Europe was an almost self-contained Bourbon fortress.

THE CONTRAST BETWEEN THE TWO SIDES was equally striking in their methods of directing war. In France only one man decided and his royal decision was law. By contrast, the Allied systems of government seemed ill-suited for swift and effective decisions on common policy.

The stubborn, indecisive old emperor in Vienna, while insistent that his younger son should wear the Spanish crown, thought that country a distant nuisance, and he did not wish the son to go there to help win it in war. He was lukewarm towards the Maritime Powers, even though they financed him. He clung to familiar and inefficient ministers and blocked all attempts at institutional reform. His council was hidebound, particularist, narrow and ineffective. The Treasury's finances were chaotic, and by tradition it defied the Imperial War Council; within a few months of renewed war the Imperial government was effectively bankrupt. Not until Prince Eugene of Savoy became president of the War Council in 1703 were matters discussed in a businesslike way.

Each of the seven Dutch provinces had its own council (Estate) which sent delegates to the federal States General, each province (whether large or small) possessing one vote. To lessen delay the province of Holland, which supplied almost 60 per cent of the nation's public finance, often floated its own policy beforehand but the whole process remained cumbersome. William had been Dutch captain general by land and sea and his authority had overborne these constraints, but henceforth the post (and that of his deputy) lay vacant throughout the war, and the States General's decisions were passed to Dutch commanders by one of the Councillors of State and a group of field-deputies selected from the provinces. But for the help of certain powerful friends, principally Heinsius, Grand Pensionary of Holland, Marlborough might have suffered even more from Dutch generals, deputies and councils than he actually did.

As in Holland so in England the death of the Stadtholder-King Commander-in-Chief threatened effectiveness, since semi-invalid Queen Anne could not undertake his role and it had yet to be seen if her counsellors could compensate for this. But she presided at Cabinet at least once a week, and she made her personal views known to Parliament, where policy was scrutinized and the expenses of the war sanctioned. The financial prostration at the close of the last war had resulted in a new coinage, a reformed banking system and better control of public revenues, encouraging confidence in English credit, which, coupled with improving trade flows, gave Anne's government the strength needed to meet without despair the costs of a new long war (£99 million in Anne's reign).

The new queen desired a government of unity without party, managed by personal friends like Marlborough and Godolphin, but the deep differences between Tories and Whigs over war policy ('blue water' and colonies versus Continental war), trade and church matters forced party government upon her. That process strained and finally destroyed her relations with the Whig partisan Sarah, and the more 'centrist' Godolphin and Marlborough.

Anne's Cabinets included the Archbishop of Canterbury, courtiers (Chamberlain, Steward, Master of the Horse), the Lords Chancellor and Treasurer, the Lords President and Privy Seal; and the Lord Lieutenant of Ireland and the heads of the Navy, Army and Ordnance when present in England. Her two Secretaries of State (Northern and Southern Departments) attended, having responsibilities for particular overseas regions and the military operations in them – Northern for Flanders, the Empire and Bavaria; Southern for France, Spain, Italy and naval operations. The Secretaries sent policy instructions to commanders-in-chief in the field, who in turn addressed to them their dispatches and correspondence.

Thus what is sometimes called 'Marlborough's war' was never directed exclusively by him. Absence, time, distance and the slow speed of communication, added to party allegiances within the Cabinet Council, would automatically have made that impossible. His views on war policy might be challenged in Cabinet; other opinions than his might prevail. But the immense influence he had established over Anne and her husband, who was 'generalissimo of all forces by land and sea' and Lord High Admiral – and the assiduity with which he sought to explain his reasoning to them both – meant that in the early years 'dear Mr Freeman's' opinions carried enormous weight with the royal couple in matters naval as well as military, supported as he was by Godolphin's regular reading to the queen of the letters he had received from Marlborough. Moreover, as his victories added to his international prestige and influence with foreign rulers, so the English ministers tended to pass decisions to him. In 1709 a young English diplomat on mission to London from head-quarters in Spain reported that the Cabinet seemed happy to accept whatever advice Marlborough might proffer on Spain, and that the duke 'enters with more earnestness and detail in all these affairs than anybody else', affairs which most ministers studied only cursorily.

This structure – Anne herself, her Cabinets, the Crown in Parliament – proved a surprisingly efficient combination. Without their efficiency Marlborough's ideas on the war's direction and conduct might never have overcome obstacles in The Hague and Vienna. But there is another aspect of the matter. With a lesser general and diplomat than Marlborough the structure, however efficient, might not have overcome Louis XIV.

FINALLY THERE ARE THE CONSTRAINTS of war as practised at this time. Clausewitz described the era of Gustavus Adolphus and Frederick the Great, two absolute monarchs, in the following very negative terms:

> Even a royal commander had to use his army with a *minimum of risk*. If the army was pulverised, he could not raise another, and behind the army there was nothing. That enjoined the greatest prudence in all operations. Only if a *decisive advantage* seemed possible could the precious instrument be used, and to bring things to that point was a feat of the highest generalship [my emphasis].

This applied equally in Marlborough's time, and too many of his campaigns (as he himself bemoaned) saw little more than marching and manoeuvre. But Clausewitz, who rarely mentions him, is less than fair. The odds which Marlborough accepted in fighting each of his great battles were never 'on' or even 'short' in themselves, as Marlborough's enormous gamble in the 1704 Bavarian campaign, and the supreme improvisation at the *Ne Plus Ultra* Lines and the siege of Bouchain against superior forces in 1711, both demonstrate.[9]

But of course armies *had* become more professional, more expensive, more valuable; the professional mercenary was giving place to the professional who was 'native born' and owed instinctive allegiance to his own monarch and flag. Mercenaries of a sort there continued to be: Marlborough spent much time hiring Hessians and others from their rulers, to whom they 'returned' on completion of contract. The French king had his Irish 'wild geese' and his Swiss guards but they were not mercenaries in the old sense, for the former were religious refugees loyal to their adopted protector, and the latter refused to serve in Germany, a distinct disadvantage in the campaign of 1704. Weaponry was becoming less unwieldy and more complicated, and therefore drill for cavalry and infantry became more minutely detailed: the two arms had to be integrated with each other, and with the artillery, lest confusion in manoeuvre should bring disaster. The engineer arm grew as sieges became more scientific. The long-service national standing army was the monarch's precious toy.

It had to be fed, and agricultural production was barely able to meet this demand in poor years. Even in good years the supply lines were fully stretched. Fortescue defined the advantage of the Low Countries and their waterways in an age of atrocious roads: 'a country where men could kill each other without being starved'. Hence the endless sweeps to bring in forage and to find pasture for meat on the hoof which so preoccupied the commanders in summer, and hence the creation of great magazines of food and fodder in winter so that the campaign could open early in the spring. More will be said of this later.

Expensive and hungry manpower is best camped in the fields of one's enemy or on territory recently conquered but not yet annexed. During Louis XIV's thirty years of aggression he had acquired or occupied a vast swathe of land on his eastern and northern frontiers, along which he had constructed an intricate and interconnected barrier of fortresses. Beyond them his armies either ravaged for food and mulcted money 'contributions' for his war chest, or reduced a zone to scorched earth as a protective *glacis*. Within the fortress barrier his armies could refuse battle while rendering assistance to any stronghold the enemy attacked. War against France would entail repeated siegework, which the genius of Vauban, the great fortress builder, ensured would be protracted even if successful.

This conception of war led Louis XIV into the disastrous command policy suggested by his advisers Louvois and Chamlay (already guilty of advocating the scorched-earth policy he had adopted). The great generals of Louis's earlier years, Condé and Turenne, had sought battle; they were too great to browbeat, but the next generation was more deferential. Louis believed he could shelter behind his conquests and strongholds, decide at Versailles policy for distant fronts and 'advise' on accepting or avoiding battle, and not worry about 'the mediocre capacity' of the generals whom he might select for command.[10] Exceptional commanders like Villars could minimize the disastrous effects of such thinking; Villeroy, Marsin and Tallard could not.

In other respects, however, fortress warfare was time effective. Among commanders of that era Marlborough was unusually keen on battle and yet in his ten famous campaigns he fought only four great pitched battles, two lesser ones and two breakthrough strokes by manoeuvre. By comparison his armies had to undertake endless sieges, twenty-seven of them major ones (eighteen under his direction or in conjunction with the equally offensively minded Prince Eugene). Sieges were expensive in men: while Allied casualties in the four famous battles came to over 44,000 men (over half of which were at Malplaquet), they were far exceeded by casualties from siegework. Taking only the campaigns of 1708–11 in the French fortress belt, over 50,000 Allied troops were killed or wounded, while others must have been incapacitated for some time at least with 'flux' and trench fever. Because a captured fortress required a garrison, the field army was to that extent weakened further. Sieges consumed time in brief campaigning seasons. Of Marlborough's eighteen sieges, two lasted six days and two over four months, but on average the eighteen sieges lasted thirty-six days each. Louis XIV, when all other hope had failed, relied on time to save him from Marlborough.

CHAPTER 5

Queen Anne's Army

FROM THE CREATION of the king's army in 1661 there had been separate armies in the three kingdoms until the English and Scottish became 'British' at the Union of Parliaments in 1707, leaving separate only the Irish establishment. Until 1707, whenever Scottish regiments went abroad they first passed onto the English establishment; regiments on the Irish establishment likewise were posted overseas as part of the English (or later British) establishment. Hence in the first years of Anne's reign it was correct to call the forces overseas 'English', a habit the French maintained into the twentieth century, and one generally used here.

The legality of a standing army was sanctioned by England's Parliament through the 1689 Mutiny Act, annually renewed, which also decreed its total size and cost. In the short peace of 1697–1701 Parliament failed to renew the Act, and so slashed the Army that whereas the Dutch retained 4,100 cavalry and 41,000 infantry as a safeguard against France, in England – where about £1 million of arrears was due to the Army, with many discarded officers and men ruined or starving – the 'establishment' was 3,000 cavalry and 5,577 infantry, with actual numbers much smaller. In 1701, the Dutch having invoked the old mutual security treaty, England undertook to recruit another 10,000 infantry. By the year end British forces worldwide stood at forty-two squadrons of cavalry and thirty-three battalions of infantry (say 29,000 men: a squadron 'establishment' reckoned at 150, a battalion at 650 men). Of these, however, twenty-two squadrons and fourteen battalions were required for garrison or policing duties in Scotland, Ireland and the colonies.

The peak of the country's military effort during Queen Anne's war – taking men of British birth only – reached about sixty-five squadrons (11,000 cavalry and dragoons) and eighty-four battalions (58,000 infantry) for all purposes. Taking infantry alone, throughout the war England and Scotland required a garrison of around twelve battalions, Marlborough's army acting as reserve: during the 1708 invasion scare ten battalions returned from Flanders. To hold Ireland the Lord Lieutenant kept ten to fourteen battalions. The West Indies and (from 1704) Gibraltar required about four battalions. The Navy used six battalions as marines (borne on the Navy vote). From 1703, when troops went to Portugal and subsequently to Spain as well, the Peninsula took an initial four battalions, peaked at twenty-six and then fluctuated between twelve and twenty battalions for some years.

For much of the war the queen's British-born forces in Flanders stood at no more than seventeen squadrons and twenty battalions, falling to seventeen battalions in late 1706 (when twenty-six battalions were in the Peninsula), but rising to twenty-seven battalions in 1709–10. The queen also employed German and Danish auxiliaries, who during their period of employment were effectively under Marlborough's control, though renewal negotiations entailed much time and patience. Marlborough's command over Dutch forces was subject to supervision by their field deputies and generals, and this limitation extended to the famous 'Scots Brigade', six Scottish battalions employed for generations by the Dutch: Marlborough had to consult their paymasters before using them. There were also contingents from German states, paid for by their own sovereigns; these were subject to their rulers' whims and Marlborough had always to watch lest other projects should call them away. The composition and hiring terms of the contingents comprising the army in Flanders meant that winter was spent at home in relentless recruiting, and abroad in hard bargaining, in meetings to arrange food contracts and fix their costs. At winter's end efforts were usually necessary to secure the auxiliaries' arrival from home on the dates stipulated and to sort them into peaceable groups in camp.

On her accession Queen Anne became head of all her forces. She appointed her husband supreme commander by land and sea and Lord High Admiral, but his poor health and personal preferences tied him to the Admiralty, and military matters passed to Marlborough, who from 1701 had been English commander-in-chief in the Low Countries. Marlborough was immediately appointed captain general of land forces in England and Wales. This appointment (worth over £5,000 p.a.) gave Marlborough powers for the training, movement and discipline of troops, and operational authority. He had no control over the Army's size, money, stores or equipment. He was part of a complex system: queen in Cabinet for policy; ministers and Parliament for the establishment 'vote'; the Treasury, Admiralty, Ordnance and other interests for implementation. But the post entitled him to give overall strategical advice to the Cabinet; when English troops went to other war theatres (such as Iberia) the local commanders-in-chief were never made captain general.

Establishments were complex. The Army comprised regiments of cavalry, dragoons and infantry; the mounted and foot guards were on a separate establishment. Theatre establishments could be confusing, units on the establishment of one theatre sometimes serving elsewhere. When during the war voluntary recruitment quickly proved inadequate, Parliament established conscription – limited effectively to imprisoned men and those out of work – but this expedient was not tried again for two centuries, for local magistrates and officials were unhelpful over quotas and numbers, and despite Marlborough's complaints little improvement was seen. Regiments were essentially 'property', a shareholding by officers who purchased their commissions and were responsible for finding volunteers up to the establishment fixed by Parliament. The colonel was chief proprietor of his regiment, dedicated to the queen's service by the terms of his commission, delegating its management to his lieutenant colonel. Beneath him field officers acted as proprietors of their companies.

'Property' implies rights. So although Marlborough issued commands, he added his compliments and an expression of his wishes. He was gentle – and he was politic.[11] His long tenure of chief command in that violently partisan era meant that the 'Marlburian ring' expanded greatly. There is no indication that he used these officers for personal ends but several had places in Parliament and others were vociferous advocates of his policies; and in the practice of the time loyalty to the administration was encouraged by hopes of military promotion. Those who differed from him politically or lay outside the magic circle (Lords Argyll, Rivers, Orrery, or General Webb MP) made close alliance with his political enemies, and provided a running commentary on his failings; they spread dissension and were rewarded when Marlborough lost favour and his clients lost places. The brief, inglorious record of his successor, Ormonde, aided by an 'anti-Marlburian ring', made a telling contrast to the great duke's ten-year governance.

An English commander-in-chief reported to one of the queen's Secretaries of State. But worming himself into this reporting structure came the Secretary at War. This official, in William's reign merely secretary to the royal c.-in-c. at the war, sat in the Commons and spoke on administrative matters for the Army there. In 1704 Marlborough chose Henry St John for the post, and when St John left office Walpole took over from him. Such major politicians vastly increased the Secretary's role and by the time of the Duke's dismissal the post was sharing functions with the Secretaries of State, and was independent of Marlborough, who for genuinely 'secretarial' services during the war had relied upon his own man, Cardonnel. The Board of General Officers, set up in 1706 to handle administrative matters (such as clothing), was seen by hostile ministers during Marlborough's decline as a further means of reducing his authority, but little came of this.

Artillery and engineers, their personnel, guns, equipment, fortresses, munitions and stores in the British Isles and colonies, were the responsibility of the Board of Ordnance, an independent office of state. Within weeks of becoming captain general Marlborough removed any potential conflict by securing the key post of Master General of the Ordnance ($£1,500$ p.a.). He restored the sound organization designed by James II, and to ensure the board's efficiency during his regular absences he brought in new, energetic men to run it. He was well served.

Pay, commissariat and land transport were in civilian hands under the Treasury, and answerable directly to Parliament. Sea transport and victualling were handled by commissioners responsible to the Board of Admiralty and Lord High Admiral. Medical matters seem to have been delegated to the Army by the Admiralty's Commissioners for Sick and Wounded Seamen, and organized on a 'benevolent' basis by the regiments themselves. Marlborough himself took a constant interest in medical matters within his own army, and furthermore created a local scheme whereby a contributory fund for widows and orphans was set up – Parliament having thought nothing necessary. He even donated his Blenheim bounty as c.-in-c. – $£600$ – to widows and orphans from the campaign.

A FIELD ARMY'S ORDER OF BATTLE was a matter of diplomatic and military calculation. A potentate sending troops to a coalition army might cavil or even withdraw his force if it was placed in a less 'honourable' position than the contingent of a less exalted ruler: Marlborough had to spend much time adjusting the claims of precedence, those of the right of the second line against the left of the first, and similar little problems.

In purely military terms, so minutely detailed and rigid had this system become that an unwilling opponent might slip away while his assailant painstakingly deployed into battle position. Marlborough paid only qualified regard to elegant coloured charts detailing the order of battle. In the Blenheim campaign his infantry took the left of their line though the right was the place of highest honour, and in 1708 he showed how fluid his ideas could be as, irrespective of the charts, he threw units one after another into the 'running' encounter battle at Oudenarde: he was the charts' master, not their servant. In practice he usually placed the infantry in the centre and in two lines, under a general of foot, grouped in the largest formation of the time (brigades of three to five battalions), with artillery posted in front. The two wings, each under a lieutenant general, grouped cavalry in two lines. More cavalry and infantry were held back in reserve.

Marlborough's infantry was mustered in single-battalion regiments (except for the 1st Guards and the Royal Scots, which each had two battalions) of twelve or thirteen companies: rarely exceeding 700 men at the start of a campaign, they soon shrank considerably. The flintlock musket (precursor of the 'Brown Bess') was now standard, to which a bayonet (progressively the socket type) was added; it fired a heavier and more penetrative ball than French muskets. Battalion musket-fire was by platoons in succession and not (as in the French Army) by successive ranks; thus a British battalion's fire 'rolled' along the front almost continuously and yet allowed reloading under cover of neighbouring platoons' fire.

To ensure improvement Marlborough exercised his whole army in platoon fire 'by signal of flag and drum under his own eye'. The first shot, carefully prepared, might well be the one good discharge; troubles in reloading (one shot per two minutes was good), misfires, bad flints or poor powder were often noted in battle. The clash between the 18th Royal Irish and Louis's Irish 'wild geese' at Malplaquet in 1709 demonstrates musketry's limitations even when massed: commencing at 100 paces (250 feet) each side fired two volleys while closing, the 'wild geese' discharging a third wavering volley before seeking cover, with the 18th then replying with their third volley. Each regiment thus fired about 500 bullets, but the 18th reported only four dead and six wounded, with almost forty enemy casualties left on the ground, an insignificant hit rate of about 2 per cent for the 'geese's' musketry and 8 per cent for the 18th's fire. This is why massed attacks like Rowe's at Blenheim could be made in serried ranks of scarlet, muskets on shoulders, right up to the barricades before coming under fire: decisive range was at 100 feet, or less. If an attack was not halted at this point by the fire of the defence, the climax could come very swiftly in hand-to-hand fighting.

British cavalry was organized in regiments of about 450 men usually in six troops – some larger regiments had nine – but its force was measured by squadrons (about 150 men). It relied upon shock rather than missile tactics and as mounted combat tends to swing back and forth and can quickly get out of hand at the gallop, Marlborough insisted on his cavalry keeping to a fast but measured trot. Nevertheless, he was ready to unleash it in full pursuit after victory – as at Ramillies. To counter French missile tactics Marlborough allowed light breastplates (but not backplates) after 1707. Dragoon regiments (still in companies, not squadrons), originally mounted infantry and used as such at the Schellenberg, were gradually assimilating themselves to cavalry.

Artillery, cumbersome, and drawn by civilian teams of drivers, was difficult to manoeuvre during battle, and its control and siting were therefore critical matters to which Marlborough gave his personal attention. Its batteries were usually of six to eight pieces: at Blenheim Marlborough and Eugene deployed fifty-two pieces in total. Artillery fire was effective at some 600 yards with solid shot, much less with grape; siege artillery of course had far greater range.

Most western armies were similarly organized, though the French were reputedly more conservative, perhaps because supremacy in the previous generation under Condé, Turenne and Luxembourg had led to complacency. They were slower than their opponents in recognizing technical changes to weaponry. They continued to deploy infantry in depth, sometimes six ranks deep, which meant that the rear ranks' firepower was wasted. They tended to rely on missile tactics for their cavalry – and shooting meant checked momentum. (In central Europe irregular light cavalry 'hussars' were much used, and the French were beginning to follow suit: but 'hussars' had an evil reputation.) France was in advance of the rest of Europe in having regular regiments of Royal Artillery: Britain did not institute this until 1716.

Food, forage and movement required constant attention. Amassing stores, providing basic food for about four days, and cooking and distributing it dominated the siting of the army's camp and its range of march. Two leading authorities, Professor Pérjès and Ivan Phelan, estimate that Marlborough's force of 25,000 cavalry and infantry on the march to the Danube was backed by a supply train of 1,700 wagons, 2,000 carters and 5,000 horses, plus the artillery train of similar numbers. They cite the daily bread requirement: 56,000 pounds or 38,000 loaves per day, requiring 25 dismountable brick ovens serviced by 100 bakers, with 100 carts for the firebricks, the firewood, the flour and other ingredients, and for the grain mills needed when milled flour was unobtainable – workmen, carters and horses themselves needing food and fodder. Twelve miles on a 'marching day' was the effective limit. Additionally there was the fodder requirement for the officers' horses, the cavalry and the transport. In the Flanders campaign of 1711 foraging even in well-watered meadow country was a major worry for the opposing armies. It could not be left to chance. It required administrative skills of a very high order, constantly applied.

The staff at Marlborough's field headquarters are usefully listed in the 'Blenheim Bounty Roll', which also gives a rough valuation of their roles and status. His principal assistant was the cavalryman Brigadier William Cadogan, quartermaster general, who acted also as chief of staff. The QMG received £60 bounty (plus £123 regimental bounty as colonel of the 5th Dragoon Guards). There was an adjutant general (a brigadier with £60 Blenheim bounty), a deputy judge advocate, a provostmaster general, wagonmaster general, a physician and a surgeon to the captain general (most of them £30), all of whom supervised subordinates. Adam de Cardonnel's service as the duke's secretary (£30) involved a massive correspondence in several languages, day after day for years on end. Dr Francis Hare (£20), chaplain general from July 1704 onwards, assisted with the war diary. Marlborough's eight ADCs with the rank of colonel or lieutenant colonel received £30 apiece.

Generals held no specific commands though they did serve on rosters as 'General of the Day' (Blenheim bounties were £360 for general, £240 lieutenant general and £120 major general, plus regimental bounties as colonels). A brigade being the largest formation, there were brigadiers (£90) and brigade majors (rewarded with £30 each). In addition the artillery train (a part of the Ordnance, not the Army), which included engineers, bridgers and pontoon units, was under a colonel (whose Blenheim bounty at £75 was £15 less than that of the fighting brigadiers).

Besides his military staff Marlborough relied upon several civilian or Treasury servants who were in post on the Continent, notably Sweet in the Netherlands and Davenant in Frankfurt; both men were constantly employed in raising credit, furnishing money and arranging supplies for the army when it was in their respective theatres.

Marlborough was famous for his care over the army's food and forage whether in camp or on the march. When in 1712 Marlborough's enemies sought to arraign him for malversation of funds over bread contracts and the contracts for hiring foreign troops, he made a remarkable statement to Parliament. He showed that the commission he received on these contracts had been used by him for intelligence payments, and that it had been authorized by the Treasury and had been granted to his predecessors. (In reply Parliament still censured him for it, then granted the same commission to his successor.) He demonstrated that the bread price for British troops was as low as for the frugal Dutch, that two different prices for the same ration of bread would have provoked a mutiny, concluding: 'the whole affair has been so regulated, and there has been so little occasion for complaint, that it is well known that our army in Flanders has been duly supplied with bread during the whole war, and has received it with an exactness that will hardly be thought consistent with the secrecy and suddenness of some of the motions [marches] that have been made'. It was true, and it did not happen by chance.

Marlborough profoundly understood the complex system he inherited. He made few changes. Nevertheless, he made it work better than ever before. He made everything work by constant supervision, encouragement and remark day after day for ten years. Nothing was too much trouble. No aspect of his army's needs could escape his notice for long, and it was for the well-being of officers, 'the poor men', and widows and orphans. Lord Ailesbury may have overstated matters slightly in saying that 'for natural good temper [Marlborough] never had his equal, ... in command he could not give a harsh word, no not to the meanest Serjeant, Corporal, or soldier', but this agrees with other accounts of his geniality and kindliness. Because as a commander he was as humane as he was inspiring, Marlborough's word of surprise or his expression of disappointment sufficed to make subordinates do better. And so it was that Marlborough's army came to respond so well.

PART THREE

The first two years of war

CHAPTER 6

The First Campaigns, 1702–03

THE DAY AFTER ANNE'S ADDRESS to Parliament her captain general, the Earl of Marlborough, with the coveted Garter as the new queen's first gift, sailed for Holland to concert strategy. War was formally declared two months later (15 May) but thereafter six campaigning weeks passed in haggling over an Allied supreme commander for Flanders: Anne desired this for her adored husband, with Marlborough commanding the English forces. The horrified Dutch made their commander Nassau-Saarbruck a field marshal to block Anne's claim, then offered a compromise: that Marlborough, without being Dutch deputy captain general, should command Dutch troops when combined with English forces in the field, but would have to consult with the four field deputies. The compromise was formally ratified by all parties on 3 July.

France had begun operations as far back as April, with three armies under Marshal Boufflers between the Channel and Cologne, and a fourth on the upper Rhine. Boufflers advanced down the Meuse/Maas and early in June surprised an Anglo-Dutch force under Lord Athlone (one of William III's trusted Dutchmen who had been preferred to Marlborough for the Irish command in 1691) and drove it to Nymegen, where the Dutch insisted on a passive defence, avoiding battle. When Marlborough finally escaped The Hague in July and reached the front, his proposals for action were blocked; certainly Marlborough's skill was yet untried but there was also jealousy and Athlone often successfully opposed Marlborough's plans.

Activity on the middle Rhine by the Imperial commander Margrave Lewis of Baden obliged Boufflers to divert troops there from Holland. Marlborough gained approval to move, marching almost 50 miles south to Boufflers's rear; the latter turned, seeking the safety of a river line, 40 miles westward. On 2 August Marlborough's army, in battle formation, saw the tired and numerically weaker French straggling across its front: a future French marshal admitted, 'we were posted in such a manner that we should have been beaten without being able to stir'. Marlborough's council of war declined to risk battle. Shortly afterwards, Boufflers attempted to regain the initiative and capture an Allied supply convoy. Marlborough concentrated; the French closed on the convoy only to find Marlborough awaiting them (23 August). Battle lines were formed and artillery began firing, but despite Marlborough's order the Dutch commander on the right wing refused to attack, the field deputies checked all action and Boufflers decamped intact – followed by Marlborough's trumpeter carrying an apology for such inactivity.

So in late August Marlborough turned to capture the forts along the Meuse, a task he entrusted to the Dutch generals. The Dutch were slow and their generals Nassau-Saarbruck and Athlone sought to frustrate Marlborough's intentions. 'If this [a ten-day delay in opening trenches to besiege Venlo] be zeal, God preserve me from being so served as you are, my friend', Marlborough wrote to Heinsius, and later he twice hinted that unless matters improved he might not return the next year. But by the end of October, with three fortresses taken and Liège capitulating, Marlborough had in four months completely freed more than 100 miles of the Meuse from Nymegen almost to the French frontier: at least for the moment, Holland had been saved. Athlone recanted: 'The success of this campaign is solely due to this incomparable chief, since I confess that I, serving as second-in-command, opposed in all circumstances his opinions and proposals.'

Returning from the front to The Hague in November 1702, Marlborough was ambushed by an enemy patrol and taken prisoner. By amazing chance he was not recognized and was allowed to go free. When he reached The Hague 'I was not ashore one minute before I had great crowds of the common people, some endeavouring to take me by the hands, all crying out welcome. But that which moved me most was to see a great many of both sexes cry for joy.' Marlborough has always been a distant figure to his own countrymen, but for one brief moment in a foreign country he prefigured Nelson at the harbour steps before his final voyage, or Winston in London during the Blitz: a talisman and a blessing whom the people he had saved wished to touch and hold.

Elsewhere matters went badly. An Anglo-Dutch expedition to take Cadiz, close to the bullion port of San Lucar and intended as a base where Allied fleets could overwinter, proved a fiasco. Returning home, the expedition's leaders, Rooke and Ormonde, partially redeemed themselves by the fortuitous capture or sinking of the Spanish treasure fleet in Vigo harbour. In Italy Eugene had fought a punishing, drawn battle in August, and had to hold on without resources. In September Elector Max Emmanuel of Bavaria had seized the Free City of Ulm on the upper Danube and declared himself on France's side. Shortly afterwards France's ablest general, Villars, inflicted a serious check on the margrave on the upper Rhine, so that only the Black Forest mountains separated Villars from Max Emmanuel and the road to Vienna.

Even so, the campaign of 1702 had been better than most of William's, and in December Anne rewarded Marlborough with a dukedom and an annual pension of £5,000. But his only surviving son died of smallpox (3 March 1703) and he and Sarah were crushed.

After a brief seclusion he resumed duty in mid March. Sarah seemed almost unhinged for a time; her personality underwent a disastrous change and she progressively became shrill, domineering and careless of others, too often making the lives of everyone a misery. Its consequences were far-reaching.

One great theme of 1703 was the growing crisis in Germany (dealt with in the next Part). In the Low Countries dissension marred Allied operations. Marlborough completed the conquest of the lower Rhine with the capture of Bonn in May, but he abandoned his plan to invade France via the Moselle because of problems with the German princes. He turned instead to his 'great design' for Flanders, trusting to co-operation from the Dutch generals Cohorn and Opdam. Marlborough would hold down French forces in eastern Belgium by threatening the Lines of Brabant, perhaps even forcing a battle. Cohorn would make a coastal thrust at the Ostend privateering base, drawing away French troops from Antwerp, which Opdam would then capture by pincer attacks. Cohorn soon abandoned the plan and went plundering inland, a matter of indifference to Antwerp's garrison which remained concentrated. Although Marlborough drew Marshals Villeroy and Boufflers back and forth in the east, Opdam's attempt to surprise Antwerp went awry and an alerted Boufflers rushed troops to Antwerp in time to shatter Opdam's army (30 June). Hearing of Boufflers' move Marlborough sent warnings, but his subsequent march to help could not make up lost time. The furious Dutch blamed him for delay, then vetoed his proposal to assault the Lines at Antwerp and pin the French against the Scheldt estuary.

Within weeks Marlborough found a weak point elsewhere in the Lines suitable for attack, but continuing recriminations led the Dutch to reject his plan and limit him to a minor siege. In mid August his next proposal to breach the Lines was also rejected by the Dutch although the English, Danish and German generals unanimously gave him written support. While the Allies finished the disappointing campaign by taking Limburg and Guelders to strengthen the Dutch frontiers, Marshal Villars had meanwhile plunged deep into Bavaria, and Marshal Tallard on the Rhine had taken Brisach and won a skilful victory at Spire (13 November) which doomed the Allied fortress of Landau. Two more routes into Germany were available to France for next year's campaign.

Portugal, forced by France into becoming the unwilling ally of the old enemy Spain, found that closing her ports to the Allies was ruining her economy. The naval predominance of the Maritime Powers led King Pedro II to join the Grand Alliance in May 1703 in return for foreign troops, subsidies, and promises of Spanish territory. Marlborough, aware of the darkening scene elsewhere, had pressed ministers to conclude the Portuguese alliance, 'for our affairs go very ill in Germany'; to assist the negotiations he accepted that some of his best regiments would go as part of a 12,000-man contingent. But fearful of being abandoned by the Allies, Pedro insisted that the Austrian Archduke Charles should come to Lisbon and be proclaimed king of all Spain and the Indies, thus also guaranteeing the land cessions. Kitchener's words of 1915 echo in the mind: 'unfortunately we have to make war as we must, not as we should like to'. Present dangers outweigh a future problem. For Portugal's importance to the Maritime Powers in breaching Bourbon trade barriers and creating a military diversion led the Allies to replace William III's Spanish 'partition' by a war-aim demanding an undivided inheritance, which would see two Habsburg brothers establishing a Vienna–Madrid 'axis', less dangerous only than one between Versailles and Madrid. It caused a major diversion of Allied land forces which could ill be spared, with campaigns in Portugal and eastern Spain absorbing more and more troops at the end of overlong supply lines. Against that, opening Brazil's gold mines meant that bullion and trade flowed once more to relieve England and Holland's economies, without which the cost of the war could not have been supported so successfully. And whereas

Land's End was some 1,250 miles from the Straits of Gibraltar, Lisbon was only some 330 miles off and could accommodate the Allied Mediterranean fleets in winter.

Marlborough now hoped for greater Anglo-Dutch naval pressure and longer presence in the Mediterranean. He looked towards Savoy where its duke, Victor Amadeus, was unwillingly yoked to France. Victor resented and feared French predominance in north Italy. Though the Imperialist armies under his cousin Eugene of Savoy lost ground in Italy in 1703, Victor held negotiations with Vienna and when Louis retaliated by seizing Savoyard troops, Victor joined the Grand Alliance (November 1703) in return for promises of land, and a subsidy from the Maritime Powers. For military support he relied upon Vienna, a nearly fatal mistake, for in 1704 Vienna faced disaster on the Danube and had no support to offer anyone anywhere.

PART FOUR

'To secure the liberties of Europe': the Blenheim campaign, 1704

CHAPTER 7

'The Affairs of Germany Require a Farther Help',

Winter 1703 into Spring 1704

BY LATE 1703 THERE WAS general gloom. Those who had advocated the 'Continental commitment' and England's part as a principal in the European war saw few signs of Dutch or Habsburg co-operation in 'the common cause', and feared rising discontent at home. In Holland there was grievous financial strain and doubts over how long she could maintain herself against France. Germany seemed in an even worse state. In March 1703 Marshal Villars had captured Kehl on the Rhine, by May he had joined the Elector of Bavaria at Ulm on the Danube and but for the Elector's disconcerting changes of plan (which caused blazing rows) their combined armies might have reached Vienna. Villars built a great entrenched camp on the Danube, smashed an Imperialist army at Höchstädt (20 September 1703) then resigned his army to a junior and more accommodating marshal, Marsin. Vienna was reprieved but not saved.

All through 1703 Count Wratislaw, the Imperial envoy to London, had pressed ministers for assistance to the emperor. He proposed a year-end meeting between Marlborough and the new president of the Imperial War Council, Prince Eugene. This did not take place, but Marlborough held long discussions with Austrian officials (with

Wratislaw present) when in October the Archduke Charles, the would-be Carlos III of Spain, came down the Rhine en route for England and Portugal. Yet in his report Marlborough said nothing of anyone's views over Germany, only that the Austrians wanted financial, military and naval assistance for the archduke's Iberian plans. The duke was certainly deeply uneasy over Germany and was tired of working in Belgium with Dutch generals, but if he had thoughts of going further than the Moselle or middle Rhine he kept them entirely secret.

With the coming of winter Marlborough returned home, depressed and dissatisfied but still speaking of serving next year. Sarah, mourning the adored son, increasingly neglected the queen and thus weakened their ties (ominously, Anne begged Sarah not to 'hinder' their living in friendship 'as we used to do'); before spring came Sarah was assailing her husband with accusations of adultery and demanding a new legal settlement. The bewilderment and misery in his letters to her early in 1704 cannot have been totally thrown off when he moved from private to public concerns, and yet at this time he was trying to establish a plan to reverse the misfortunes suffered by the Alliance in the previous year, and somehow bring the partners to one mind. The discussions he held with Heinsius's envoys, with Godolphin and with Wratislaw required the most careful and cautious handling.

Marlborough was in The Hague for much of January and February 1704, taking soundings, maintaining his Continental contacts, and receiving from and sending to London a series of reports, requests and instructions. His help was sought on problems too important to ignore but all distracting. He was asked by the English ministry about finding troops to support the Protestant Cevennes rising inside France, and so he spent some time on negotiations to hire Prussian and Hessian troops, a negotiation that eventually came to nothing. There were fears that the French would invade Scotland, and he had to consider which of his regiments might have to be placed in readiness for recall.

Marlborough in these weeks also devoted much thought to the problems and prospects in the southern theatre. He was generally averse to setting out some world vision: his are occasional comments, almost in parenthesis. But that he had that vision is clear – for instance, his concern for Newfoundland fishing rights and the need to exclude the French from that area of the Atlantic. He recognized that Savoy was the fulcrum for the war in the south, swinging the balance towards the Alliance now – just as Victor Amadeus's quiescence late in the war enabled France to collect a sufficient army in the north. Writing to the already hard-pressed Victor in February 1704, Marlborough promised that he himself intended to act so powerfully as to prevent any French assistance going to Italy or the Empire, that the queen intended to send a strong fleet into the Mediterranean to assist Savoy's land schemes, with most of the fleet then to overwinter at Lisbon. In late March Marlborough agreed with Godolphin instructions for Admiral Rooke. The great French naval base of Toulon was to be seized jointly by Rooke and by Savoyard forces advancing from Nice. Sicily's ports should then be attacked and then Naples, all to assist the Austrians against the Spaniards. France's grip on the inland sea would be broken, the Cevennois rebels encouraged, and Allied movements in Italy, Sicily and along the eastern coast of Spain could take place unhindered by French naval action. This great scheme was acceptable to Victor Amadeus, and so when Marlborough marched from Holland on his German expedition it was in the belief that France would be distracted on several fronts at once.

In early summer 1704 Savoy drew back from the plan. By then Marlborough was in Swabia, and his letters neither make comment nor pass judgement on this disappointment. He promptly set out his views on what could be saved. As the Brest fleet was reportedly sailing for the Mediterranean, he proposed that Rooke should be reinforced to support operations on the Spanish coast. (Neither he nor anyone else planned the seizure of Gibraltar, and Rooke took it by a happy chance.) But Marlborough's main visions were always the destruction of France's Mediterranean naval base, and the acquisition of a safe port within that sea – a policy underlying the abortive attack on Toulon in 1707, and partly achieved by the British capture in 1708 of Minorca, under 300 miles from the French coast. His early sea service had taught him the complexities of sea operations, he had seen Minorca, and he understood the 'multiplying factor' of naval, military and diplomatic power in combination, an understanding which has earned him the highest praises of two outstanding historians of seapower, Sir Julian Corbett and Admiral Sir Herbert Richmond.

In the north two questions remained unresolved despite the weeks ticking away. The first was who should command in the German theatre, an appointment about which Vienna was as obsessed as it was undecided. The emperor's eldest son might have proved a socially impressive generalissimo, but he was unwilling to serve. The king of Prussia was keen to join as an independent commander, a prospect which put fear into the emperor. Queen Anne would not hear of George of Hanover. Prince Eugene was intent on leaving Vienna's War Council and returning to Italy. In mid January 1704 Marlborough let Wratislaw understand that he was ready to lead some forty-five battalions and fifty to sixty squadrons to the Moselle or the Rhineland, and he subsequently wrote to the principal commander in Germany, Margrave Lewis of Baden, asking for views on which river valley should be the preferred theatre. Lewis, a German noble, slightly younger than Marlborough but with longer command experience from the Turkish wars, was jealous of his junior, Eugene, and had quarrelled to the point of total rupture with the commander of the Dutch contingent attached to his Rhine army. His lands being sandwiched between France and Bavaria, he was half suspected of links with Elector Max of Bavaria. Marlborough had formed a poor opinion of Lewis's skill and commitment in 1703, but he was indispensable on the Rhine and could materially affect for good or ill operations in Swabia and Franconia. Marlborough courted and flattered him, although telling Wratislaw that he would expect a command independent of Lewis.

The second problem was Holland's fears for its southern borders. Marlborough was sympathetic to the Dutch over their growing financial exhaustion, the evidence of which he said was visible in the streets, and he warned Godolphin that more of the financial burden would have to be assumed by England, since the two countries' fates were intertwined. But in military matters Dutch fears would nullify his plans. The split between their general and the margrave made them wish to withdraw their troops from the middle Rhine and they were fearful about Marshal Villeroy, who, with sixty battalions and ninety-one squadrons, was restoring French positions in Flanders and Brabant. Marlborough differed from the Dutch over the marshal's probable intentions, but although he felt Villeroy was unlikely to attack, the duke ordered Cadogan to ensure Allied magazines were fully replenished in good time. To cover that frontier while leaving himself some freedom of movement he floated the idea of two Dutch contingents, one of 'position' in Flanders under Dutch generals, the other under himself 'on the Moselle'.

Marlborough in his discussions with his closest confidants in London had only mentioned Germany's Moselle and Rhine fronts. He told Wratislaw that the former would be the main theatre. Judging from his correspondence he was prepared only to speak of matters which required immediate decision, and of course he was careful not to stir fears unnecessarily in Sarah's mind. But on 12 February 1704 came two significant declarations, one to Sarah, the other to Mr Secretary Hedges. Writing from The Hague he warned Sarah that 'the affairs of Germany require a farther help. My only hope is that we have a just cause, and that God Almighty will enable us, some way or other, to secure the liberties of Europe.' That final phrase implied that he meditated something vast and truly decisive, but exactly what he still did not say, and 'Germany' is a broad term. But on that same day Marlborough, in his letter to Hedges, wrote the name 'Bavaria', ostensibly in a diplomatic context; for the Prussians had opened talks with the Bavarian Elector, seeking to woo him over to the Allies, and Marlborough shrewdly suspected that the Elector would draw out the discussions and subtly outwit them. He had written to Berlin praising this initiative while offering to help; in parallel he also pressed Queen Anne, through Hedges, for independent powers to treat directly with the Elector. He had fixed on his military mission.

During his weeks at The Hague Marlborough was also busy handling financial questions. He loved and understood money; he had been a most successful governor of the Hudson's Bay Company during a period of expansion and rising dividends, 1685–92; he studied and profited from the Amsterdam money market. This gave to his military and diplomatic ideas an additional dimension unusual among his military contemporaries, and one which he used wisely in preparing for his long march. He negotiated on the market an urgent loan to Swabia and the emperor, security for which was the emperor's quicksilver-mine production – a favour which later ensured local co-operation when his troops were marching across Germany. In London Marlborough attended Godolphin's departmental meetings on finance for operations in 1704. He was also present when contracts with the entrepreneurs Machado and Medina for bread and 250 bread wagons were agreed, those present including Blathwayt the Secretary at War, Pauncefoot the deputy paymaster general, Sweet the paymaster from Amsterdam, besides Marlborough and Cardonnel and Medina.

In March Marlborough dropped some of his reticence with the Dutch, mentioning his negotiations with Prussia, Württemberg and Hesse to hire more troops. He now disclosed to Heinsius the Prussians' Bavarian negotiations, adding that as German rulers thought a Moselle campaign was essential, the queen had given him full powers to decide with the Dutch how many of her troops could go to the aid of the Empire. For Wratislaw and Godolphin and Marlborough had now concerted terms.

On 2 April Wratislaw presented a memorial to Queen Anne requesting that she should send Marlborough to concert with the Dutch on 'the speediest method for assisting the Empire', or at least 'to conduct part of her troops to preserve Germany' from total ruin by French armies. The queen's reply promised using every effort with the Dutch to ensure urgent assistance. On 4 April Marlborough sent both documents to Heinsius for communication to the States General, and he applied pressure for an end to vagueness and indecision by emphasizing that unless 'the reduction of the Elector of Bavaria' was achieved, 'all things must go wrong', also that England would have taken the decision unilaterally had he not insisted that Holland be consulted. To Hop, the Dutch Treasurer, he wrote that the queen was 'so determined to do everything for the common cause that if public funds are inadequate [for providing troops] she is ready to use her own money'. On 8 April Godolphin authorized a remittance to Amsterdam of £100,000 campaign money. On 20 April Marlborough, his staff and Wratislaw reached Holland.

But would the Dutch co-operate? For ten days Marlborough encountered solid opposition. They insisted that the main army should be on the Meuse with only a smaller one of 15,000 men on the Moselle. The stress was intense. He was racked by nervous headaches. Funds promised from London were slow in coming, and Marlborough had to negotiate with local bankers for a three-month loan, explaining to the Treasury in London the complex expedients to which he was reduced, for he was already in arrears when he should have possessed a month's funding in advance. Margrave Lewis failed to send his strategical ideas for a Rhine campaign, though intelligence did come of Bavarian preparations and of French concentration in Alsace under Tallard. After long debate the only Dutch decision was merely not to withdraw their forces from the Rhine.

This could not continue. On 2 May, backed by Heinsius and three of the better Dutch generals, Marlborough brought the interminable speeches to a stop: it was the queen's command, he said, that he should go to Coblenz [at the confluence of the Rhine and Moselle] with his English troops and those in English pay. There was silence. Next day the Dutch graciously accepted his decision. They did at least permit him to take those foreign units for which they jointly paid.

What the States General never knew was that on 29 April Marlborough had written to the queen and Prince George (the letter was ostensibly to Godolphin) that once at Coblenz he intended to march 'for the speedy reducing of the Elector of Bavaria'; adding three days later that 'when I shall come to Philippsburg [on the Rhine, 13 miles south of Heidelberg] if the French shall have joined any more troops [to] the Elector of Bavaria, I shall make no difficulty of marching directly to the Danube' and that as it is entirely for the queen's service, 'I do no ways doubt that Her Majesty will approve it, for I am very sensible that I take a great deal upon me'. To the Secretary of State Marlborough in his official dispatch of 2 May merely wrote of 'my resolution of going to the Moselle' and it was not until mid month that he confided to another Cabinet minister that his 'real intentions' – to be kept secret from the Dutch until he should have passed Coblenz – were to go 'much higher into Germany, even to the Danube … I should not be thus rash in taking all this upon myself were I not very confident that, if I did not make this march, the Empire must be ruined … If unlucky I must endure the malice of my enemies.'

Sarah had let him leave England without a word of comfort. On 2 May he wrote that 'I intend to go higher up into Germany … Whatever happens to me I beg you will believe that my heart is entirely yours, and that I have no thoughts but what is for the good of my country. Remember me kindly to my dear children.'

CHAPTER 8

'Over the Hills and Far Away',
May and June

THE ENGLISH CONTINGENT had already begun to march on the assembly point at Maastricht and the duke joined them there on 10 May. In addition to handling the details which accumulate as a campaign begins, Marlborough attended to Dutch worries, and sought to insert himself into the Bavarian negotiations. To reassure the Dutch he left them not only their Scots Brigade but six English battalions and fourteen squadrons. Fearing that the Prussians would prove no match for Elector Max Emmanuel's adroitness, Marlborough obtained Anne's authority to treat personally with the Elector, and the Dutch granted him general authority to act as he thought best in this matter 'without their being acquainted with the particulars'. Meanwhile, when deferentially asking the Prussian king for his ideas about the Moselle, Marlborough remarked that it would be the greatest pleasure in the world if the king felt he could be of service in the Bavarian negotiations.

Although at the time his army began moving from the Netherlands towards some unknown destination the queen and Godolphin were party to his plans, the Cabinet had not been told, and of course nor had Parliament. The risk was overwhelmingly Marlborough's. He was deliberately marching an English army farther from its base than any since the Black Prince's Spanish expedition more than three centuries earlier. For the first part at least it would be a flank march across the north-eastern bastion of the French frontier, from which he might be attacked in strength. His personal contacts made him think that the German provinces through which he was to march and where he planned to purchase supplies would be able and willing to meet his needs. He hoped that once in Bavaria his and the emperor's joint pressure would induce the Elector to change sides and push the French back to the Rhine. But the emperor was bankrupt and unreliable in performance of his obligations, while his principal commander, the Margrave Lewis, kept alarmingly silent as to his views and intentions: all that Marlborough possessed was Wratislaw's word of honour that there would be full co-operation. If Marlborough should not succeed in Germany his career and even his life would be at the mercy of Parliament; should he suffer defeat his army might be irretrievably broken and scattered.

Clearly Marlborough had faith in himself in marching so large a proportion of the English Army into southern Germany. But if his expedition were to meet disaster the emperor would be defenceless against the French, Bavarians and Hungarians, the Dutch would face invasion or a 'diktat' peace, and the prospects for England – with Louis planning to restore 'James III' by invasion – would have been as desperate as those of the summer of 1940. Taking English infantry as a yardstick: there currently existed four battalions of Guards and twenty-nine senior line battalions (i.e. raised before 1695), plus twenty-two battalions raised since 1701. The West Indies garrison had three battalions (all senior), there were six battalions (one senior) aboard the fleets, Portugal had seven battalions (five senior) and was to lose two senior battalions by capture in June 1704. None of these forces could be called back quickly. Distant Bavaria would now account for another fourteen (of which one was newly raised), representing 25 per cent of total infantry and 40 per cent of the Guards/senior category. In Flanders there indeed stood six battalions (one senior) doubling as cover for Holland and emergency reserve for England, but apart from them there remained to guard the British Isles (where England's extremity was Highland Scotland's and Ireland's Jacobite opportunity) only nineteen battalions (nine new), invalid companies and the militia. The Navy might have saved Britain from invasion but France would have dominated Europe, its money markets and all trade. These infantry figures are a measure of the risk Marlborough chose to take 'for the common cause'.

At least the duke's mind was relieved of one anxiety, for Sarah suddenly realized the dangers he was facing, and sent a letter of love and reconciliation which he received on the day he started for Maastricht. 'This dear dear letter' transformed him and, with her subsequent loving letters, must have sensibly affected his perceptions and his inward resolve during the setbacks of the campaign: 'Love me always as I think you now do', he replied, 'and no hurt can come to me.'

A PURELY CHRONOLOGICAL ACCOUNT of the Blenheim campaign would produce a daily kaleidoscope of negotiation with German potentates and Dutch statesmen, the provisioning arrangements during the slow advance upriver and over the hills to the Danube, delicate and shifting relations between equal and independent high commanders, disagreements and disappointments over strategy, and all complicated by opposing plans and movements by the French and Bavarians. For the 1711 campaign (see Part Six) the mind of the commander is best studied daily moving between concerns as they distractingly arise. For 1704 it may be easier if the strands of narrative are disentangled, and this chapter deals with topography, the *étapes* of Marlborough's march, marching times and distances, and welfare on the march. What assessments and suspicions the French formed, and how they reacted, are dealt with in the next chapter.

In planning his march Marlborough started from German maps and the advice provided by his Allies, and in certain localities such as

Heidelberg he drew upon his own knowledge of western Germany, having campaigned there under Turenne thirty years before. Once embarked on the march he supplemented and improved this information with eyewitness reports from Cadogan's little group, who were reconnoitring ahead of Marlborough and the cavalry, and we see the duke repeatedly passing to the infantry and artillery trudging after him information on roads and steep places. The duke's maps were marked with the contemporary march scale, the league (3 miles), and comparison with modern surveys shows that this scale varied only slightly (between 2.5 and 3.5 modern English miles). The maps were also reasonably accurate for the main rivers and towns; the wealth of supplementary information on them may well have been due to Marlborough's careful statement of requirements and his wise expenditure of intelligence money for cartography. The relation of villages to each other was less accurate and the distances and bearings far from reliable, and sometimes streams could flow in the wrong direction. No heights or gradients were shown, nor any roads, though political boundaries were marked. These maps were therefore indicative, not definitive; but all travellers knew this and relied upon experience and reliable reporters for the necessary correction.

The geography of Marlborough's march needs to be kept constantly in mind, and since he was generally marching upstream the description will follow rivers from their mouths upwards to their sources, against the true flow. The brief first stage was *down* the River Meuse/Maas from Maastricht and then eastwards over heath and moorland to Bedburg, where the Rhine is at about 250 feet above sea level. From Bedburg south to Coblenz the mountains of the Eifel and the Westerwald confine the river and road. The Moselle wriggles out of the Eifel at Coblenz, having started west of the Vosges and passing Metz and Luxembourg. From this junction the Rhine ascends in a great curve south and then east until it is joined by the River Main at Mainz, but Marlborough was able to cut the arc of the great river by routes across hills upon whose steep flanks cling vineyards. South of Mainz the Rhine flows straight for over 50 miles in a wide, flat plain, bordered by an escarpment to its east: at that time the plain was marshy with occasional river crossings, all strongly defended. The northern edges of the Black Forest barrier soon begin to hem in this plain, and here German defences relied upon the riverside fortress of Philippsburg and somewhat further south the 7 miles of Margrave Lewis's defensive lines across the plain from Stollhofen to Bühl. Only if these fell could the French safely move northward round the Black Forest into Württemberg; likewise, a German army in these positions posed a threat to the French in Landau and Strasbourg on the west bank of the Rhine.

Some 18 miles north of Philippsburg the Rhine is joined by the River Neckar, which flows west from the escarpment into the plain. Following the Neckar upstream a traveller will find it gradually turning south-east and then south, before continuing south-west to its spring only a short distance east of the Danube's source in the Black Forest. Only a line of low mountains, the Swabian Jura, separates the basins of the two rivers. In its central section the Neckar offers a useful north–south corridor. Marlborough took the chord of the Neckar's arc by cutting straight across country from the lower river until he met it again high on this central stretch. Further south upriver and just as the Neckar turns west, one of its own tributaries, the River Fils, comes from the south-east and meets it at Plochingen. The Fils and its streams mount to their sources in the eastern Swabian Jura, the last line of heights before the Danube valley: a traveller who has mounted the Fils until reaching the pass of Gieslingen close to its source finds himself at this point only 17 miles from Ulm on the Danube.

Much of the country between Coblenz and Mainz comprises hills at some 600 to 800 feet altitude. The Rhine escarpment in the next stretch stands some 500 to 700 feet above the flat plain, and once across that wall at Wiesloch (about 600 feet) and into the country

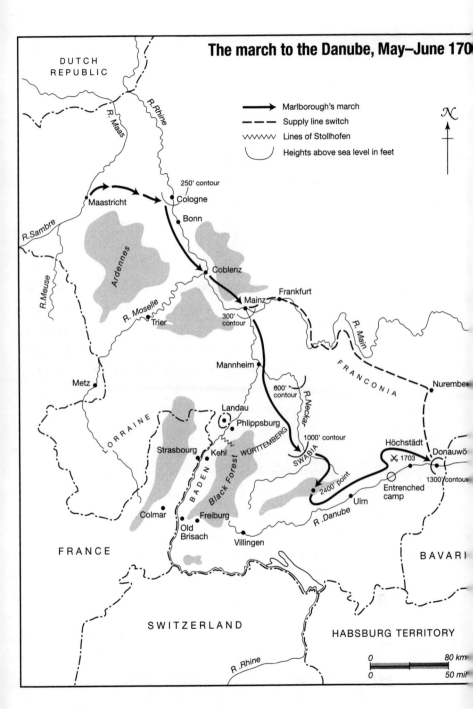

The march to the Danube, May–June 170[

→ Marlborough's march
- - - Supply line switch
ⵡⵡⵡ Lines of Stollhofen
◡ Heights above sea level in feet

𝒩

DUTCH REPUBLIC

R. Maas
R. Rhine
R. Sambre
R. Meuse
Maastricht
Cologne
250' contour
Bonn
Ardennes
Coblenz
R. Moselle
Trier
Mainz
Frankfurt
300' contour
R. Main
Mannheim
FRANCONIA
Metz
Nuremberg
600' contour
R. Neckar
LORRAINE
Landau
Phlippsburg
1000' contour
Strasbourg
Kehl
WÜRTTEMBERG
Höchstädt
✗ 1703
Donauwö
BADEN
SWABIA
Black Forest
Entrenched camp
1300' contour
2400' point
Colmar
Freiburg
Ulm
R. Danube
Old Brisach
Villingen
FRANCE
BAVARI
SWITZERLAND
HABSBURG TERRITORY
R. Rhine

0   80 km
0   50 mil

96

inside the great bend of the Neckar, the roads run at about 700–850 feet through hills and small valleys. The River Fils joins the Neckar at about 780 feet and in the next 20 miles it rises to about 1,300 feet, an average gradient of 1 in 200, though the hills on either side rise steeply in places. Only in the final 5-mile climb to the pass of Gieslingen at more than 2,000 feet is the going really difficult: after that the descent is relatively easy, for the Danube at Ulm flows at about 1,500 feet. As Hilaire Belloc pointed out in his study of Marlborough's campaigns, gradients and pulls as at Gieslingen are not unfamiliar to modern hikers in England, and he instanced Leith Hill above the Surrey Weald; Dunster to Dunkery by the Avill valley, or Robin Hood's Bay to Blea Rig on Fylingdales similarly come to mind.

The Romans had driven military roads beyond the Rhine in their wars with the Teutonic tribes, but the dilapidations of 1,400 years had been worsened by generations of French and Imperialist armies passing along them, burning the villages and crippling the rural economy. The 'roads' along which thousands of Marlborough's infantry, cavalry, artillery and impedimenta stumbled and staggered were beaten earth tracks along which wooden-wheeled carts and wagons pulled by horses or oxen, and droves of cattle and sheep, had travelled: irregular, swampy in places, churned up – and also liberally caked in animal droppings. Baked into dust and firm ruts in dry weather, in wet they must have become sloughs or minor streams.

The queen's forces comprised fourteen battalions and nineteen squadrons. To this must be added the Allied contingents. Estimates vary as to the English strength: Fortescue put it at 16,000; C.T. Atkinson at 14,000 all ranks (using the Blenheim Bounty Roll, plus Schellenberg losses, plus wastage on the march). David Chandler put the starting strength of the *total* force (all nationalities) at 21,000 all ranks (thirty-one battalions, sixty-six squadrons), and Ivan Phelan in his logistical study accepted this, and further estimated well over 2,000 chargers for officers and staff and cavalry, and 10,000 horses for supply wagons and the train. This included thirty-eight English and eleven Dutch field guns, plus some howitzers (Fortescue cites a newsletter saying fifty-two guns); there was no heavy siege artillery with the expedition since the Austrians had undertaken to provide that. The state of the tracks by the time the rear formations reached them is almost impossible to imagine. Heavy equipment, the hospital and stores had already moved from Holland, initially by barge.

The bulletins published by the army record that it left Maastricht on 15 May, reached Bedburg on the 18th (in total 35 miles), moved up the Rhine valley to a site west of Bonn (25 miles) by the 21st, having rested on the 17th and 19th. The concern that French troops might cross into southern Germany, and the state of the roads along his line of march, obliged Marlborough as early as 25 May to divide his forces; he himself rode ahead with his cavalry the sooner to join with the Imperial forces in the south, while the foot and artillery followed on more slowly in several parallel columns under the command of his younger brother General Charles Churchill. On that day Marlborough and the cavalry were near Coblenz (another 34 miles), while the infantry were marching upon Andernacht, 10 miles north of the city. He had written to the Elector of Trier on 19 May that in eight days he should reach Coblenz, and requested him meanwhile to construct a bridge over the Rhine to speed the march; to save the local population from harassment he sent ahead a senior quartermaster to concert delivery of supplies for the troops. By the time he reached Coblenz two bridges of boats spanned the Rhine, near the old stone bridge across the Moselle. Up to this point an observer could assume that the Moselle was indeed Marlborough's objective; certainly his soldiers thought so. Only when the troops stepped onto the temporary bridges did it seem that Alsace and the upper Rhine might be the duke's destination, and this idea was encouraged by Marlborough, who ordered another bridge of boats to be assembled near Philippsburg, facing France.

From Coblenz the duke's forces took the chord of the arc across the hills and valleys, latterly in very bad weather. The cavalry came down from the hills to Mainz on the 29th and the remainder of the expedition arrived a day later. On the last day of May 1704 the cavalry crossed the River Main, the remainder of the army crossing four days later, much impeded by the state of the roads. Private Deane of the 1st Guards noted these as the worst marching conditions within memory.

South of Mainz Marlborough's army moved up the Rhine at the foot of the escarpment until it came to where the River Neckar flows west from the hills. The cavalry found awaiting them a bridge of boats on the Neckar at Ladenburg (6 miles north-west of Heidelberg) and crossed it on 3 June, then camped while the auxiliaries came in. On 7 June, thirty years to the month since he had last been there, Marlborough and the cavalry rode to Wiesloch, only 10 miles east of Philippsburg but perched on the high escarpment. Now he left the Rhine valley and swung south-east into country of rolling hills and streams. At long last the troops knew where they were going, 'High Germanie'. The secret of their destination seems to have been well kept from Marlborough's army, as the memoir-writing soldiers testify.

Marlborough again cut the chord of an arc, for he continued east to Gross Gartach and then turned upstream along the Neckar to Lauffen, where he crossed to the eastern (right) bank nearly 60 river miles above Ladenburg. On 9 June in fine weather which turned into extreme heat he continued upstream to Mundelsheim, camped, and there, at 5 p.m. on Tuesday 10 June, Marlborough first met his future comrade Prince Eugene of Savoy. The duke was now only 50 miles from the Danube at Ulm.

On 11 June he continued to Gross Heppach, staying there till the 14th, after which he left the Neckar at Plochingen for the route to the pass of Gieslingen. Here his German contingents joined him. On the 16th he marched to Gross Seissen. At this stage the weather changed again, bringing continual cold and rain for over ten days, and while Marlborough could at least have a fire in his quarters, 'the poor men' were subjected to cold, sodden camps and the inevitable sickness. It was in these conditions that the army hauled itself up the 700 feet to the pass at Gieslingen, a task requiring two days for some 7 miles (21–22 June); for the artillery labouring behind, the conditions must have been indescribable.

Once beyond the pass Marlborough met with the main Imperial forces under the margrave. The two armies moved down towards the Danube. Danish and Prussian units also joined the duke, and by the last days of June plans were being concerted for the invasion of Bavaria. The long approach march was over.

MARLBOROUGH'S DISPATCHES show how constant was his attention to the fitness of his men on this march. In May he was careful to rest the 'equipage' [wagons and train] when he found them 'extremely harassed' by weather and roads. Because he himself travelled with the cavalry there is little recorded on their problems, but on 3 June Marlborough asked his brother about the condition of the infantry and the places Charles planned to reach each night, and sent him advice on the best route to follow; on the 8th he advised him on how to conciliate a local ruler, and also asked him to establish how many replacement shoes his men would need, told him how to order them from the English agents at Frankfurt, and where they could be delivered; on the 18th, having previously warned his brother not to overstretch his men and horses on the march, he gave instructions for the artillery to hire as many contractors' horses as possible for the long pull up and over the Swabian Jura; on the 20th he gave further route details, repeated the need to take the mountain tracks slowly to 'ease' the men, warned him that there had been complaints made about a dispute between Charles's men and some local authorities over summarily requisitioning vehicles ('it will not look well that we should impose any hardships' on friendly people), and gave new instructions on baggage restrictions for officers;

the next day the duke sent instructions on hospital facilities and transport for the sick. When he assured Godolphin that he was taking all possible care of the men's wants he was telling no more than the truth.

For it is not the length of the march to the Danube, and certainly not the time it took, that is so remarkable: it is the superb condition of Marlborough's army at the end of its long trek. Yet it was neither by good luck nor by chance. Over a century later Clausewitz was to write of marches by Continental armies in the Napoleonic Wars, by which time roads had improved somewhat, and he emphasized the almost inexorable wastage, sickness, physical deterioration of man and beast, of carts and equipment, from lengthy marches. He cited the fifty-two summer days up to 15 August 1812 when, between the Niemen and Smolensk (350 miles), the *Grande Armée* suffered 10,000 casualties in minor operations but lost 95,000 men in wastage along the road – 'about one-third of the whole army'.[12] He cited a two-fifths wastage in Blücher's army in central Germany in 1813. In 1825 Wellington criticized the unnecessary 'over-marching' to which Napoleon subjected his army in 1812; later he commented on the Prussians' heavy wastage after Waterloo during the two-week march on Paris. That was the vicious Continental practice. Both Marlborough and Wellington ensured a more economical use of men, lighter wastage and a fitter fighting force.

The contrast is evident from Tallard's experience in June 1704. It has been said that his 160-mile advance from the Rhine to Augsburg in central Bavaria would have registered a greater daily mileage than Marlborough if he had not stopped six days to besiege Villingen (i.e. taking twenty days, or 8 miles per day if we exclude those six days). But 'fitness' and not 'speed' was what concerned Marlborough: for Tallard's wastage along the route amounted to one-third of his force. The experienced Prince Eugene was struck by the health, smartness and 'lively air' of Marlborough's cavalry when he saw them at Gross Heppach on the 24th day after 220 miles of march.[13] Diarists and memoir writers who marched with Marlborough's infantry single out the careful planning of their marches, of the well-appointed camp-sites ready to receive them, of the general sense of thoughtful attention in the arrangements. Captain Parker's remarks are rightly famous:

> We frequently marched three, sometimes four days, successively, and halted a day. We generally began our march about three in the morning, proceeded about four leagues, or four and half each day, and reached our ground about nine [12–14 miles in 6 hours]. As we marched through the Countries of our Allies, Commissaries were appointed to furnish us with all manner of necessaries for man and horse; these were brought to the ground before we arrived, and the soldiers had nothing to do, but to pitch their tents, boil their kettles, and lie down to rest. Surely never was such a march carried on with more order and regularity, and with less fatigue both to man or horse.

Parker was writing after the lapse of many years, and Private Deane preferred to emphasize the hardships when commenting in his journal:

> it hath rained 32 days together, more or less, and miserable marches we have had for deep and dirty roads and through tedious woods and wildernesses and over vast high rocks and mountains, [so] that it may be easily judged what our little army endured and what unusual hardships they went through. And to help, everything grew to be at an excessive dear rate that there was scarce living for a soldier ...

But the fact remains that at the end of its 300-mile approach march Marlborough's army, which had started from Holland in May with 21,000 men, had lost only 1,200 men sick (plus a few deserters), and was fresh and fit for hard fighting in southern Germany. That is a record not approached by any other army of the time.

CHAPTER 9

'The Watch on the Rhine',
May and June

WHEN MARLBOROUGH LEFT THE HAGUE on 5 May, the question of command in Germany was still unresolved. Margrave Lewis maintained a total silence on this and all aspects of the campaign. Wratislaw knew that Marlborough was indispensable and that he would not serve under Lewis, but the emperor was notoriously incapable of reaching decisions on such matters. Together the duke and Wratislaw sought to force the margrave's hand, Wratislaw delivering a letter from Marlborough disclosing his intention of marching to Bavaria, but emphasizing that in some twelve weeks he would have to return to Belgium with his forces: 'around the end of July'.

The Dutch had understood that Marlborough was marching no further east than Coblenz and the Moselle, and had let him depart with the queen's troops plus her (and some of their) auxiliaries, subject to leaving six English battalions in Flanders. But the States General were fearful of a French attack from Flanders, and Heinsius therefore extracted a promise from Marlborough that the troops would return downriver if the French should attack; and Marlborough duly arranged for the assembly of a flotilla of boats capable of carrying his troops back at 80 miles per day. What he would have done if such a call had been sent him is a question now beyond answer; but had he obeyed, the fate of the Empire might have been sealed. For a northern counterstroke was an option favoured by Marshal Tallard. On 2 May, the very day Marlborough told the Dutch of his Moselle decision, Tallard in Strasbourg had written to Versailles reporting growing rumours of Marlborough and the Dutch marching into the Empire to overwhelm the Elector of Bavaria. Tallard suggested that, though his patron Villeroy was better informed than he on matters in the north, French thrusts down the Moselle towards Jülich or down the Meuse and then to Aix-la-Chapelle would cause the Dutch to call everyone back from the German expedition. Fatally, Louis XIV decided that Villeroy should do nothing except make his Belgian defensive lines more secure. Villeroy, never a bold general, failed to act positively when proof of Marlborough's march did reach him: initially he sent about 5,000 troops to watch the Moselle; only belatedly did he himself move, and even then not against Belgium but towards the middle Rhine.

For the next two months the merits of defending the Rhine as against those of taking Bavaria were to complicate and threaten Allied plans. Lewis of Baden broke silence just as Marlborough's troops left Bedburg, reporting that Tallard had moved towards the Lines of Stollhofen, possibly the commencement of a major French offensive into Germany. The ever-accommodating duke diverted Dutch, Hanoverian and Hessian units to his assistance for a few weeks, but he particularly instructed their commanders to rejoin him near Philippsburg by 8 June, warning Wratislaw in Frankfurt that if Lewis kept these troops it would 'entirely derange the whole plan of campaign' and that he counted on Wratislaw's word that he would keep the margrave under control and prevent all that could counter the plan. To the existing problem of command was added potential conflict over strategy.

In reality, Tallard's moves towards Stollhofen were mere feints. On 13 May, two days before the margrave wrote his appeal to

Marlborough, Tallard's main force of 18,000 men crossed the Rhine some 60 miles south of Stollhofen, slipped past Freiburg and took the tracks into the Black Forest. In five days he brought a vast convoy – nearly 10,000 infantry (mainly recruits), 2,400 cavalry, a company of trained armourers, 200 draught horses, equipment and a large sum of cash – 42 miles of mountain tracks to Villingen, a remarkable feat. At Villingen on 18 May he met the Bavarian Elector and Marshal Marsin, who had marched 75 miles westwards with 30,000 men and many wagons. Tallard was pursued by the margrave, but with a delay of at least two days and by a longer route; an Imperialist force from the Danube joined Lewis at Rottweil, only 10 miles north of Villingen, on 19 May. Lewis now had 40,000 men and none of the impedimenta burdening the French, but by error and mischance he never quite caught up with the convoy hastening on to Bavaria. As a result, the balance in the Danube valley was even more weighted against the emperor.

Marshal Tallard returned to the Rhine valley, and now fell prey to Marlburian deception and poor French intelligence. The decoy pontoon bridges Marlborough had placed on the Rhine at Philipps-burg alarmed Tallard, so he took care to cover Landau while awaiting Villeroy's arrival. On 4 June, the day after Marlborough's expedition finally disclosed its ultimate destination by turning away from the Rhine and crossing the River Neckar, and on the day when the duke wrote to the English government that 'I now expect in ten days to be upon the Danube', Tallard wrote to Marsin in Bavaria that there could be no question of Marlborough going to the Danube, for the wastage of troops from straggling, sickness and the attacks of the peasantry had too much reduced his strength. This information was confirmed by 'deserters', who may have been primed for the purpose; it drew upon French experience of a hostile peasantry and their assumption that Marlborough must encounter the same enmity, would adopt French methods of requisition, and would inflict the same severe French march routines as Tallard.

If this misreading was helpful to the Allied plans, Lewis's sense of pride and grasp of priorities were not. When Marlborough learned of Tallard's junction with Marsin and the Elector at Villingen he warned London and The Hague that the Empire now risked complete destruction, that it was essential that he reach the Danube, but that the margrave (who was now deep inside Germany) wished him to command on the Rhine instead. Marlborough now saw a new combination to be desirable: one army posted to hold Stollhofen, a second to act in southern Bavaria from a base between Ulm and Lake Constance, a third to enter northern Bavaria through Donauwörth: the second and third forcing Elector Max to come to terms before any further reinforcement could reach him from France. But energy was vital and Lewis's dilatoriness was ominous. Even his trustworthiness in Bavaria was coming into question. Marlborough's preferred solutions were diplomatic and military: diplomatic in that he pressed the queen urgently for plenary powers to negotiate independently and conclude a pact with Elector Max; military in that Wratislaw and he emphasized to the margrave and to the emperor that the Rhine command was so important to the empire that either Lewis (as senior Imperial general) or Prince Eugene should command there. As Lewis was jealous of Prince Eugene, this was a bait to encourage the margrave to take the 'senior' (and passive) command – but the duke was prepared for Lewis to command in southern Bavaria provided Marlborough should command in the north: and either way he was resigned to detaching a large contingent of his German auxiliaries to strengthen the Rhine. In the event Vienna ruled that the margrave should stay on the Danube while Eugene went to the Rhine.

If Wratislaw had failed in this, he yet brought consolations. He recognized that a bankrupt empire needed to acknowledge the value and price of a rich England's assistance, a value of which Marlborough was always conscious yet too wise to mention. He brought a letter in which the emperor declared his wish to create Marlborough a Prince of the Holy Roman Empire with lands and a vote in the Diet. Marlborough at once referred this to the ministry at home, but though he was desperately keen to accept the honour he had the self-command to insist that the moment was premature. Secondly, Wratislaw was able to assure him that though he was stuck with Lewis, the margrave's weaknesses were known to Vienna.

With Wratislaw came Eugene on his journey to the Rhine, and at last the two great commanders met. At this date Eugene had the longer and more distinguished fighting record and a reputation for victory in battle which Marlborough as yet did not possess, though the duke's experience of the toils of coalition command was probably rather greater. Marlborough employed deference and charm and quiet questioning to establish how far they could work harmoniously together. Instinctively their ideas on this campaign coincided. They liked and trusted each other, Eugene being struck by the administrative generalship which had maintained the fitness of the English troops on so long a march. He may even have been seduced by what Lord Chesterfield termed Marlborough's 'art of pleasing ... [which] he enjoyed and used more than ever man did': for we find Eugene writing a few weeks later that this Englishman was 'of high quality, courageous, extremely well disposed, and with a keen desire to achieve something, all the more as he would be ruined in England should he return empty-handed. With all these qualities he understands thoroughly that he cannot become a general in a day, and he is diffident about himself.' For his part Marlborough privately likened Eugene to his old ally the Duke of Shrewsbury ('the King of Hearts') but 'with the advantage of seeming franker'. Eugene's description of the state of affairs in Vienna and Germany alerted Marlborough that 'everything here is in a worse condition than I could have imagined, although I thought them very bad' and the Duke sent a cipher message to Godolphin that the emperor had given Eugene full powers to remove the margrave from command should he not act with zeal. So the fiery and abrupt Eugene and the charming and diplomatic Marlborough awaited the margrave's arrival to concert plans and test his resolve and good faith.

The next two weeks tried everyone's patience to the utmost. Eugene left for the Rhine after several days of delicate tripartite talks, taking with him the reinforcements offered by Marlborough. The forces destined for the invasion of Bavaria were now so reduced that Marlborough's earlier scheme for the two armies to operate as pincers from north and south had to be abandoned. Instead they had to be combined into a single army, with overall command being held on alternate days by the margrave and by Marlborough.

There is disagreement among historians regarding exactly what this alternating command really meant. In June Marlborough repeatedly stated to his correspondents and in the army bulletin that it meant 'each should have his day of command alternately while they are together', but three months earlier the minutes of the Vienna War Council had noted that the margrave had been ready only 'to divide' the command if the armies came together and 'to share' it in battle, with only the choice of the daily password or 'parole' alternating. In April and May the duke had been emphatic that his forces should not come under the margrave and that he himself should not serve under him, but these remarks refer surely to a permanent or 'duration of campaign' position. In the end a compromise was reached, possibly forced on the two generals by the proximity of an enemy sometimes only 'two leagues distant', a day's march away. It may be likened to a partnership in which by agreement one 'manages' and the other 'sleeps'. The separate instances of 25 June and 2 July 1704 seem conclusive: Lewis took command at midnight on 24–25 June for one day and promptly imposed a day of rest on the combined force; and as 25 June and therefore 1 July were Baden's days, so it confirms the statement in the semi-official 'Dr Hare's Journal' that it was 'his Grace's turn to command the army the next day [2 July]' when the

Schellenberg was attacked. But in both instances it is recorded that the commander of the day sought his partner's agreement concerning what he wished to do, and indeed no army could function within a day's march of the enemy if the intentions of one day were to be turned upside down the next. On 25 June all that was lost was one day's activity, a deferment that was worrying but might to some extent be rectified the next day; on 2 July no commander for the day could have risked a major battle without his partner's full agreement. (Moreover, Marlborough had experienced the same rotation of daily command when alongside the Duke of Württemberg at the siege of Cork in 1690, as a compromise between the English refusal to recognize the precedence of foreign commissions and the German aristocrat's dislike of conceding place to a mere English parvenu, though that parvenu had been appointed by King William himself.)

Marlborough's and the margrave's forces met and combined on 22 June, and though the margrave's was the smaller force yet the duke conceded to him the prestigious right of the line. Plans were laid to seek battle with the Franco-Bavarian forces north of the Danube and just east of Ulm in the next three days – requiring an approach march of just over 20 miles. At the moment that the margrave took over command for his day (25 June) he told Marlborough that he wished to rest the army for a day to mature a plan to take the Elector at a disadvantage. Wratislaw brought Marlborough the plan and recorded the duke's dismay and astonishment at its feebleness. The Dutch General Goor (who had long and bitter experience of service under the margrave) told Marlborough that Lewis had tried to prevent the approach march altogether. Far from taking the Elector at a disadvantage, the day's delay allowed him to retreat to his vast entrenched camp at Dillingen–Lauingen on the Danube. The duke saw himself in danger of being frustrated and even marooned in southern Germany by the very general the emperor had chosen for him, while by 29 June Wratislaw reported that Marlborough, though he would 'never break out publicly against the Margrave, but will on the contrary caress him on every possible occasion', was coming to the view that the next few days would show whether the margrave's actions would require his arrest or replacement by Eugene. For by then Marlborough determined to have forced the Danube crossing.

It is impossible to say whether Margrave Lewis meditated treachery or was merely unable to accept sharing command with either Eugene or Marlborough. That Lewis proposed dividing forces, leaving Marlborough to watch the entrenched camp while he himself with some more of Marlborough's units marched downstream to attack Bavaria, may indicate mere incompatibility. But in any case Marlborough suppressed his doubts. Now that Charles Churchill's infantry had come out of the mountains into the river valley, and as other detached units of Germans and Danes trickled in, Marlborough intended leaving the sparse lands of Swabia and the upper Danube, moving eastwards to a second supply line which had been established through Frankfurt and Nuremberg and which was in all respects easier to maintain. It would also bring him closer to the borders of Bavaria, the north-western gate of which was Donauwörth, some 15 miles downstream of the entrenched camp.

As early as 8 June the Duke had told Godolphin of his intention of taking Donauwörth: it was the final stage on the new line of communication from Nuremberg. Armed at last with Queen Anne's authority to conclude terms with the Elector, Marlborough in the final days of June insisted to Lewis that Donauwörth should be taken, the Danube crossed, and a conclusion sought with the Bavarian ruler. He added that the cold and heavy rains which had fallen for a fortnight would likewise make the Rhine less passable, thus depriving the Elector of succour from France and shaking his resolve. In the face of Marlborough's determination Lewis dropped all objections.

Until mid June the preferred French strategy was to threaten Mainz and central Germany rather than push directly to Bavaria. But an appeal from the Elector and Marshal Marsin beseeching help reached Versailles on 22 June, having been sent while Marlborough's army was still on the Neckar and well short of the pass through the Swabian Jura. Versailles reacted promptly and new orders reached Marshals Villeroy and Tallard in Alsace on the 27th. Villeroy was to feint against the Stollhofen position while Tallard was to move south to Freiburg, pass the Black Forest with fresh reinforcements and supplies, and march down the Danube. Tallard was dubious. He had undertaken a similar journey in May and it had cost him dear in men, horses and wagons. Yet once more he acted energetically, moving south from Kehl (opposite Strasbourg) on 1 July, and by the 5th had collected his convoy and was near Freiburg and approaching the mountains which rise 2,000–2,500 feet above the Rhine valley. If Versailles's scheme should succeed, Eugene would be kept tethered to the Stollhofen lines by Villeroy while Tallard's reinforcements would increase the numerical advantage on the Danube against the Allies, bolster the Elector and maintain pressure against Vienna.

Such were the French intentions as Marlborough prepared to force the passage of the Danube at the start of July 1704.

CHAPTER 10

The Schellenberg,
2 July 1704

MARLBOROUGH'S IMMEDIATE OBJECTIVE, the bridge over the Danube at Donauwörth, was protected by the town's considerable defences, themselves overshadowed to the east by the 'bell-shaped hill' Schellenberg. This is a north–south ridge which extends for about 1.5 miles north from the Danube, bounded to east and west by south-flowing streams some 2 miles apart. At its northern end the hill stands at almost 1,700 feet and at that epoch was protected by dense woodland; in the middle is a saddle 400 feet wide which constricts the crest; south of the saddle the ground broadens and rises again to about 1,600 feet at the southern summit or boss. From the southern boss the ground falls very steeply 300 feet to the Danube. Just south of the saddle were the remains of an earth fort built by Gustavus Adolphus after capturing the hill in a two-day battle in 1632.

The eastern face of the hill is the easier flank to climb, for the slopes rise at about 1 in 12 though gradually steepening towards the summit. The western face rises more steeply from the Kaibach stream for 250–300 feet and at an average 1 in 9 gradient. From away north-west the River Wörnitz snakes round the southern marshy edge of the fortified town of Donauwörth; the Kaibach joins it here just before they are absorbed by the great Danube. The town's north-eastern defences were overlooked by Gustavus's fort some 1,600 feet distant above a slope of perhaps 1 in 7. Together town and hill controlled the road south and its successive bridges over the Wörnitz and then the Danube. Yet should the hill somehow be lost the town would be dominated from the crest. Given that in 1703 Villars had recommended the hill's refortification, it is curious that little or nothing had been done by the Elector or Marsin.

In late June 1704 the Allied joint army had moved close to Marsin and the Elector's entrenched Dillingen–Lauingen position in the hope of enticing the Franco-Bavarian force to give battle, and though this ploy failed, it kept the defenders bunched inside the camp. Only when the Allies moved away north-east did it become clear that the camp was not in danger and that troops could be spared from it to attend to the Schellenberg. In the final days of June the Elector detached a force of 14,000 men to Donauwörth under the Bavarian Field Marshal Count d'Arco, comprising 7,000 veteran Bavarian infantry, three French infantry regiments, twelve squadrons and fifteen cannon. It arrived on 1 July. The stone bridges at the streams and the River Wörnitz were broken so as to impede the Allies. The local peasantry were conscripted for additional labour. Even so, work on the Schellenberg went slowly, the first efforts being on the eastern face where the slopes were easiest, with the men subsequently working round north. The western gap between the old fort and the town was left till last, as it was covered by cannon from both points. The entire front would probably measure some 3,000 yards, but the half-finished north-west sector where the worst of the fighting was to take place was only some 300 yards long. D'Arco must have considered (rightly) that the Allies could not reach the eastern flank until at least nightfall on 2 July, by which time that face would be complete and his labourers would be improving the western defences. He placed a garrison within the self-contained defences of the town, and since the road from the town over the Wörnitz/Danube could be a bottleneck, he

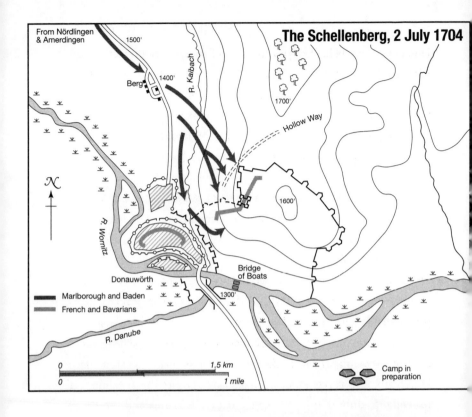

From Nördlingen & Amerdingen

1500'

R. Kaibach

Berg

1400'

1700'

Hollow Way

N

1600'

R. Wornitz

Bridge of Boats

Donauwörth

Marlborough and Baden
French and Bavarians

1300'

R. Danube

0   1,5 km

0   1 mile

Camp in preparation

threw a boat-bridge across the Danube from the southern toe of the Schellenberg to the south bank, where he began to lay out a vast camping ground to receive the main Franco-Bavarian army. By 3 July the position could well be impregnable, and it would seem that this was the timescale d'Arco allowed himself for the works.

None of this could be kept secret, and as Marlborough always paid well for intelligence he was quickly in possession of the salient facts. The Allied force, still lacking Württemberg's contingent of Danish cavalry (despite Marlborough's repeated messages to him), now comprised 68 battalions, 171 squadrons and 48 guns (of which Marlborough's contribution was 44 battalions, 86 squadrons, 34 field-pieces and 4 howitzers). The promised Imperial heavy artillery had never materialized, much to the duke's private vexation. Their force was not strong enough for major siege operations, and within days the

114

Donauwörth/Schellenberg position would require nothing less. Marlborough had sent Cadogan with a reconnoitring force to study the defences, and when, at last light on the evening of Tuesday, 1 July, Cadogan returned to Amerdingen, to which the army had just marched that day, his report was so clear that even Lewis accepted Marlborough's opinion that a prompt assault was necessary. Consequently, that same night the duke warned the commissaries and surgeons to bring the hospital from the rear and to establish it at once on the main line of communication at Nördlingen (17 miles from Donauwörth).

Wednesday, 2 July was the duke's day to command and he used every minute. Amerdingen camp was at least 15 miles from Donauwörth, and the roads were very bad. While it was still dark Cadogan was sent ahead with cavalry, 400 pioneers and thirty-six pontoons to clear the way, level obstacles and make river crossings. At the first streaks of dawn there marched a specially picked contingent of 5,850 infantry from the duke's own forces under the trusted Dutch General Goor, three regiments of the margrave's Imperial grenadiers, and thirty-five squadrons of horse. This was Marlborough's intended storming force. At 5 a.m. the main army and the artillery (with orders not to unharness even if halted) set out in two columns stretching back over several miles, the baggage being kept far in rear to avoid congestion. By 8 a.m. Cadogan, who had left the pontoons and quartermasters 3 miles back at Ebermergen on the Wörnitz with orders to lay out camp, had breasted the last high ground, 200 feet above and a mile distant from Donauwörth, and was faced by enemy troops holding the village of Berg covering the north-western approaches. Marlborough arrived at 9 a.m. to inspect the Schellenberg and was soon joined by the margrave and other senior officers. As they carefully studied the position they came under sustained fire from the enemy artillery.

By noon the advanced detachment had struggled forward almost a dozen muddy miles but they were not to camp at Cadogan's site;

Marlborough rested them briefly, then got them over the Wörnitz by an undemolished bridge and pontoons. The main body followed on. By about 4 p.m. parts of the main army were assembling around the village of Berg within range of the enemy, the cavalry having returned from an expedition to the nearby woods to cut fascines (bundles of brushwood) for the assault. A couple of hours later Colonel Blood's artillery had taken position in Berg. That village was well sited for bombarding not only the town, which lies 100 feet lower, but also the hill the trenches of which, though 200 feet higher, were also within range: a French battalion commander at the critical sector recorded that cannonfire accounted for five of his officers and eighty men even before the infantry attack came up. But the decisive arm had to be infantry. There were only two hours of daylight left for that decision, thus precluding any plan for marching round to test for weak points, or for feinting.

Until well into the forenoon d'Arco, high up on Schellenberg, had expected the Allies to halt at the Ebermergen camp, which he could see Cadogan had marked out: it was a full day's march from Amerdingen in the present conditions. Only at noon did he realize that the Allies were still moving upon him. With their intention no longer in doubt d'Arco had to decide whether to stand on a position which might wreck the attacking force but from which there was no easy escape route if the defences failed, or precipitately to withdraw his force intact, hold the south bank of the Danube and link up with the Elector and Marsin, but thereby abandoning the well-filled magazines inside Donauwörth. He knew that the margrave was a stolid rather than an intrepid commander, and while Marlborough already had shown great ability in the seventeenth-century skills of manoeuvre, marches, feints and siegework, nobody yet knew that the queen's favourite was to prove himself a dauntless and inspired battlefield commander. Hence d'Arco's decision to stand and fight was both understandable and worth the risk. Fourteen battalions of his infantry and sixteen guns were massed along the north-western sector and in the old fort, the sector where he saw Marlborough's force would attack.

Marlborough is rightly termed a considerate commander; a man combining outstanding skill, geniality and warm-heartedness. But when this 'considerateness' is stressed by comparison with other British commanders of later epochs, who by reputation were harder or less genial, then caution is necessary. For Marlborough was ready to sacrifice men in murderous assault, to thrust them repeatedly at fortified positions and massed fire, to see them maimed and perish there, if by so doing he could smash open the defences in front of them or weaken the enemy front elsewhere for a decisive thrust. In these circumstances his 'considerateness' was cut off as by a guillotine, for in these costs was the price of victory to be paid.

So it was at the Schellenberg. His dispatches tell us only that he was resolved to attack it at once; they give no indication of any detailed plan. His inspection had told him that the unfinished works between the woodland on the north and the old fort were the weakest part of the defence, as well as being nearest for his advancing army. The climb might take some fifteen minutes, rendered easier by the lower slopes offering shelter from fire from above (though not from the town), and Blood's guns could assist with covering fire until the leading line should reach the shoulder and enter the fifty to eighty paces of 'killing ground'. The men's fascines should block the ditch and with luck the infantry would dash over the parapet and break through the defences before casualties brought them to a halt. Cavalry following close behind would then sweep along the broad hilltop and complete the affair. Meanwhile, as leading units of the main force arrived they would form up as a reserve behind the cavalry. As soon as the margrave's column should arrive it would extend the front westwards, easing the pressure on the initial front and drawing away defenders from Marlborough's sector.

Thus without waiting for the entire army to form up, Marlborough assembled along the Kaibach stream a force of sixteen battalions under Goor. The artillery duel intensified overhead. The cavalry handed the fascines to the infantry, and the leading four lines of infantry began their climb, preceded by a 'forlorn hope' of English Guards, the scarlet coats of the English brightly visible on the left wing close to the northern woodland. Immediately behind them moved two lines of cavalry, and while their primary role was to exploit any breakthrough on the crest, they may well have had a secondary one to form a wall to stop any retreat by the infantry. Behind them again were eight more battalions from the main force, with a further eight held in reserve. Round-shot, then case-shot, then musketry ravaged the attackers, and by misfortune a 'hollow way' across the front and below the crest was mistaken for the main defensive ditch so that the fascines were cast in there, too early, and the surviving infantry found themselves checked when, breathless, they reached the final ditch. Riddled with bullets and torn by cannon-shot, the assault wavered. The enemy rushed forward with sword and bayonet to complete the butchery. The Guards stood firm though most of their officers were casualties by now, and the Royal Scots and the 23rd Foot held with them until the enemy fell back to their earthworks. The attackers regrouped in the hollow way, their standards just visible to the enemy. Then a second assault was launched, backed by the cavalry, which certainly on this occasion blocked any efforts at retreat. In turn the wall of cavalry, was heavily punished, but nevertheless stood firm. It was now 7.30 p.m. and after ninety minutes the Allied attacks, if magnificent, were so far giving no hopes of victory. Indeed, so heavy was the carnage that the Scots Greys as dragoons eventually had to dismount and support the infantry on foot simply to maintain the line. Renewed rain added to the difficulties and the misery. To Marlborough it must have seemed that nightfall would bring total failure.

The margrave meanwhile had formed up on the right (west) of the Allied army and was advancing with his troops towards the slope which lay between the town and Gustavus's old fort. Marlborough at this very time sent a small patrol of his own to feel out the defences on that sector. It returned with the amazing news that the sector was virtually deserted, for in fact the defenders on the western face of the Schellenberg had been taken away to help in the main battle, so that this sector now relied entirely on the protection of the Donauwörth garrison's musketry and cannon. Marlborough at once sent his eight-battalion reserve to storm the unguarded slope while he personally organized another frontal assault through the mud, and over the wounded and corpses. But the margrave's force was already marching up and along the slope in as formed an order as the ground permitted. The four battalions inside the town were either too badly placed or too slack to observe and fire on the Imperialist columns, and the Donauwörth cannon inflicted only a few casualties. Lewis's attacking troops threw their fascines into the ditch and crossed the empty works. They still had not fired one shot. Once upon the crest the margrave wheeled left and advanced on the flank and back of the defenders, who, themselves tired, were desperately preoccupied by Marlborough's newly launched third frontal assault. Some cavalry attacked the Imperialists but were driven off, and suddenly the French and Bavarians realized that this grey-white uniformed mass marching upon their rear with shouldered arms was not a friendly reinforcement but the most deadly of foes – as yet unshaken by battle.

Even so, the close-range volleying and hand-to-hand battle continued for several minutes, the British and Dutch infantry struggling forward through the shambles, with the Scots Greys on foot beside them, while the Imperialists struck in savagely from their flank. Then the bewildered and exhausted defenders broke and moved back towards the southern boss of the hill. Instantly the cavalry rode after them, cut them down and turned the defeat into a rout; the Greys remounted and joined their colleagues in chasing the fleeing enemy down the eastern slopes. Marlborough was with his cavalry and fully master of the crest before the light had faded: his infantry he ordered to regroup round their colours. The remaining fugitives plunged down towards the Danube or ran towards the town.

The German forces maintained the pursuit, the Imperialist cavalry hastening to seize the bridge of boats, trapping the baggage, and hunting the fugitives to their deaths in the fields, marshes and river; so shaken was the town garrison that it only reluctantly opened the gates to its defeated comrades, and actually abandoned the town the next morning. So precipitate was that withdrawal that the Allies secured the town and magazines before the houses could be fired or the stores destroyed, and as a result enormous quantities of food and forage, thousands of barrels of powder and three heavy guns and seventeen copper boats fell into Marlborough's and Baden's hands.

It was definitely victory: the objective had been taken, the town and magazine secured intact, the bridges seized; thirteen colours, sixteen brass field-pieces, all the enemy tents, and much booty and valuable plate were captured. But it had been at a high price. Of the three senior Imperialist officers, the margrave and one other were slightly wounded and the third died of wounds. The Dutch lost the splendid Goor and another general. In all, eleven lieutenant generals were killed or wounded, with four major generals and twenty-eight brigadiers, colonels and lieutenant colonels, a tally indicative of the leadership needed in the repeated assaults. Many officers had had horses killed under them. From the official accounts compiled at the time for the information of the Allied governments, from the British 'Bounty Roll' drawn up at the campaign's end, and from the various calculations of historians, it would seem that Marlborough and Lewis of Baden attacked with some 25,000 men in total, the worst of the brunt being endured by some 6,000 British infantry, dragoons and horse and a smaller number of Dutch. Nearly one-third of the British infantry engaged fell as casualties, the total British loss being 29 officers and 406 men killed, and 86 officers and 1,031 men wounded. Of the brave 82 in the 'forlorn hope' only 17 remained. The Dutch lost nearly 600 killed and 1,000 wounded. Estimates of d'Arco's initial strength vary between 10,000 and 14,000 (Marlborough put it at above 12,000), with only 3,000 to 5,000 escaping. The Danube, flowing strongly after weeks of rain, drowned many of those who fled down the south face; those running away east fared best. Very few prisoners were taken: an exchange of prisoners later in the month dealt with only 216 unwounded and an unrecorded number of wounded men.

As to generalship, if the plan outlined above was indeed what Marlborough had in mind (and historians have tended to describe what happened rather than try to fathom what the duke intended should happen), the lack of time made it a fairly simple exercise in brute force and will power. It suffered one disastrous accident: the dumping of the fascines in the hollow way which ruined the attempt to sweep over the entrenchments, kept the infantry stationary under murderous fire, and checked all momentum. It enjoyed one uncovenanted advantage: the extraordinary inactivity of the town garrison coupled with the diversion of enemy troops from the western face, which gave the Imperialist force the key to the summit – whether Marlborough's eight reserve battalions might by themselves have achieved on that western slope all that the massed Imperialists did, cannot be guessed.

THE ELECTOR IMMEDIATELY ABANDONED his camp in the Danube valley, retreated south-east to the River Lech, broke down its bridges and took shelter inside Augsburg, midway between Donauwörth and his capital, Munich. Max Emmanuel thus still appeared defiant. The Prussians had made no progress in their negotiations with him. Augsburg's fortifications were of such strength that the Allied army, lacking adequate siege artillery, could not threaten it. And now came new if half-expected worries for Marlborough. For in mid afternoon on 2 July, as the duke prepared his assault of the Schellenberg, he received news from Eugene that Villeroy and Tallard had decided to send to Bavaria a reinforcement of fifty battalions and sixty squadrons of their best troops. The Allies had won a battle, but not the campaign.

CHAPTER 11

Tallard Advances:
Marlborough Burns Bavaria, July

ALTHOUGH MARLBOROUGH and Lewis of Baden congratulated each other on their victory and followed it by marching into Bavaria, the month of July brought them frustration and disappointment.

The duke had written to the queen on the morning after the battle of 'this happy beginning' and of 'the unparalleled courage of your troops' and to the Secretary of State: 'all our troops in general behaved themselves with great gallantry, and the English in particular have gained a great deal of honour in this action, which I believe was the warmest that has been known for many years'. The margrave declared that he would fall in with Marlborough's every recommendation for the common cause, and the duke noted that all the officers were happy to obey his orders 'without knowing any other reason than that it is my desire'. These assurances and observations undoubtedly reflected the majority view in the combined army. The queen wrote a letter of congratulation. In Vienna there was delight and the emperor repeated his wish to make Marlborough a prince. In Rome people spoke of Marlborough continuing down into Italy, for in that theatre the Duke of Savoy and the Allies were in difficulties. There were, however, other opinions. Captain Richard Pope of Schomberg's Horse (7th Dragoon

Guards) dissented from 'the view of all Europe', for he termed it 'a considerable advantage' rather than 'a victory', and 'purchased at a dear rate'. But in fact 'all Europe' was not of one view. Elector George of Hanover was saddened by the casualty list, sarcastically remarking that proper measures had not been taken because of 'the mistakes made by that great general Marlborough', who had been saved from disaster by the margrave. The Dutch struck a victory medal with Lewis on it but not Marlborough.

In England, though the Whigs were pleased, the Tories had already expressed their fears over Marlborough's great march into Germany, saying openly, 'if he fails we will break him up as hounds upon a hare'; now they asked what good was capturing one hill in a country where there were so many. Only the Whigs expressed much satisfaction. An informed English observer based on the Continent had already summed up the essential problem to a friend: 'If the Elector of Bavaria is reduced, it will stop the mouths of his [Marlborough's] enemies, and they will not be able to hurt him in England. But if he fails, he must be railed at in Holland, and accused in England, for the loss he must suffer in such an expedition, and I much apprehend the consequence everywhere.'

Knowing that Tallard was marching to join Marsin and the Elector, Marlborough had to break or bring over the Elector within the next two weeks by material inducement or physical coercion. The duke had no belief in Prussian negotiating abilities, and together with Wratislaw he now took over the talks with Max Emmanuel, even though he suspected the Elector's good faith. Max was offered every inducement in the names of the emperor and the queen: the restoration of territory and even its enlargement at the expense of other rulers, money to restore the damage of war, a highly lucrative contract with England for the employment of Bavarian troops with the Austrian armies in Italy. Only two provisos were demanded: no claim to a kingship, and no release of Marsin's army for further service.

The inducements were generous because the means for coercion were so few. Marlborough himself was suffering from crippling shortages of bread and of artillery. Despite the capture of Donauwörth's magazines and urgent messages for vehicles to be sent from friendly states, the flour and wagon shortage continued and 'the troops I have the honour to command can't subsist without it [bread], and the Germans that are used to starve can't advance without us'. In addition, though Lewis assured the duke that twenty more cannon would reach them by 7 July, nothing of the sort occurred.

Thus when the Danes finally reached Donauwörth on 5 July, just as the combined army was crossing the Danube and marching towards the Bavarian frontier at the River Lech, the first priority was to find means of subsistence. The town of Neuburg 20 miles downstream from Donauwörth had surrendered and been occupied, and if Marlborough could take the little fortified town of Rain, 3 miles south of the confluence of the Lech with the Danube, then the army could camp safely within a triangular area of plain protected at each angle by a defensible town. Rain was not strong, and yet so weak in cannon was the besieging army that the operations extended over seven days, the first siege guns arriving from Nuremberg on 14 July and the garrison surrendering only on the 16th. This weakness was not lost on the Elector.

On the morrow of the Schellenberg Marlborough deemed it unlikely that Tallard's reinforcement would reach the Elector and Marsin; he seems throughout to have been less concerned by a possible junction of enemy forces to his south than of Tallard striking at the English line of communication north of the Danube, reoccupying the abandoned camp at Dillingen and Lauingen, and creating a second front. To avert this the duke levelled the Elector's old camp on the north bank before pushing towards Augsburg. He accepted that with Villeroy staying on the Rhine Eugene would have to divide his forces, but he knew that Eugene would personally command the wing intended to shadow Tallard, and that he could trust him implicitly.

When Eugene asked for an additional thirty squadrons the duke immediately sent them, so that the mobile wing under Eugene, though numerically inferior to Tallard, amounted to twenty battalions and sixty squadrons: at times Marlborough seems to have thought that this would of itself divert or stop the French expedition. If so, he was wrong.

How was Max Emmanuel to be coerced to change sides before he learned of Tallard's expedition, as soon he must? Too poorly gunned to smash Rain quickly, even to hope of assaulting Augsburg, or occupying the capital at Munich, Marlborough deliberately ordered the systematic burning of Bavarian towns and villages.

Marlborough was a humane man. He wrote to Sarah that Bavaria had been untouched by war for sixty years and 'these towns and villages are so clean and neat that you would be pleased by them'. While on his march to the Danube he had been scrupulous in paying for supplies and protecting property, and he sought to avoid disputes between the local populations of Swabia and Franconia and his troops. But to break the Elector's will he began a campaign of blackmail against the Elector and terror against the defenceless civilian inhabitants of Bavaria. Some historians have argued in extenuation that systematic devastation had been common in much of Germany in the Thirty Years' War two generations earlier and when the French had ravaged western Germany in Louis XIV's earlier wars; that Suchet's actions at the siege of Lerida in 1810 or Sherman's in Georgia in 1864 showed the nineteenth century capable of atrocities, and that the twentieth century could far surpass this savagery against land, food, water supply and civilian life.

The extent of the damage in 1704 was certainly much less than in those instances, but buildings were burnt down, crops seized, the people forced to flee. Trees and woodland were spared – as were the Elector's properties in order to turn his people against him. The evidence of Chaplain Noyes of the Royal Scots is that substantial plundering and burning did occur, though the extent of this went far beyond orders, and he added that irregular 'hussars' were the worst culprits. Captain Parker wrote that '372 Towns, Villages, and Farmhouses were said to have been laid in ashes …a shocking sight'. Tallard, though French policy in the Palatinate in 1689 gave him no right to say such things, wrote of 'barbarism worse than the Turks', but it is significant that the French Colonel de la Colonie, who rode over parts which were reportedly totally devastated, saw that the reported slaughter and rape had not occurred, that much still stood and that there was far less damage than he had expected. That stands to the duke's credit. However, although Wratislaw did not object to Marlborough's tactic, both the emperor and the margrave most certainly did.

In looking at the morality of the policy we are back with the nurse's excuse for her illegitimate baby in Marryat's *Mr Midshipman Easy*, 'If you please, ma'am, it was a very little one.' What of its efficacy? Marlborough knew on 2 July of Tallard's approach. He therefore had to break the Elector within days, before news of Tallard's progress reached him. Given this, the duke did either too little or too much. *Schrecklichkeit* might have succeeded within that narrow space of time; 'semi-frightfulness' worked too slowly on the Elector's resolve, while inflicting unjustified suffering on the people. Did Marlborough's half measures pay? By 16 July even he was worried that 'it may at last do ourselves hurt for want of what we destroy' – and, of course, had the campaign ended in his defeat and the scattering of his men as 'heretic' fugitives in Catholic Bavaria, one may imagine what punishment would have been meted out by the peasantry.

Though one may find reasons – the inability of Vienna to honour its desperate promises of the spring, the lack of siege guns, the 'want of everything', the lack of support for Marlborough's army after his great gamble and long march – the fact remains that the burning of Bavaria was an act of desperation marking the failure of war by normal means, a confession of strategic near-bankruptcy. It was not total bankruptcy, however, for on 9 July the Elector sent word that he wished to see Wratislaw. When that nobleman arrived at the rendezvous he found only the Elector's secretary, who nevertheless insisted that his master would accept the Allied terms and come to sign them the next day, 14 July. Marlborough informed London of this but warned that he doubted the Elector's integrity. Nevertheless, the burnings were suspended. The Allies seemed to have won the main objective in their campaign.

Two factors upset everything. To protect his own farms and palaces the Elector had dispersed Bavarian troops so widely that the French were dominant in Augsburg. Marsin refused to let his army be subject to any treaty, frightened Max Emmanuel that Wratislaw might kidnap him, maybe even himself threatened to take the Elector hostage. And fatefully, after a six-day journey, Tallard's letter was handed to the Elector on 14 July informing him of the relief expedition. The Elector, whose incessant havering and bargaining were notorious, immediately sent the waiting Wratislaw a message declaring that his honour forced him to reject the Allies' offers.

Could the first of these developments have been allowed for? Probably not. It was possibly beyond the Elector's power to have disarmed and interned Marsin's forces, but in May 1704 Tallard's return to France through lands where the French were hated had cost him very dear at the hands of the peasants, and this time Marsin would have been pursued by Allied armies superior in numbers; on this occasion Marsin might well have become marooned and been forced to capitulate. As to the second factor, Tallard's message, Marlborough was wrong to discount the likelihood of Tallard's reaching Bavaria a second time (had Tallard not taken certain decisions en route he might have been with Marsin by late July instead of early in August), but there was little more that he could do to force Max to sign. Messages do slip past cavalry patrols.

One aspect of Tallard's message merits a digression because it discloses a weapon Marlborough constantly employed. Tallard had received his orders on 27 June and had left Strasbourg on 1 July. He might have written at once, but did not, preferring to wait until leaving the Rhine plain and entering the Waldkirch defile into the western Black Forest. His courier then took almost seven days to cover the 150 miles to Augsburg (14 July). Yet Marlborough's network of agents was so excellent that he, though at least 130 miles away, had by Wednesday afternoon, 2 July, received news of the secret decisions taken at enemy headquarters inside Strasbourg on Friday, 27 June. Such speed and accuracy are the best answers to that vindictive House of Commons vote which in 1712 condemned Marlborough's use of secret service money as 'unwarrantable' (despite the duke's having the queen's own signed warrant for it).

By 14 July Tallard was coming down from the mountains, burdened with 2,500 carts of supplies, all the impedimenta necessary to his large force and with four 24-pounder and eight 16-pounder cannon. He reached the decrepit fortifications of Villingen town and decided not to march past but to secure them as protection for his communications; then he could continue the 85 miles to Ulm in safety. But the garrison commander was obstinate and the siege, instead of lasting one day, lasted six. Eugene with some 18,000 men had time to pass the mountains and reach Rottweil, only 10 miles away, and Tallard abandoned the siege on 22 July and swung away down the Danube valley. He reached Marsin and the Elector at Augsburg on 4 August, having maintained a fast rate of marching (as mentioned in Chapter 8) but having lost one-third of his strength, while 'the German sickness' destroyed many of his cavalry horses. And for all that he had squandered the precious advantage over Eugene with which he had started, as only one day after his arrival at Augsburg Eugene's army came to Donauwörth – and on 6 August Marlborough and Eugene met once more. But that still lay in the future.

Marlborough at the age of 40, the year of Cork and Kinsale;
Sarah called him 'sunburnt'. Portrait by Kneller. (Althorp)

Marlborough, aged 61, discussing plans for the siege of Bouchain with his chief engineer, Colonel Armstrong. (Bridgeman Art Library/Blenheim Palace)

OPPOSITE PAGE
TOP LEFT Sarah Churchill, Countess of Marlborough, in her thirties. (National Portrait Gallery, London)

TOP RIGHT Prince Eugene of Savoy. (Bridgeman Art Library/ Heeresgeschichtliches Museum, Vienna)

BELOW LEFT Camille d'Hostun, Comte de Tallard. (National Portrait Gallery, London)

BELOW RIGHT Louis-Claud-Hector, Duke of Villars. (Bridgeman Art Library/Château de Versailles)

Marshal Tallard about to doff his hat in surrendering to Marlborough at Blenheim, 13 August 1704. The village of Blindheim is in the distance on the left; the mills are in the middle-distance behind the grenadier. Note also the cumbersome artillery-pieces. (Blenheim Palace)

The siegeworks at Bouchain, 1711. Marlborough's tented camp is shown beyond and below. (Blenheim Palace)

In mid July the burning recommenced and with it a slump in relations between Marlborough and the margrave. Both the duke and Wratislaw suspected that Lewis maintained a link with the Elector and it was at Marlborough's insistence that Imperial troops were sent by the margrave to assist in burning along the road to Munich. The promised artillery was still wanting and without that the fortress and magazines of Augsburg would be impregnable. On 23 July Marlborough moved the army close to that city – to Friedberg, only some 4 miles away – to isolate the Elector, perhaps to tempt him out. The margrave apparently lost interest in all this and pressed instead for the siege of Ingolstadt, a strong city on the Danube, 30 miles downstream from Donauwörth. Concerned at the devastation – and possibly at the friction within the high command – Vienna proposed that the emperor's eldest son should take supreme command of both armies. Marlborough appeared agreeable to this, feeling that he could handle the young man, but noted that Lewis had reservations; the idea came to nothing, but this may have been because the emperor learned that Eugene was about to reach Bavaria and take a hand.

By 27 July the duke was expecting Tallard to join the Elector and Marsin within days, and he concluded that little could be achieved in the region of Augsburg. Very belatedly thirty siege cannon were being collected at Neuburg and if they were used for the margrave's preferred scheme at least that would strengthen the Allied hold on the great river all the way to the Austrian border.

Eugene heard of the worsening personal relations, and while he preferred Marlborough to Lewis, he condemned them both for lack of any strategy. Marlborough had lamented the death of the Dutchman Goor, having found him an invaluable and experienced subordinate of positive views during their short time together; Eugene heard of this, and thought that Goor's loss had made the less experienced and 'diffident' duke 'more than a little hesitant in his decisions'. Certainly Marlborough was not much comforted to find that after all his own

efforts and all the promises made to him the emperor was now diverting Austrian troops to Italy for personal advantage. He was also
concerned lest Villeroy should thrust into Württemberg and menace
the lines of communication with Holland. All this may have added to
his sense of uncertainty. Eugene did not share these worries. Unable
to stop Tallard's expedition himself, he thought that Marlborough
and Lewis should have stopped it and, not having followed that course,
that they should now menace Augsburg and seize all produce so as
to force a battle. For Eugene imagined (somewhat incorrectly) that
Augsburg's magazines must be empty. Marlborough was indeed slow
to recognize the probability of Tallard getting through, but a sweep
of all produce had already been one result of the systematic devastation. Eugene thought that marching close to the fortifications of
Augsburg would force the Elector to come out, but that assumption
was not necessarily true, and in fact Marlborough was stationed in
battle formation reasonably close (4 miles). Perhaps more importantly,
Eugene took no account of the Allied artillery shortage or the imbal-
ance between the food reserves in Augsburg and the scanty rations
reaching Marlborough.

In such a milieu, semi-isolated and conscious that there were too
many dubious friends and secret enemies influencing Allied policy,
aware that his initial plan had become stalled, Marlborough had need
of all his reserves of courage and self-belief. July's correspondence is
somewhat careworn, taken up with the treatment of troops wounded
at the Schellenberg, anxiety over the shortage of provisions (he uses
the word 'dearth' more than once) and the delays in obtaining bread
and wagons, concern over events in Italy. But he managed to brew
beer for his men. Additionally he had to sit down and study Godolphin's apprehensive letters over the campaign in Portugal and the
domestic squabbles in England, and make out and encipher some
suitable comment and advice in reply.

It is scarcely surprising that at mid month Marlborough suffered nervous headaches and sickness for several days together. It is some-times said that he was a hypochondriac and an inveterate grumbler but his health and state of mind at this time have to be set against the cumulative strain of three years' endeavours and frustrations, of plans repeatedly sabotaged by colleagues' inaction or opposition, of a German crisis over which he had risked everything and for which the promised help was not forthcoming, possibly (at least in his mind) because of treachery and an unforgiving Opposition at home ready to break him and even put him on trial if he returned without decisive victory. For a man at bay his complaints are remarkably mild.

After its promising start July had witnessed Allied bafflement and indecision, tentative searches for strategies to suit two 'alternating' commanders who not only disagreed in their views but increasingly disliked working together. The policy of burnings had not secured the hoped-for decision. And to the frustration of near stalemate was added the worry that through Tallard's advance the initiative was passing to the enemy. But on Tallard's heels was coming Prince Eugene, and Marlborough applied himself to persuading that kindred spirit to break the impasse.

CHAPTER 12

French Advantages Thrown Away:
Allied Unity Restored,
Early August

THE FIRST TWELVE DAYS of August were marked by a gradual shift in the balance of advantage. A mass of nearly 60,000 French and Bavarians was compactly formed south of the Danube, whereas Allied forces, though strengthened by Eugene's arrival on the north bank, remained relatively dispersed. It was essential that the Allies should tempt the enemy into accepting battle if the campaign was not to end in failure, and the wisest course for the French would have been to let time do their work, stay within entrenchments and steadfastly refuse battle. That was certainly one course proposed within the French command. What the Allies could not have hoped for actually occurred: an almost total breakdown in relations between the Elector, Tallard and Marsin, a breakdown presaging disaster. By contrast, at this very time Marlborough persuaded Eugene that they should restore unity of purpose within the Allied contingents by separating themselves from the margrave, even at the cost of reducing their two forces to augment his. Lewis's enthusiasm for the siege of Ingolstadt provided the solution. The great partnership of Marlborough and Eugene, conceived in June, now came into being.

A tally of Marlborough's achievements and failures at the end of

July would have included one expensive victory which had severely punished the enemy army. Against that, burning the countryside had failed to break Max Emmanuel's will, Marsin remained in Bavaria and the duke now expected that Tallard would reach Augsburg around 2 August, thereby creating a preponderant mass. There was no sign of a promised Imperialist siege train. The margrave and he were at cross purposes on most matters. The principal causes for hope lay in other events. Fears for the Rhine valley had diminished because Villeroy's army there was stationary and indeed distracted by some welcome activity by the Dutch general Overkirk in Belgium. Eugene's decision to divide his forces and come to the Danube with one part gave a degree of protection to Marlborough's lines of communication, and his battle-mindedness could help to overcome the stalemate which the margrave's attitudes imposed.

Starved of the promised Imperialist siege artillery, Marlborough now called up the Dutch siege train of twenty large cannon from its station at Mainz, intending with it to reduce the last enemy fortresses on the Danube at Ingolstadt, Ratisbon and then Ulm, so that the river line could provide a series of bridgeheads into Bavaria and deflect enemy plans for an advance on Vienna. To conclude the campaign on so minor a key would seal his fate in England, and meanwhile little support or encouragement could be expected from Vienna or his fellow commander Lewis of Baden. It is a measure of the stress and distrust Marlborough felt about Lewis that while he wrote to Eugene of his call for the Dutch siege train, he kept it secret from the margrave, judging that any hope of receiving the Imperialist artillery still promised by Lewis would disappear if the latter thought someone else would make good the shortage.

If Lewis was averse to battle, he appeared enthusiastic about taking Ingolstadt. There followed a complicated exchange of views between the three commanders about this project, the size of force required, and the method of covering the siege force from French attack. Quite possibly nobody was sincere. Eugene and Marlborough certainly found Lewis's proposals lacking in several respects. Wisely the duke said nothing to the margrave himself but opened his mind to Eugene, and Eugene used Marlborough's arguments as though they were his own. Though Lewis's forces were nearest to Ingolstadt Lewis nevertheless suggested that Marlborough should command the siege force. Marlborough did not reply. Wratislaw ascribed silence to Marlborough's fear that the besiegers would be at risk if they trusted their security to the margrave as field commander. This was the position when Tallard at last joined Marsin and the Elector.

Tallard's arrival led the Allies to break up the camp at Friedberg and by the evening of 5 August Marlborough's force was 20 miles to the north-east, at Schrobenhausen, halfway to the Danube, with Lewis himself still further north, at Neuburg, examining stores and preparations for the siege of Ingolstadt. On this day Eugene's 18,000 men had arrived at Donauwörth and had then moved 4 miles west upriver to camp at the village of Münster in the opposite direction from Ingolstadt. The next day Eugene, accompanied by a single servant, rode to the duke's camp and on the 7th Lewis joined them. Marlborough declared his preference for the covering role, and asked who should command the siege, Eugene or Lewis. The margrave argued that he was better placed for this than was Eugene. Thus it came about that he resigned the mobile command to the men whom he almost certainly regarded as his rivals. The resulting dispositions resembled a triangle, with the margrave undertaking his siege (at the north-east angle), and with Eugene and Marlborough interposed between him and the enemy armies to the south-west, Eugene on the Danube (at the western angle) and Marlborough not far from Eugene (at the southern angle).

Lewis departed with twenty-four battalions and thirty-one squadrons on Saturday, 9 August, collecting the siege train from Neuburg. Some news of enemy movements now came in, and as a precautionary reaction Marlborough's contingent marched west towards Exheim, a mid position only 8 miles from Rain and 20 from Eugene's force. Eugene then bade the duke farewell and left to rejoin his troops. Scarcely had he departed than the duke received another and very different situation report. The French were coming out.

Following Tallard's arrival the Franco-Bavarian generals commanded a body of over 55,000 men and would have had considerably more but for the Elector having dispersed thirty battalions and twenty-two squadrons (at least 16,000 of his troops) to garrison outlying points at risk from Marlborough's marauders: this dispersal of the Elector's troops affected French planning, and to this limited extent the burning of Bavaria may be seen as having had some strategic effect. Further detachments took the services of seventeen battalions for the protection of Ulm and Augsburg, though these were not first-class troops. Nevertheless, the overall situation seemed satisfactory. Marsin and Tallard argued that their junction had forced Marlborough out of central Bavaria towards the river and Franconia, and eased the plight of the Elector's subjects. They thought that Marlborough would therefore seek battle, and that their interest was to avoid it. Even if their combined force remained inactive, each day that passed without a battle placed their enemy increasingly at a disadvantage. If they moved back to the north bank of the Danube, this would so menace Marlborough's communications that he would be further embarrassed and outmanoeuvred.

Two factors undermined this strategy. First, French intelligence was poor: when Tallard neared Augsburg he informed Marsin on 1 August that he had no idea where Eugene's army was, yet that fiery and active prince had never been much more than 25 miles from him, though keeping always to his north; uncertainty on whether or not the three Allied generals were together or separate would continue to confuse French plans. Secondly, the Elector, though contributing only five battalions and twenty-three squadrons to the combined host and later ordering four more battalions and four squadrons to join him from Munich, proved a disruptive and headstrong colleague.

However, there was unanimous agreement on the initial step to go north beyond the Danube. Moving from Augsburg down the left bank of the River Lech on 7 August, the Franco-Bavarian force then swung west and on Saturday, 9 August reached the Danube opposite the old Dillingen–Lauingen position.

The Danube at this point has open ground to the north of the old camp. A little downstream, after Höchstädt, the country broadens out to create an amphitheatre large enough for armies to deploy in, but at the eastern end of this plain the hills start to close in at Schwenningen. For the next 7 miles eastwards almost to Donauwörth the flat ground between the hills and the north bank varies from an initial 1.5 miles at Schwenningen to about 500 yards near the big town, and these bordering hills rise on a gradient of perhaps 1 in 10 to a height of some 130 feet above the river. On the east side of Donauwörth the Schellenberg itself falls steeply to the Danube, so that once beyond Schwenningen there is very little room for manoeuvre. A series of streams and small rivers flow south at right angles into the Danube, thus slowing east–west movement along the bank, and there were many marshy patches, even in summer. This was the area which preoccupied the commanders of the opposing forces from Saturday, 9 August onwards.

The Franco-Bavarian army crossed the Danube on Sunday, 10 August. Marlborough had demolished the Dillingen–Lauingen entrenchments a month earlier; there was no time to undertake the work again, nor it seems did the Elector, Marsin and Tallard consider this a serious problem: what was a source of disagreement was whether to wait for the Bavarian reinforcements before going further, or to march to Donauwörth as the Elector demanded. For, contemptuous of a 'waiting game', relying on his personal status and considerable military experience, he ridiculed the two marshals' lack of enterprise. Bitter words were exchanged. The magnitude of the French contribution settled the immediate question, but the triple command remained a source of time-consuming debate and indecision. As a compromise it was decided to move to the broad plain beyond Höchstädt. On Monday, 11 August the Allied outposts at Dillingen and Höchstädt were captured, some 180 men being taken prisoner. On Tuesday the 12th a new camp was laid out just under 3 miles east of Höchstädt, between the villages of Blindheim[14] and Lutzingen and just west of the little River Nebel. Very little information had come in as to the Allied armies' strength or whereabouts.

Matters went differently on the Allied side. On the Saturday Eugene and Marlborough had separated before either had received word of the French moves. The reports immediately brought them back together for a conference, as a result of which the prince hastened to Münster, sent troops to restore the Schellenberg defences and then moved his baggage to it, thus covering the crossing to Rain and the south and guarding the magazine in Donauwörth and the line of communication northwards. The prince himself remained at Münster. For his part, Marlborough, having informed the margrave of developments and assured him that the besiegers would always be protected and even reinforced if necessary, issued orders for substantial reinforcements to march to Eugene in the early hours of the following day.

At 1 a.m. on Sunday, 10 August, Charles Churchill marched with twenty battalions and the artillery train, crossed the Danube by a special bridge of boats east of the Schellenberg and by evening was only about 6 miles short of that position, while the Duke of Württemberg with twenty-seven Imperial squadrons had reached Donauwörth. The main army, reduced to twenty-eight battalions and eighty-five squadrons, prepared to follow. Outlying detachments at Neuburg were called in. But during the afternoon Eugene saw the French advancing en masse along the Danube towards Höchstädt, with scouts already beyond that town. He judged his eighteen battalions insufficient to offer resistance and ordered them and part of his cavalry back to Donauwörth and the camp above it, while himself remaining at Münster with twenty squadrons of dragoons. Anxious not to be 'trapped between the mountains and the Danube', he called for the duke's immediate assistance. The message reached Marlborough, 10 miles away, at 11 p.m.

Dividing his forces into two columns, the duke sent his second-line infantry along Charles Churchill's route, while he took the first line and the cavalry across the Lech to Donauwörth. By 6 p.m. on Monday, 11 August, the two commanders and their contingents had met west of Donauwörth; only the Neuburg detachment and Colonel Blood's artillery had yet to come – and Blood, by maintaining a magnificent rate of 3 mph, arrived at daybreak on the 12th. Meanwhile the enemy had frittered away their time. They had had two options: to push hard for Donauwörth and destroy Marlborough's link with Swabia; or to stand between Dillingen and Höchstädt and so to entrench themselves that the Allies would lack the superiority necessary for an attack. They opted for neither.

Thus at dawn on Tuesday, 12 August, the situation was that the French command in Höchstädt had failed to appreciate Eugene's weakness or to penetrate his screen, and did not know that the margrave's force (and the siege train) was not with the main army. They seem to have given no thought to what the enemy might choose to do and had no agreed plan of action. Instead they were marking out an extensive camp on the broad plain east of them. Marlborough and Eugene, on the other hand, had successfully concentrated without interference from the French, and were in total agreement that they should push west, take post in the broad plain on the eastern bank of the Nebel, and prepare to advance on the enemy at Höchstädt and seek battle.

Given that Marlborough's force needed some rest and that the enemy was quiescent, the initial plan for the whole army to advance was altered to a strong reconnaissance, while pioneers laid bridges and levelled obstructions so as to widen to the utmost the army's frontage for the advance. The two commanders, with up to 5,000 horse, had intended to reach the Nebel but before they could debouch into the broader plain they saw that the enemy were already moving about. They climbed the church tower at Tapfheim (4 miles from Blindheim) and scanned the ground with 'perspective glasses' until they had assessed the enemy's strength and probable intentions. What they saw confirmed their decision to seek battle. They withdrew to the army.

They had been observed, and in turn the French generals had seen Allied tents in the distance. A French cavalry reconnaissance went out and soon encountered the pioneers at work, covered by a picket and cavalry; four prisoners were taken and questioned, from which it was gathered that the margrave was present and that the army intended retreating *north* to Nördlingen. It was not noticed, apparently, that multiple routes were being cleared along the Danube bank *westward*. Marlborough and Eugene were called from their dinner and they ordered several columns of Prussian and English infantry (1st Guards, and Rowe's brigade of the 10th, 15th, 21st, 23rd and 24th Foot) to advance as far as Tapfheim and secure the entrance to the wider plain. This was achieved by evening, too late for further action. Rowe's enlarged brigade, a Hessian brigade and some cavalry remained on guard there overnight, commanded by General Wilckes of the Dutch service. As evening deepened, orders were issued for the assembly of the whole army in the small hours in readiness to march before dawn on the 13th.

CHAPTER 13

'Within the Memory of Man There Has Been No Victory so Great as This':
John to Sarah, 14 August 1704

MARLBOROUGH SPENT PART of the night in prayer. Then in mist and darkness the drums called the army together and by 2 a.m. on Wednesday, 13 August 1704, the approach march began in eight parallel columns along the constricted riverbank: two of Imperialist foot, then two of their cavalry, two of Marlborough's foot and two of his cavalry. On reaching Wilckes's outpost line, that force joined eleven other battalions to form a twenty-battalion ninth column on the left under Lord Cutts. Marlborough's many pioneer bridges facilitated a rapid deployment into open country and by 5 a.m. the army was fanning out on the plain as the sun behind them burned off the last of the mist. In the distance lay the waiting field of battle.

To the south the Danube wound in loops, at places through marshes and at others beneath bluffs some 15 feet high. Between the villages of Blindheim on the river bank and Oberglauheim just over 2 miles away to the north-west the ground rose by no more than 35 feet. Both lay behind the marshy Nebel brook. In the mile and a quarter between Oberglauheim and Lutzingen to the west where the hills close in, the rise was a further 25 feet. Thus for about 3 miles inland the plain was easy though the hanging woods on the steep 400-foot hillsides thereafter created a natural barrier. From east to west the plain had similarly easy gradients: from the Nebel bed to Höchstädt, a distance of nearly 3 miles, the ground rose by no more than 30 feet.

The Nebel's streams emerged from the hills, combined above Oberglauheim, wandered south-east, past the houses of Unterglauheim amid the marsh, then past two stone mills (which, as they spanned the water, could be forward defences or crossing points) to the great river. A stone bridge existed at Unterglauheim and another further south where 'the great road' to Höchstädt crossed above a marshy islet near the first of the two mills. Blindheim stood several hundred yards back from the Nebel, having the parallel Maulweyer brook actually flowing through it. All the villages were typical of Bavaria: stone churches, houses with walled gardens, narrow streets, barns,

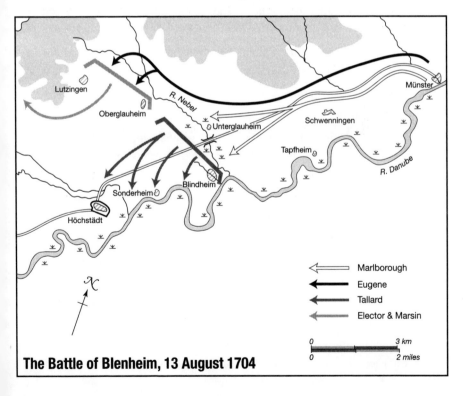

The Battle of Blenheim, 13 August 1704

Marlborough
Eugene
Tallard
Elector & Marsin

0   3 km
0   2 miles

and plots with thick hedges. So far no work had been done by the French to put these places into a state of defence.

As the Allied armies advanced, the French in their open camp behind the Nebel gazed with astonishment at the apparition, but even so Tallard at 7 a.m. complacently wrote to Versailles that although the enemy could be seen 'in battle array at the head of their camp ... it looks that they will march today: the local rumour is to Nördlingen' – apparently abandoning the Danube and their position in Bavaria. Indeed, so relaxed was he that foraging parties had been sent across the plain and the stone bridges left intact. But the Allied host continued to advance. The foragers fell back and began to break the bridges; company and battalion officers began to call out their men. Then suddenly the high command realized the truth, and aides and messengers began to dash about with orders. At 9 a.m. the Elector, Marsin and Tallard fixed their dispositions, while the French cannon fired at the distant enemy.

The German elector and the French marshals chose not to fight as one army. They were personally at odds, Max Emmanuel and Tallard particularly disliking each other. They had taken no steps to integrate their two forces into a single order of battle and there was now no time left to correct this. Moreover, Tallard's horses were suffering from 'the German fever' and it was dangerous to mingle them with the Elector's and Marsin's units. In consequence, Tallard held the Nebel from the Danube almost to Oberglauheim; Marsin and the Elector commanded from Oberglauheim to the hills. Twelve horseless squadrons of dragoons held barricades on the extreme right by the river; nine battalions occupied Blindheim, which they loopholed and barricaded; sixty-eight squadrons of horse stood between Blindheim and Oberglauheim, on firm ground well back from the Nebel. Behind Blindheim were seven more battalions, with a further eleven in rear; behind the massed horse were nine battalions of infantry. Marsin and the Elector massed twelve Bavarian battalions and two French (lent by Tallard) in Oberglauheim; then filled the upper plain with sixty-seven French and Bavarian cavalry squadrons drawn up in two lines; and placed twelve battalions of Bavarians in left rear of the cavalry, near the Elector's headquarters at Lutzingen. Ninety cannon were placed along the front, with the heaviest concentrations at Blindheim and Oberglauheim.

Such dispositions increased the commanders' problems. Two armies implied two axes of defence: stress could pull them apart. The reserves were mainly at the far southern and northern extremities, with too few in the centre where the armies touched. The bastions of Blindheim and Oberglauheim were too far apart to protect each other with musket-fire (a point made by Wellington to Stanhope in 1837), but relied upon cavalry cover. There were even two battle plans. Marsin and the Elector wished to fight 'forward', close to the Nebel to deny it to the enemy; Tallard intended to hold firmly to Blindheim but to encourage the Allied troops across the stream below Ober-glauheim and then, before they could establish themselves, sweep down with his massed cavalry, and from the two villages then to enfilade the enemy fugitives caught in the stream. It was risky: too few Allied troops across would not lead to the enemy's total defeat; too many across and the Allies might become too cohesive. Every-thing depended on Tallard's skill in judging numbers and in split-second timing, and on superior tactical practice.

The Allies were likewise in two armies, but their generals had no differences. About 7 a.m. the two commanders went to a knoll with their principal generals to point out the ground, hear the informa-tion of a general who had fought Villars at Höchstädt in 1703, study the French dispositions and identify the units by their colours, and then state their intentions. These were expressed in the broadest of terms – and unlike the French plans they were issued by the two com-manders speaking as one. They had noted the enemy's division into two armies and the probable weakness at the junction. Eugene would command on the sector north of Oberglauheim and seek to break through the enemy cavalry's wide front and pin down the northern reserve; Marlborough would attack the southern flank and if he could not take Blindheim would at least draw Tallard's reserves there, while a force of intermixed cavalry and infantry should force the centre where the link between the two enemy armies could be broken. The initial reaction was uneasy. The scheme was too bold. Chaplain General Hare, who was an observer, wrote the next day that 'almost all the generals were against my Lord's attacking the enemy, they thought it so difficult' and Major General Lord Orkney likewise 'confessed' that had his opinion been sought, given the French position and numerical strength, 'I had been against it [the attack]'.

Eugene's contingent swung north-west, parallel with the Nebel and skirting the hills, but came under continual flanking fire from French cannon. The ground was broken and scrubby, the march much impeded. It took until noon for Eugene to deploy as he wanted, with the Prussian prince of Anhalt-Dessau (latter famous as the 'Old Dessauer) commanding ten battalions of Prussian and Danish infantry on his extreme right and with some sixty squadrons in his centre and left, all backed by a further eight battalions and fourteen squadrons in second line. Because Eugene's force was smaller than Marlborough's and in more difficult ground, its task was to hold (if possible, overcome) the forces in front of it, leaving Marlborough free to attack and manoeuvre on the broader plain.

As Eugene departed so Marlborough's contingent advanced, and it is a remarkable proof of how division paralysed the French high command that it ignored this opportunity to attack either Eugene's straggling columns or Marlborough's force in an attempt to defeat them in detail. Marlborough pushed troops forward towards the burning mills and sent Cutts further to the south with a column of Anglo-Hessian-Hanoverian brigades close to Blindheim. It became clear that the Nebel banks were steeper or more marshy than had been seen from a distance. Pioneers went forward to lay five plank bridges and repair the stone ones, and the French cannon began to fire at 9 a.m. Marlborough rode forward and personally placed two batteries, one English, one Dutch, across 'the great road' to the stone bridge, then proceeded to place all the others 'and stood by to observe the range of the guns and the effect of their fire'; a prolonged artillery exchange then began.

The duke's troops continued to arrive and deploy in battle array, but nothing could be done until Eugene should be ready. Field prayers were said. For several hours the stationary army had patiently to endure a pounding from the enemy cannon and the duke ordered his men to lie down. Marlborough rode along the line to steady them. He was clearly identifiable on his white horse by his uniform, star and Garter sash; whether by chance or by aim he was nearly killed, Hare writing: 'One of the first cannon shot came between his horse's legs and beat up all the dirt into his face, but God be thanked he received no wound.' Eugene was late. An anxious Marlborough sent Cadogan to find out what was happening. Maintaining an outward calm, the duke sat down in view of his men and ordered something to eat until, between noon and 1 p.m., Eugene's signal came.

Marlborough had massed his scarlet-clad English opposite Blindheim. At his extreme right near Unterglauheim were ten of his continental battalions under the Prince of Holstein-Beck. Between these wings Marlborough mixed horse and foot in an unusual formation in four lines: in the first line seven battalions, in the second thirty-six squadrons, next thirty-five squadrons, and in the fourth line eleven battalions. This central mass gazed across at Tallard's cavalry waiting in the distance.

Cutts launched a strong but steady-paced infantry attack on Blindheim. Rowe's English brigade suffered heavily in vainly trying to breach the walls and barricades, and was then charged by French cavalry. But the Hessians advanced, blasted the cavalry, attacked the village and in turn were charged. Cutts threw in Ferguson's English brigade, but still could make little progress. Units regrouped, mingled and continued to attack. The village caught fire and many wounded on both sides were trapped by the flames. So little alarmed was Tallard by the strength of this attack that he left his headquarters near Blindheim, abandoned temporarily his own army's sector, and rode to Lutzingen to see the commanders of the northern army. He left his army leaderless and made a 3-mile journey – from which no plans or decisions resulted.

Cutts's attacks had not only diverted the enemy from enfilading Marlborough's movements in the centre but had drawn more and more of the French infantry reserve into the village, to the point where they were so crowded – twenty-seven battalions and the twelve dragoon regiments – that they could scarcely use their weapons. How had this blunder occurred? Either Tallard had relinquished control of his reserve to a subordinate local commander, or his orders as to releasing the reserve were opaque, or in his absence nobody fathomed his intentions. It was fatal.

By contrast, Marlborough, when he saw that Cutts was not making progress, ordered him to call back his fourth (Hanoverian) brigade and instead encircle the village at a distance. When in turn the garrison tried to break out, Cutts's men 'mowed them down'. Thus the garrison was 'contained' by a force only two-thirds their strength.

In the centre Marlborough's mixed force under his younger brother Charles, preceded by three squadrons under Colonel Palmes, waded the Nebel and crossed by the bridges without opposition. Seven élite French squadrons moved against Palmes's three, but while wheeling for position they were charged by him and routed, a disaster which shook confidence throughout the French army. Palmes in turn was forced back when enemy reserves came up, but he had gained time for the troops to form up after the crossing. The duke next sought to subdue the fire from Oberglauheim on his right by launching

Holstein-Beck's infantry at it. Marlborough's own first line of infantry, having made safe the west bank of the Nebel, opened to let through the cavalry of his second line. Tallard's cavalry now charged, and indeed broke the Allied cavalry's cohesion and drove it back. But Marlborough's unusual formation which had so puzzled Tallard now proved its tactical value, for as the Allied cavalry fell back through the gaps between the battalions, infantry fire blasted the French cavalry and checked it. Then the duke's third line of cavalry pounded into the French horse and forced it back. In desperation Tallard ordered infantry to come from his right wing. None came; Blindheim had swallowed them all and from the village only desultory shots annoyed Marlborough's flank.

However, Holstein-Beck's attack failed disastrously at Oberglauheim. His two leading battalions were routed and he was mortally wounded, his appeal to the Imperialist cavalry on his right for assistance going unanswered. To the north Eugene was fighting desperately. He had launched his cavalry in a great charge and the Anhalt-Dessau had taken some Bavarian artillery close to Lutzingen, but a counter-attack had swept them all back beyond the stream and recovered the guns. A second attack was checked by fire from Lutzingen and Oberglauheim. The cavalry were blown and too shaken to renew once more, and Eugene therefore led the infantry on the far right to a third attack against Lutzingen, leaving Oberglauheim untaken.

The next day Hare admitted: 'before three I thought we had lost the day'.

To check the destruction of Holstein-Beck's force Marlborough had personally requested Eugene's (leftmost) brigade of Imperial cuirassiers and Eugene, though desperate, released it. Its charge halted the rout. To master Oberglauheim's garrison the duke now brought some guns forward to decisive range and wheeled three battalions onto its southern front, while with some cavalry and Holstein-Beck's reassembled infantry he created a force which he personally led against the village. Though Oberglauheim's garrison held out, it was unable henceforth to impede events on the plain further south.

About 4 p.m., with yet more cannon in close support, and relying upon his 'intercalated' infantry-and-cavalry formation to produce both fire and shock, Marlborough launched a new attack in the centre. The cavalry combat swung back and forth, then some French infantry fire checked the Allied horse, upon which Orkney with nine battalions of the second line, including the third (Hamilton's) English brigade, struck. Colonel Blood brought nine cannon over the plank bridges and opened fire at short range with grapeshot. The duke's remaining cavalry then charged and the French cavalry, having already halted to use their pistols against the charge, broke and disintegrated. Not even the French household cavalry withstood Marlborough's attack. Tallard called on Marsin for help from Oberglauheim, but Marsin was preoccupied with Eugene and refused aid – a contrast to the co-operation on the Allied side. No help came from Blindheim. The French infantry reserve behind the cavalry was decimated by Blood's fire and then cut to pieces by cavalry and infantry.

The armies of Tallard and Marsin (and the elector) had been cut asunder. Marlborough rode along the front and, rising in his stirrups, ordered the general pursuit of Tallard's army, while at the same time calling a mounted detachment under Hompesch to turn against Marsin's flank and trap him. Marlborough's cavalry swept across the plain towards Höchstädt. Some thirty squadrons of French horse were trapped by a bend in the Danube a mile west of Blindheim and plunged to their deaths down the high bluffs into the river. The isolated Tallard, whose eldest son was mortally wounded, now sought to return to Blindheim but was recognized and taken prisoner at about 6 p.m.

Meanwhile, Eugene had rallied his cavalry and was preparing a fourth attack. Though it was Marlborough who controlled and developed the moves which brought eventual victory, it was Eugene who had lent vital assistance and who, with only half Marsin's infantry strength and inferior numbers of cavalry, had pinned down the enemy in the north. With the centre torn open the Elector and Marsin recognized that they must disengage before encirclement should overtake them. They set fire to their strongpoints and made a swift and successful retreat by small paths across moor and marsh away from the river to safety. In murky light Hompesch's mounted detachment from the south and Eugene's men from the north-east saw each other, and the delay in ascertaining that each was not a French force further delayed the tired pursuers and aided the escape.

Earlier, around 5 p.m., Orkney moved south from the cavalry-combat ground and extended the encirclement of Blindheim which Cutts had begun. He brought four guns to fire into the village from the north. Bitter fighting gradually opened ways into the village but though some of the garrison tried to break out and were driven into the Danube, others continued a stubborn and desperate defence. The local commander had abandoned the garrison without naming a successor and drowned swimming the Danube. At about 8 p.m., with both sides exhausted, Orkney negotiated a ceasefire. He was astonished to learn of the vast superiority of numbers the thin British cordon was containing, but with a mixture of boldness and bluff he secured a full capitulation.

Holding so many prisoners – and rage and shame among the proud soldiers of King Louis made them dangerous – the duke insisted on their rapid separation and upon his army resting on its arms all night. The sutleress Mother Ross described the prisoners she saw marched off: 'some having no shirts, some without shoes or stockings, and others naked as from the womb', but she added that 'each man, prisoners and all, [was] allowed a pint of beer and a pennyworth of bread and cheese'.

LORD ORKNEY REMARKED ON 17 AUGUST that the duke 'had been everywhere from one attack to another, and had ventured his person too-too much'. It was only later that the Tory partisan, the Revd Dr Swift, who never saw war and preferred not to risk his name on his publications, insinuated that Marlborough lacked courage in battle. That would have surprised Dr Hare, who wrote to his cousin on 14 August that 'My Lord Marlborough was everywhere in the action to encourage our men and exposed to infinite dangers', and Captain Pope of Schomberg's Horse likewise wrote (16 August), 'my Lord Duke exposed himself as much as any officer or soldier in the army, and much more than most of the generals'. Throughout, Marlborough had been at the critical points, choosing units and placing guns to avert disaster, leading them to the attack, massing them in skilful formation to ensure success, never losing his temper or his nerve, always encouraging his men. Unlike the Elector, Marsin and Tallard, he always had a reserve available at the critical moment. And his generals understood what he wanted and worked in accordance with his orders and wishes – a very different situation from that on the French side.

Tallard, in his frank report a few weeks later, warned 'never to have more than one commander for a [combined] army' and blamed much on the Elector's attitude and Marsin's toleration of it. These illuminating comments, however appropriate to French marshals and German princes, will not bear application to the Allied side, where two independent English and Savoyard–Austrian generals worked so loyally and harmoniously together to achieve victory against odds. Tallard's own faults were threefold: first, not to fight at the edge of the Nebel – for as Tallard believed that a waiting game could ruin the Allies' campaign, had he stopped Marlborough from passing the stream it could at the very least have produced a drawn battle and thus a French strategic success; secondly, not to control his reserves adequately; thirdly, to leave his own, decisive sector to visit his colleagues' less important one for discussions which produced no agreement – and no aid when he needed it later.

In 1933 Belloc judged that Marlborough's persistent attack on Blindheim was 'an error'. No subsequent historian has addressed this charge, so a few words here may be in order. Marlborough had personally seen how the French forces were massed, had counted their regimental colours and studied their artillery dispositions, had seen the stone walls and hedges protecting Blindheim. He could calculate that his infantry attack would be against odds with only a small strip of dead ground to give cover in front of the fortified village. But he also saw that Oberglauheim was too distant to give support, and that the centre was vulnerable and already too reliant upon cavalry. To exploit the central weakness required maximum pressure on the flanks, and a pressure maintained persistently; feints and mere 'bickerings' would not achieve this. If heavy casualties were part of the price of victory, it should be paid. It is true that by mid afternoon, with the outcome in the centre still uncertain, Marlborough called for less aggressive tactics in front of Blindheim but that was an adaptation and not a rejection of his original concept, for in essence the assaults had swallowed all Tallard's reserves. Neither in concept nor in outcome was this an error.

Blenheim was a battle where a general's instinct for ground, his eye for the enemy's least mistake, and his ability to reshape plans and adapt to circumstances made the difference between disaster and overwhelming victory: a victory, in Orkney's words, 'entirely owing to my Lord Duke'. Orkney underrated the services of Eugene, the splendid partner in the grim wearing-out battle in the north, but victory turned on the centre and south and those sectors were Marlborough's.

The opposing forces have been variously computed and scarcely any two estimates agree in every respect, but it may be said that Marlborough and Eugene with 166 squadrons, 66 battalions and 66 guns, totalling some 52,000 men, attacked a good Franco-Bavarian defensive position held by 56,000 men, in 147 squadrons and 82 battalions, and with 90 guns.

The Allied casualties cannot be exactly stated, partly because the categories (such as exactly which units are comprised within terms such as 'Anglo-Dutch pay' or 'Imperialist forces') are uncertain and because some British regiments did not distinguish between Schellenberg and Blenheim casualties or state their initial strengths, but the following casualty figures are probably not far out: a total 12,500 including British 2,250, Dutch 2,000, Danes 1,000, Imperialists 4,200. Against this the French suffered some 20,000–24,000 casualties exclusive of the 14,000 prisoners taken by the Allies, which indicates a loss of up to 38,000 men: two-thirds of their army. Tallard's army was virtually destroyed, and this estimated scale of loss is supported by two reports: Marsin stated that he began his long retreat with only 62 squadrons and 31 battalions (20,000 men), and the mayor of Ulm reported that 7,000 wounded were carried with him.

The Allies captured about 90 guns and 27 mortars, 129 colours, well over 100 standards and virtually all the equipment and paraphernalia in the tents and camp. In fact, so vast was the haul of prisoners and equipment that the Allies were hobbled by them for some days. This immense tally of casualties, prisoners, colours and booty was dwarfed by only one thing: the impact of the victory in France and across Europe.

CHAPTER 14

The Aftermath of Blenheim

AS THE SUN SET ON THE BATTLEFIELD Marlborough pulled a
tavern bill from his pocket and wrote to Sarah:

> August 13, 1704
>
> I have not time to say more but to beg you will give my duty to
> the Queen and let her know Her Army has had a Glorious Victory.
> Monsr Tallard and two other Generals are in my Coach and I am
> following the rest. The bearer my Aid de Camp Coll Parkes [*sic*]
> will give Her an account of what has passed. I shall do it in a day
> or two by another more at large   MARLBOROUGH

Parke sped across Europe, handing Sarah the note on 21 August. She
immediately sent him on to Windsor where the queen rewarded him
with 1,000 guineas for the news. Lord Tonbridge followed with Marlborough's official dispatch to the Secretary of State, dated 14 August.
The news transformed the European scene, and the queen's reply in
her own hand, written on 22 August, conveyed not only her affection
for Marlborough but her gradual realization of the implications for
her ministry:

> You will very easily believe the good news Col Parke brought
> me yesterday was very welcome, but not more I do assure you

than hearing you were well after so glorious a victory, which will not only humble our enemies abroad but contribute very much to the putting a stop to the ill designs of those at home. I will not give you my account of what passes here, knowing you have it from other hands, but end this with my sincere wishes that God Almighty would continue his protection over you and send you safe home to the joy of your friends, none I'm sure is more truly, and without any compliment so, than your faithful servant.

ANNE R

The Prince congratulates your great success and safety.

Few subjects have in one day given such lasting glory to their sovereign's reign. Few have earned so justly the heartfelt and affectionate compliments of their sovereign.

Marlborough's first concern was to get the wounded into care. There was no thought of instant pursuit of the enemy, for the numbers of prisoners and the problems of feeding and housing them practically immobilized the victors: to share them out and send them to the various Allied princes became an overriding priority if the victors themselves were not to starve. He gladly passed half of them to Eugene, who had been denied many prisoners because of Marsin's successful retreat. Additionally, the commanders had to write to all the confederate princes and powers about their contingents' share in the victory, and they also had to pacify Margrave Lewis for his exclusion from the battle and persuade him that he should abandon the siege of Ingolstadt, now irrelevant, in favour of a march on Alsace. It is scarcely surprising that Marlborough was exhausted by so many weeks of excitement and stress, had to be bled, suffered much from 'heated blood' and was thankful for a day or two's relative calm.

The Duc de Saint-Simon at Versailles recorded in his memoirs how the victorious generals treated their prisoners: Eugene 'treated them harshly; the Duke of Marlborough with all respect, all kindness, with the most attentive politeness in all things, and with a modesty perhaps even greater than his victory'.[15] Marlborough was particularly considerate towards Tallard, whom he had known as ambassador to London in 1697–1701, inviting him to dine, providing a guard of honour for his lodgings, and allowing him to send the French king an account by a personal messenger and then by letter: a courteous gesture which not only ensured that Marsin and the Elector's accounts would not stand unchallenged but also that disharmony should spread at Versailles (Saint-Simon remarked on how nobody had been willing to inform the king of the defeat). The duke expressed to Tallard 'his sorrow that this misfortune should fall on him'. Tallard rose to the occasion, remarking 'that since it was so, he thought it his happiness to have fallen into his Grace's hands'.

Marlborough's mind was already busy with prospects and problems: how to complete the French expulsion from Germany, how to prevent Prussia from turning away towards the Great Northern War, how to succour the Duke of Savoy in Italy, how to end the Hungarian insurrection, and how to keep the emperor to his promise over a certain principality. These can be treated in reverse order.

In June a desperate emperor had sought to please Marlborough by offering him the title of prince, with land and with a vote in the Imperial Diet; Blenheim having saved him, he reduced the offer to the title only. Marlborough graciously, persistently and ultimately successfully held out for the full original promise and so he became Prince of Mindelheim, an estate cut from the fugitive Bavarian Elector's lost dominions (at the peace, when Marlborough was no longer in a position of power and the Elector was, the duke lost the estate but kept the title). Blenheim also made the emperor less conciliatory to the Hungarian rebels, whose intransigence probably equalled that of the Habsburgs: the duke's best advice went unheeded. If the Habsburgs now felt able to divert troops from the Hungarian front, it was to pursue purely dynastic ambitions in Italy, where they nourished tastes for Naples and Milan. Yet Savoy-Piedmont remained under threat from large French armies. Marlborough privately argued for hiring 8,000 Prussians (to be paid 2:1 by England and Holland) to serve in Piedmont, but the idea hung fire. It would have helped considerably in diverting Prussia from involvement in the separate war raging in Poland and the Baltic, which currently seemed likely to attract her energies: hence the duke's later visit to Berlin. He was also determined to clear western Germany of the French, and here at least he could do something.

The army began to march on 19 August and passed through crowds of well-wishers on its way to the Rhine. This welcome was all the greater because of the breakdown of order among the retreating French: one of their officers wrote of 'the fires and clouds of smoke rising from the villages and châteaux along our route ... our people burned and pillaged and committed some frightful atrocities, but no one could restore order – *or even seemed to want to*' [my emphasis]. Marlborough's army reached Philippsburg on 5 September, and moved over the Rhine towards the French fortress of Landau, before which Chaplain Noyes expected a third great battle. This prospect did not shake the army despite the losses at the Schellenberg and Blenheim, so great was its faith in the duke. But the French were in no condition to fight, and retreated 'in consternation'. Meanwhile, the remaining French garrisons in Germany gradually surrendered, unblocking stores and releasing the train; and with supply routes fully open Lewis was asked to command the siege of Landau.

Whether through pique at being excluded from a part at Blenheim, or through inefficiency, or want of equipment, Lewis only secured Landau's surrender after a siege of fifty-four days, on 8 November. Initially Marlborough and Eugene were to cover Lewis, but the duke noticed Villeroy's total passivity on the Rhine and decided to resurrect his earlier Moselle scheme. On 20 October he moved north through bad country, and in bad weather occupied Trier on the 29th and then invested the fortress of Trarbach on the lower Moselle, which he took on 20 December. This autumn campaign foreshadows the year 1705, when the margrave was to show himself at his inactive worst, but it also indicates how far-seeing were Marlborough's strategic ideas and how energetic he continued to be even after a campaign as exhausting as Blenheim – and how this energy passed into his tired troops.

Nor was this all. After setting in hand the siege of Trarbach the duke left to visit the courts of northern Germany. From Wissembourg he and his secretary and a large escort travelled to Frankfurt, Kassel and then to Berlin. Jolting over bad roads in a cumbersome coach, the duke complained of sore sides and aches, but he maintained a gruelling pace, Cardonnel writing, 'we travel fifteen hours in the four and twenty, night and day', over 400 miles in sixteen days. At Berlin allegiance to the common cause was reaffirmed, defection or diversion talked away, and a plan for 1705 discussed. He returned via Hanover, where he charmed and delighted the Electress Sophia, and finally reached The Hague. Congratulations and praise were showered on him. Only in England had there been evidence of party spite.

The Tory Admiral Rooke's tactically indecisive sea battle off Malaga (24–25 August) had left Marlborough dissatisfied, 'but the less is said of this the better': not until much later did it become clear that it had been a strategic victory, with France henceforth no longer willing to risk battle for naval supremacy in the Mediterranean. Marlborough had thought (18 August) that Blenheim would 'entirely settle and quiet everybody's mind' at home, and old John Evelyn's diary account of the solemn thanksgiving at St Paul's in September indicates that many minds were not merely settled and quiet but happy and elated. But some Tory critics said that 'it was true a great many men were killed or taken [at Blenheim], but that to the French King was no more than to take a bucket of water out of a river', a comforting and helpful remark of the sort that British successes often provoke among a certain breed of men. Marlborough had no gift for witty or biting phrases: his words were sober, his work with mere deeds. He could only remark, 'if they will allow us to draw one or two such buckets more, I should think we might then let the river run quietly and not much apprehend its overflowing and destroying its neighbours'.

Marlborough reached London on 25 December 1704. He brought with him Marshal Tallard, sixteen French generals and nineteen senior officers, and all the colours and standards which had been his army's agreed share after Blenheim. Not until his return to London could he receive the full thanks of a sovereign intent on vesting the royal park at Woodstock on him, together with an Act for the construction of a new palace there to commemorate the greatest victory on land since Agincourt. But first Marlborough received the thanks of Parliament, that of the Commons deliberately linked with Rooke's action at Malaga. The Lords were more gracious and applauded his saving Germany: 'The honour of these glorious victories, great as they are (under the immediate blessing of Almighty God), is chiefly, if not alone, owing to Your Grace's conduct and valour. This is the unanimous voice of England, and all Her Majesty's allies.' Then the duke briefly replied, praising 'all the officers and soldiers I had the honour of having under my command; next to the blessing of God, the good success of this campaign is owing to their extraordinary courage': words which fittingly close the year of Blenheim.

PART FIVE

High tide and the turn,

1705–10

CHAPTER 15

War Policy and the Campaigns of 1705–9

IF MARLBOROUGH HOPED IN 1705 to build upon the success of the previous year he was disappointed. His Moselle scheme was not backed by the German princes and Margrave Lewis seemed even more ill-disposed. While Marlborough tried to push measures there, hoping to move via the Saar and the Moselle into Lorraine, a French offensive in Belgium retook Huy and the city of Liège from the Dutch army. Abandoning his plans, Marlborough hastened west and retook both places. In July he outwitted Villeroy, who was holding the Lines of Brabant with 70,000 men, and by feints and counter-marches broke through at Elixheim in a brilliant operation. This might have led to a general engagement but the Dutch proved obdurate and little more resulted than levelling part of the Lines. Even so, Marlborough's action had drawn French troops from the Rhine front, where the ablest French marshal, Villars, had been dangerously active. In Spain and Portugal Allied arms made apparent progress, but in north Italy Eugene had been able to achieve little towards helping the Duke of Savoy. Perhaps the best development was that Emperor Leopold died and was succeeded by his eldest son, Joseph, who admired Marlborough.

In preparing for 1706 Marlborough was determined not to be tied to Imperial generals in Germany, and was actively planning to take English troops south to fight alongside Eugene. A French success against the mortally sick margrave thwarted this, for it led the Dutch to insist that the duke remain in the Low Countries. Here Villeroy was venturing forth in search of Marlborough. They clashed in open, rolling country where the duke won perhaps his greatest victory, at Ramillies (23 May 1706), by unbalancing the French in their dispositions and swiftly transferring his own attack to their weakest point. Villeroy lost almost 20,000 men and over fifty cannon; Marlborough's casualties were under 4,000. A whirlwind pursuit across Belgium seized Brussels and the vital supply port of Ostend and left Marlborough controlling most of the waterways leading into France: next year might see France invaded. In Piedmont Eugene defeated and killed Marsin at Turin and drove the French out of Italy across the Alps. From Portugal Lord Galway advanced and took Madrid for the Habsburg claimant, Archduke Charles, 'Carlos III', but Allied forces from Catalonia marched too belatedly and Galway, faced by widespread hostility, abandoned the capital, united with the Catalonian contingent and retreated to the east coast.

The year not only marked the high tide of Allied successes, but exposed the Alliance and Marlborough to increasing strain, for the recovery of Belgium for the Habsburgs raised questions of its future government and the definition of the 'barrier' promised to the Dutch in the Grand Alliance Treaty; henceforth, secondary objectives in the treaty fomented dissension between the partners, and the differences between the Austrians and the Dutch soon embroiled Marlborough in conflicting claims which permanently soured relations and led each disputant to blame or suspect him for not siding with them. Worse, at home Sarah's growing estrangement from Anne, and her relentless advocacy of the Whig party to a queen who abhorred 'parties', was slowly poisoning relations between the monarch and her old friends Godolphin and Marlborough. This was the more serious because

Robert Harley, a former Speaker and currently a Secretary of State and the third partner in the ministerial 'triumvirate', was gradually and silently moving against them and seeking to create a privileged place by backstairs influence. Further afield, in Spain Felipe V emerged as stronger and more popular everywhere except in Catalonia. The Habsburg cause there steadily declined, though the Allies became more vociferous in its support.

The victories of Ramillies and Turin had achieved the first of the late King William's objectives, the ending of French supremacy; and his second, a settlement of the Spanish succession upon 'partition' lines, was certainly being considered by Louis XIV in 1705–6. Louis may have been sincere, but his forty years' record for chicanery made all his negotiations understandably suspect to the Allies. Moreover, the need to open diversionary fronts in 1703 had extended Allied objectives: 'no peace without Spain' was a political imperative for the emperor, the English ministers and the Whigs, though Holland was lukewarm over this and the Tories increasingly hostile. The Allies were trapped between their 1701 agreement to 'common' peace terms and an excessive demand. So Louis's approaches failed.

The year 1707 was one of frustration. In the north the Allies had to spread garrisons across Belgium and this enabled a large French army to keep Marlborough's weaker force marching and counter-marching. He himself was distracted by Prussian fears that the Swedish king might make war in Germany, and he was obliged to spend several weeks travelling across half Europe to see the king and ascertain that his priority was fighting Russia. In Germany Villars overran and raised contributions from southern Germany after capturing the Lines of Stollhofen. In north Italy the Austrians annexed territory and signed a private agreement releasing blockaded French troops for service elsewhere. The Austrians also helped to ruin an attack on Toulon, Marlborough's greatest objective in the southern theatre. They suddenly diverted part of their army south to capture

Naples, their remaining troops and the Savoyards were late in marching from Italy, and the British contribution (the fleet) could do nothing to offset this. France gained time to strengthen Toulon's defences, the siege was started but abandoned almost at once and the scuttling of the French Toulon squadron was the only gain.

More ominously, troop requirements for Iberia were proving insatiable. A longer campaigning season than in Flanders, a harsher climate and the great distances (Madrid is 300 miles from either Lisbon or Barcelona, 180 from Valencia) caused greater wastage, while resupply took much longer. By 1707 Gibraltar, Portugal and Spain's Mediterranean coast absorbed six English cavalry regiments and twenty infantry battalions as against the seven and seventeen in Flanders. When in April Lord Galway was overwhelmed at Almanza, losing fifteen battalions, virtually all Spain save the east coast was free from Habsburg control. Almanza implied that 'no peace without Spain' was unattainable.

Throughout 1708 stalemate continued on the Rhine and Moselle. In the spring a Jacobite expedition against Scotland distracted British attention but came to nothing. It had been one part of a larger French plan which hoped also to capitalize upon discontent in Belgium over Anglo-Dutch administration. Slightly too late, in July a Franco-Belgian conspiracy secured strongpoints in western Flanders for the French army, including the vital communications hub of Ghent. Marlborough marched from south of Brussels and was joined by Eugene from the Moselle. They won a great running encounter victory over the French at Oudenarde (11 July) – the opposing forces being equal in numbers but the casualties only 4,000 Allies against 15,000 French – penned the defeated army in a corner of the coast, and promptly turned south to France. Marlborough wished to march on Paris: dropping reliance on his old supply lines, he proposed that an expedition from England should take Abbeville, which would become the supply port for his march. This was too daring for Eugene and the

Dutch, who insisted that the rest of Belgium had to be cleared, and so the remainder of the year until December was taken up with the siege and capture of Louis's cherished fortress city of Lille and secondary operations connected with this undertaking.

That same year Imperialist forces began to arrive in Spain, but accomplished little. Marlborough's old dream of Minorca was endorsed as a strategic priority by the Cabinet, and in September it was captured by British forces, giving the fleet dominance over the waters between Spain, France, Italy and Africa.

The year 1708 also saw the break-up of the Marlborough–Godolphin–Harley triumvirate, Harley going into opposition and the Whigs securing control of the ministry. It had proved impossible to maintain a controlling balance between the Whigs and Tories, and the two ministers were increasingly driven to adopt policies which were anathema to Queen Anne. Sarah had lost virtually all influence with Anne, who relied increasingly on Harley's confidante Abigail Hill (Mrs Masham);[16] Sarah's tantrums undermined Godolphin's position when he sought to reconcile the two women and – though Anne respected him above all her servants – even estranged the queen from the duke. To this he himself later contributed by a catastrophic misjudgement, through his perennial sense of insecurity. Throughout 1709 Marlborough repeatedly asked Anne for the post of captain general for life. Cromwell's memory was too fresh, Marlborough's prestige with his troops was too great, and the queen first hedged and then demurred. Marlborough's warnings that without such an appointment he might resign left her angry and unconvinced.

A desperately exhausted France sought peace in 1709 and conceded to the Allies almost everything that they could desire, save for two articles in the Allied draft terms. The Allies demanded too much and pressed Louis too far, and for this tragic mistake Marlborough must bear his share of blame since he thought the king would refuse them nothing, and his assessment of France's military weakness must have convinced the other negotiators. It is an indication of a decline in his judgement. The two unacceptable articles were that within a stated period Louis XIV must somehow dispossess Felipe V of the Spanish throne; and that if that cession was not made within the stated period – during which time the Allies would occupy key fortresses in northern France, thus leaving Louis totally defenceless – then war would resume. This last point meant that the Allies, but not the French, could improve the balance of advantage during a 'stand-still period', and was plainly prejudicial. But the crux was in the other article, for though Louis would in any event have been averse to marching against his own grandson (Marlborough sympathized over this), the French by this time probably no longer had the power to depose him by force. Felipe had become an independent monarch with considerable popular support inside Spain. He was determined to keep that throne; and the Iberian campaign of 1709 further strength-ened him. Louis rejected the articles. In June military operations resumed, though talks continued into mid 1710.

Outside Flanders little of importance occurred in 1709, but there Marlborough and Eugene continued the siege campaign against the fortresses on the Franco-Belgian border. They were challenged by France's main army, led by Villars, with Boufflers as his second in command. The resultant battle of Malplaquet (11 September) saw 110,000 Allies drive 80,000 French from entrenched positions but at a cost of 24,000 casualties (the French lost some 10,000). It permitted the Allies to complete their siege programme, but it showed how bravely France still could fight, and the casualties shocked England and Holland, where the war was increasingly seen as futile and unnec-essarily prolonged.

With a crumbling position in England, diminishing support from the queen, without comfort when at home and increasingly exhausted by his duties in the field, Marlborough prepared for the campaign of 1710.

CHAPTER 16

The Campaign of 1710:
The Ruin of Marlborough's Domestic Position

THE CAMPAIGN OF 1710 **PRODUCED** no decisive outcome, but as it paved the way for Marlborough's greatest achievement as a manoeuvre general in the following year, the sombre events of this year deserve more than a brief mention. Although Marshal Villars had boasted to his master that 'If God gives us another defeat like this [Malplaquet], Your Majesty's enemies will be destroyed', the risks behind such a claim, and its hollowness, were exposed by the care with which the supreme command at Versailles avoided battle. Marlborough's spies reported that Villars 'had not been able to keep his word to the King of France in giving a battle'; but Marlborough thought that if they should venture one, 'this country being all plains, it must be very decisive. I long for an end of the war, so God's will be done'. But when Villars did advance and the Allies turned to face him, the marshal drew back again. For much of the year the French stayed behind their existing earthworks, and at the same time were urgently constructing a great rearward line, the *Ne Plus Ultra* Lines from the English Channel to the Ardennes, as a final barrier against Marlborough's and Eugene's armies.

The duke's plan was for a thrust along the waterways to Douai on the River Scarpe and, that place once taken, to besiege and take

Arras, thus clearing the road to Paris and isolating the territories of the Pas de Calais. In addition Marlborough intended a landing further south along the Channel coast at the Somme mouth below Abbeville, so that the French western flank would be continually under threat. By making an unexpectedly early start to the campaign, Marlborough and Eugene surprised the French and by feints and hard marching, broke through the 40-mile Lines of La Bassée which ran from Aire-sur-la-Lys to Douai, pressed on to the plain of Lens and opened the siege of Douai. Villars threatened them near Lens but withdrew when battle was offered, and Douai, despite its extensive water defences and a determined garrison, fell at the end of June. A reinforced Villars had, however, thrown himself into Arras and was now too strongly placed for the duke to risk an attack and so the Allies moved west, besieged Béthune and captured it by the end of August. Then the Allies moved yet closer to the coast, taking first St Venant (late September) and Aire (early November), and thus by these three sieges almost isolated the Pas de Calais. Strategically the campaign had achieved much less than Marlborough had hoped, the one real prospect of battle at Lens had come to nothing, and sieges were slow and yet still costly in men and munitions. What had been achieved was the opening to the Allies of the waterways of the Lys and of the Scarpe and Escaut (Scheldt) as far as Douai, so that in 1711 the advance might be continued along several rivers.

When the duke returned to England just after Christmas 1710, nearly all the foundations of his power at home had gone, and he could no longer count upon any acceptance of his belief that time would ensure decisive victory for British arms. War-weariness and a poor harvest had turned people against the Whig government and its policy of 'no peace without Spain'. A government prosecution of a Tory clergyman, Sacheverell, for a foolish and insulting sermon (in which Godolphin was libelled) proved a disaster for the government and in the aftermath the most unpopular of the Whig ministers,

Sunderland (John and Sarah's son-in-law), was dismissed. That straw in the wind led the French finally to break off the desultory peace talks which had continued in Holland since early 1709. In August 1710 Anne summarily dismissed Lord Treasurer Godolphin in a curt and graceless letter. The Whigs were outmanoeuvred and dismissed successively and a new ministry came in, dominated by two men of very different and ultimately incompatible persuasions, Robert Harley and Henry St John. Harley, the new Chancellor of the Exchequer, had become the most inveterate enemy of Marlborough in recent years. St John, now a Secretary of State, was young, unprincipled and ambitious; Marlborough had treated him like a son, had secured for him the post of Secretary at War, a post which he resigned in 1708 to follow Harley into opposition, both of them agreeing on the need for an early peace.

Circumstances rather than desire had led Marlborough into the Whig camp; unlike Sarah he was not naturally at ease among them, and for their part the Whigs had used his prestige without really trusting him. Their party was swept away in the General Election of October 1710, which gave the Tories a crushing majority in the Commons. Even before this Marlborough had suffered deliberate royal snubs: early in 1710 some senior officers had already been appointed without his being consulted; and his objections to the promotion of the worthless Jack Hill (brother of Sarah's supplanter as favourite, Abigail Masham) were curtly rejected. After the election political interference in the Army's administration increased. Harley suggested to the queen that all generals and admirals and captains should be appointed annually and the commands of all regiments dispensed of by the crown – proposals which would have placed control entirely in the hands of ministers, with dire consequences for the efficiency of the fighting services. One of Marlborough's critics with the army, Lord Orrery, sought and received through Harley the queen's authority to take leave without his commander's permission, and by like means he was promoted major general after only eighteen months as a brigadier. In November 1710 several of Marlborough's most trusted officers were cashiered by the government on an informer's report of their drinking in private an anti-ministerial toast, and the letters of dismissal were sent to the duke for him to deliver unopened. Furthermore, his personal entourage were progressively stripped of their emoluments. He himself was subjected to pinpricks, snubs and patronizing condescension.

Worst of all, on reaching home Marlborough for the first time – and to his real anger – heard all the details of the irreconcilable breach between Sarah and the queen: how Sarah had even written to Anne alleging that the queen and Abigail shared lesbian inclinations. It is almost impossible to imagine his feelings, caught between his adored wife's fury and the insulted and alienated monarch by whose favour he held office. It must have been an excruciating homecoming. His attempts at explanation and excuse failed, even though he knelt at the queen's feet: Sarah had to give up all her places. Faced with this he could make only the most abject of submissions to Anne and carry out her orders in this matter while his wife raged at home. To Lord Dartmouth he 'complained of his wife who, he said, acted strangely, but there was no help for that, and a man must bear with a good deal, to be quiet at home'. He grimly remarked to the queen's physician that in being dutiful and submissive to the queen he also 'longed to have his wife quiet'; and it is a sign of Anne's residual affection for him that when the physician repeated this the queen 'melted' and said she 'was sorry to see him so broken; that there was no thought of putting him out'.

That, however, was exactly what Marlborough believed her new servants intended. They had made unavailing approaches to the Elector of Hanover to take Marlborough's place as c.-in-c. They used the occasion of an inquiry into the conduct of operations in Spain to criticize his colleagues and praise his critics. In 1710 an Allied thrust from Catalonia briefly took Madrid again, until widespread hostility and strong Bourbon armies forced it back. During the retreat an isolated British force of eight squadrons and eight battalions (but mustering only 2,500 men) was overwhelmed at Brihuega (December). This so decisively affected opinion at home that the Marlburian and Whig policy for Iberia was judged bankrupt. So powerful was the swing that in the early months of 1711 the Tories set on foot an inquiry into the way Marlborough's army's bread contracts had been awarded and executed, and moneys spent. But for the moment there was caution: Harley thought that Marlborough's dismissal could trigger a run on the funds and shake England's financial standing abroad. St John, however, was seeking the duke's outright humilia-tion and wrote to him with barely concealed insolence. The duke warned his family and friends that his correspondence was being opened and examined: nothing important should be written unless a safe hand could be found to carry it. To add to his problems, Sarah, who said she cared nothing for ministers' opinions, continued to write freely until her much tried husband had to tell her that she had 'already forgot his earnest request'. To his foreign correspondents' enquiries about what was passing in England he made only veiled allusions or simply declined to give them any real answer ('I shall hold over all account of my troubles till we next meet', or 'what you have written about our embroilments shows me that you are fully and accurately informed').

As so often in the past Marlborough wrote of his war-weariness and the pleasures of retirement, but it is impossible to judge whether he really did intend resigning. For the Dutch, Austrians and Hano-verians, the thought of Marlborough's removal from command was deeply disturbing. At home the displaced Whigs and his old friend Godolphin beseeched him until he promised that he would continue to serve, despite the change in circumstances in England. With a mind full of foreboding he left England early in 1711 for his final campaign.

PART SIX

The supreme manoeuvre: 'Ne Plus Ultra' and Bouchain, 1711

CHAPTER 17

The Complications of Deceit, Disorganization and Smallpox,
Spring 1711

MARLBOROUGH RETURNED TO THE HAGUE in the first days of March 1711, leaving a hostile court and a comfortless home for the comparative peace of his army. Unknown to him, the ministry in London was playing a double game over France. Several months earlier Versailles had made secret suggestions for a separate peace with England, and by the time Marlborough left England Harley was covertly preparing a welcoming reply. The consequence was that while English ministers sought early progress in negotiations and used French fear of the duke to gain a bargaining advantage, the French considered that Marlborough's dismissal would equate to a major victory and sought every means to avoid the risk of engagement in the coming campaign. He himself judged that this must be a campaign to smash the last barrier and march on Paris, fearing that he would incur displeasure if he made no progress and yet be condemned if he was suspected of risking casualties.

In January 1711 French defensive preparations were so advanced that an alarmed Marlborough instructed Cadogan, who had remained in the Low Countries, to push ahead with provisioning and attending to the state of forward outposts in order that the campaign should start as early as possible. But such activity meant disbursing money, and since Godolphin's dismissal the British government had begun to slip ever further behindhand in this and other respects. The energetic Whig Secretary at War, Robert Walpole, had been replaced by the lacklustre Tory Granville, and Marlborough's correspondence all through February and March was full of requests for greater activity – over officers returning to duty, recruits, supply of clothing, better co-ordination with the Commissioners for Transports, even for properly drawn-up orders. For the first time in the war the commander-in-chief had to write protesting at the way the War Office was being run and the Army neglected, using phrases such as: 'As it is of the last consequence, I am willing to repeat it to you again that HM's pleasure may be immediately signified accordingly' and 'I am persuaded that you will do your utmost in forwarding this service ... and must particularly recommend to you the hastening over of the clothing ...' and 'I ought not to take those bare minutes [of a committee on Army matters] for my direction, but that whatever HM agrees ought to be digested and signified by proper orders'.

Other problems of diplomacy, money, men and royal *amour-propre* added to Marlborough's cares in March 1711. So backward were preparations in the Low Countries and so great the drain on troops to fill the 'corps of neutrality' (a composite force, largely funded by Britain, to maintain neutrality in Germany, where the Great Northern War was again threatening to spread) that upon arrival Marlborough judged that the Allies were still unready. Moreover, lack of 'subsistence money' for various German contingents made it impossible for them to join, and Marlborough had to beg an advance of funds from London to overcome this additional complication. He believed that the Allies' recent prize of Douai might be threatened, for which he was ready to hazard a battle. He ended a formal letter to Eugene, who intended leaving Vienna in mid March, with a sentence in his own hand: 'Prince, in God's name, hasten your coming to the utmost.'

Marlborough then wrote to the Duke of Savoy advocating an attack on Dauphiné. Given his concern at Allied weakness in Flanders, it is interesting to find that he declared that the Allied strength in the north would attract all available French troops away from the south; he may well have hoped that a Savoyard démarche would weaken the northern front; but rather than conclude that this was Marlburian duplicity it seems probable that he was arguing for that classic strategy of alliances at war with central powers, multiple simultaneous attacks from all sides.

He now received a body blow from London: late in March Colonel Richard Kane arrived with instructions for five infantry regiments to leave Flanders for an expedition against Quebec. Marlborough had to comply. The expedition was St John's personal project, never discussed with Harley nor planned with the proper involvement of the Admiralty. The five battalions were sorely missed in the subsequent Flanders campaign and their absence undoubtedly depressed prospects for battle. In the result the expedition, badly led by Admiral Walker and Mrs Masham's useless brother Jack Hill, never reached Quebec, ending in September with shipwreck in the St Lawrence, uselessly costing many lives. The venture had been strategically futile and harmful to Marlborough's prospects in Flanders; furthermore, St John proved unable to account for most of the funds disbursed for it.

Nor was the loss of these five regiments the last hitch in Marlborough's campaign plans. On 10 March he had written to the king of Prussia asking that the Prussian contingent should join him at Maastricht by 2 April at latest, and he was exchanging friendly letters with its commanders when he learned that the king had taken umbrage with the Dutch and English governments over quite other matters and refused to let his troops march. April continued the trial of Marlborough's famous patience. His personal appeals to all parties in the Prussian dispute did secure the release of the Prussian troops, but their march was several weeks late. Other contingents were gathering, but slowly. The British government was tardy in providing cash at The Hague, which meant that if the army took the field before its arrival, large troop detachments would have to be sent to escort the money across Flanders. Prince Eugene was detained in Vienna until a Turkish emissary should come with guarantees of peace on the Austrians' eastern frontiers. Only on 26 April did Marlborough's campaign open, nearly a month late in a year when he could not afford delay.

By this time Europe had undergone a dynastic earthquake. The dauphin died of smallpox. News of his death reached Marlborough on 21 April, at the same time as news that Emperor Joseph in Vienna likewise had contracted the disease. The duke had barely had time to warn ministers that if the emperor should die, 'it must put all our affairs on this side in great confusion', when letters reached him at Tournai on the 28th telling of Joseph's death. At once all plans had to be recast. Eugene had been travelling from Vienna to The Hague when he heard the news and was at once ordered to the upper Rhine to serve there as Marshal of the Empire. Imperial forces in Belgium were likely to be recalled to Germany. To add to Marlborough's woes an alarmed Polish king demanded the return of his Saxon contingent from Belgium.

One of the stated objectives of the Grand Alliance had been to stop the union of the French and Spanish crowns.[17] Partition, not union, had been the initial solution; although Allied acceptance of the Archduke Charles as king of Spain had meant that victory would leave two Habsburg brothers ruling the Holy Roman Empire, the Austrian hereditary lands outside the Empire, Spain, much of Italy, and the Indies. The experience of the years of Joseph's rule had been that Vienna was fully prepared to snatch at the lands his brother claimed and that mutual jealousy would keep them at odds. But Joseph's death meant that the Archduke Charles ('Carlos III of Spain') would almost inevitably be elected to the Holy Roman throne, thus again unbalancing Europe – and indeed he was promised the unanimous support of all the Electors within two weeks. The Allies had now to decide what position to take about the Allied claimant to the Spanish crown, and in this Marlborough professed himself baffled. He feared that the French claimant would now further strengthen his hold on the Spaniards; he could only suggest that the Maritime Powers should insist that if the Duke of Savoy (with a distant reversion under the terms of Carlos II's will of 1700) claimed the succession, he should be required to assist fully in the operations against France.

Harley had been temporarily incapacitated by an assassination attempt, leaving St John free to act alone. Furious at Vienna's continued obstruction and (with far less justification) contemptuous of Dutch claims, he decided to throw over the Grand Alliance treaty obligation to negotiate peace in common. On 22 April he secretly sent to France England's own outline suggestions for peace, including the acceptance of Felipe V as king of Spain. These the French were to present to the world as peace proposals originating from themselves, and when they did so St John mentioned them to the Dutch as perhaps meriting a little consideration. The unsuspecting Dutch left the matter to their English allies, who thereafter immediately pressed ahead with separate, substantive and secret negotiations. The secret policy was thus at odds with that of the Dutch and Austrians, and with the 'official' policy which Marlborough was still following.

CHAPTER 18

Marlborough Probes the
Great French Defensive Lines,
May 1711

THE TERRAIN FOR MARLBOROUGH'S last campaign was for the most part open and relatively flat, well watered, and quite fertile. The many waterways upon which Marlborough's army depended ascend from Belgium into northern France and their protection was vital to his operations. From Ostend a canal carried traffic to Bruges and thence to Ghent, where it met the confluence of two north-flowing rivers, the Lys and the Scheldt (Escaut in France), each of which was a vital supply route. Boats could mount the Lys via Courtrai and Menin, and then continue to St Venant and Aire-sur-la-Lys in a western branch, or to Béthune to the south, or to Lille and Lens by a third branch, the Deule. By taking the Scheldt, supply boats would pass through Oudenarde and Tournai as far as the junction of the Scheldt with another river, the Scarpe. South of this point the Scheldt/Escaut was in French hands, mounting via Valenciennes to Bouchain and Cambrai (the last fortress on the way to Paris), with a tributary, the marshy Sensée, flowing from the west to join the Escaut at Bouchain. The Scarpe, with a little tributary the Gy, flowed east through Arras and Douai, Marchiennes and St Amand, till it curved north to join the Scheldt, and a canal linked the Deule near Lens and

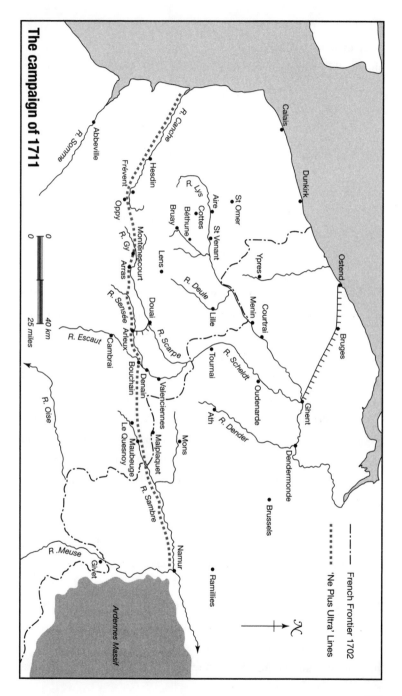

The campaign of 1711

French Frontier 1702
'Ne Plus Ultra' Lines

Scale: 0 — 25 miles, 0 — 40 km

R. Somme
Abbeville
Calais
Dunkirk
Ostend
Bruges
Ghent
R. Canche
Hesdin
Frévent
Oppy
R. Lys
R. Gy
Montenescourt
Arras
Bruay
Béthune
Cottes
St Venant
Aire
St Omer
Ypres
R. Deule
Menin
Courtrai
Lille
Lens
R. Sensée
R. Scarpe
Douai
Arleux
R. Escaut
Cambrai
Bouchain
Denain
Valenciennes
Tournai
R. Scheldt
Oudenarde
Dendermonde
Ath
R. Dender
Mons
Malplaquet
Le Quesnoy
Maubeuge
R. Sambre
Brussels
Namur
Ramillies
R. Oise
R. Meuse
Givet
Ardennes Massif

181

the Scarpe at Douai. All these places on the Scarpe, save for Arras, were by now in Allied hands. A little canal went south from Douai to the small French-held village of Arleux on the Sensée, and was important as helping to provide Douai with water both for its defences and for drinking: this canal was to play a part in coming events. A glance at a map will show how great were the advantages Marlborough could extract from control of these waterways.

This control was not absolute, however. In the far west of Belgium the French had a garrison at Ypres, only a few miles from Courtrai and Menin: an attack on the River Lys from Ypres could paralyse Marlborough's western arm. Further away the French had garrisons at Dunkirk, Calais and St Omer, which could both support Ypres and threaten Aire and St Venant. But the supreme command at Versailles had placed such constraints on Marshal Villars that any forays could not be more than tactical or 'spoiling' threats, the main intention being to stop any southward Allied advance by defence of the vast new '*Ne Plus Ultra*' Lines.

These Lines ran from the sea to the Ardennes, a total distance of some 160 miles, being a combination of defended riverbank, marsh, earthworks, formal town defences and individual forts. Garrisons held certain fixed points and could be supported by a mobile army which would shadow the movements of any attacking force for, unlike in the case of the lines of 1914–18, manpower was insufficient to man all positions everywhere simultaneously. From the mouth of the River Canche on the Channel coast the Lines went east upstream to Hesdin, Frévent, then 10 miles over downland from Oppy to Montenescourt, where the eastward-flowing waters of the Gy could be dammed and cause flooding along its course down to Etrun, where the Gy met the River Scarpe. The Scarpe protected the north face of the fortified town of Arras, but, as that river soon continued into territory which Marlborough now controlled, the Lines switched by 'a wet ditch' to a parallel river slightly to the south, the marshy Sensée. These marshes, which extended down to the fortress of Bouchain, 25 miles east of Arras, were strengthened by small fortified posts at the few ferry crossing points (*bacs*) and at a causeway through the morasses. From Bouchain the Line was linked to a separate river system, the eastward-flowing Sambre, running through Maubeuge and Charleroi and meeting the Meuse from Givet, then continuing until it met the pro-tection of the Ardennes massif. River, wet ditch, flood meadow and marsh, in themselves considerable obstacles, covered most of the sector west of Bouchain; only the downland between the Canche and the Gy presented a front facing dry ground, and here the earthworks were formidable. With lateral roads behind this long line of defences, the French army could be moved fairly swiftly from one sector to another, and given the siting and strength of the vast works it is not altogether surprising if the ever-boastful Villars told his king that Marlborough could 'get no further' (*ne plus ultra*). In Villars's mind French forces should spend the summer harassing Marlborough's supply lines, launching raids towards Brussels, confusing the enemy with constant marches, while sending troops from his front to assist Louis XIV's plans for unsettling Germany in the aftermath of the emperor's death.

Marlborough finally reached his field headquarters on 30 April, joining a force of about 269 squadrons and 142 battalions (the con-tingent of the queen's subjects being 17 squadrons and 22 battalions). Almost at once bad weather set in, but the force moved south and camped at Warde, a few miles north of the Allied fortress of Douai, where it remained for the whole of May. Since Marlborough had already lost one of his seven campaigning months, this prolonged inaction may seem surprising. Wellington famously remarked that Marlborough faced even more difficulties with his allies than he himself underwent, and so fundamental is this to an appreciation of Marlborough the commander that the instances of 1711, repeatedly affecting his concentration, need recounting.

Throughout May the Duke was hobbled by continuing difficulties arising from the threatened recall of the Saxon contingent by their ruler (the king of Poland), despite the terms of the signed contract for the year. Even when the threat was resolved, that ruler's failure to send 3,000 recruits needed to bring his contingent to its proper strength was, if not disastrous, scarcely helpful. Though the Saxon disruption was the most serious, it was not the only worry; Marlborough had reason in complaining to Holland that unless it paid the Danish contingent the (overdue) pay for which the Dutch had contracted, the troops would refuse to march. Next, the mood in Belgium was causing concern. The provinces had been under Anglo-Dutch administration for the Habsburgs since the great victories of 1706. Sentiment there among some local leaders had become secretly (and sometimes openly) pro-French; the council was refractory and continually objected to paying its dues for the Imperial forces contracted to it. Throughout this year Marlborough had to press for money and subsistence for these men, and to meet shortfalls by payment from the English cash reserve. He was also obliged to watch against conspiracies and the risk of French advances on Brussels from the Sambre and Meuse sector.

Marlborough's patience and care went further than merely seeing to the welfare of his own troops; he actively sought good relations between the army and the civil population on both sides. The following instances come from one sample day, 14 May 1711. He had to express displeasure to an officer who overlooked the need for troops to guard a convoy of 282 bread wagons due to leave Brussels on the next day (15th) and he gave instructions on which troops should be put to that service. He patiently answered a complaint from Belgian officials that some 250 supply wagons and their drivers were not furnished with forage and food; this, he explained in most conciliatory terms, was always a matter for the local authorities and not the army. From occupied French Hainault had come complaints that the

Prussians were unlawfully retaining wagons, and the duke, having made two successive enquiries among senior commanders, replied that the matter had now been seen to. Another complaint, from the occupied Lille–Douai region, was answered thus:

> Gentlemen, I have received your letter and am very concerned to read your complaints that drivers of the supply wagons are cutting corn and rye in the places they pass through. I shall give very strict orders against this in order to stop it, but as regards the pasturage in the fields it is impossible to stop them at least letting their animals graze, since we cannot supply them such forage from our depots. I am, Gentlemen, entirely etc, MARLBOROUGH

All this may seem – in the circumstances may have been – unduly conciliatory. Yet if the object of war is to secure a peace free of hatred and desires for revenge, then there was wisdom in such consideration and courtesy. It certainly contrasts with French military practice towards occupied lands and conquered civilians under the *ancien régime* and the Revolutionary and Napoleonic wars, and with German practice in the nineteenth and twentieth centuries.

Despite concern for the quiet of the country behind him, Marlborough had every intention of continuing his advance into France. His plan in the previous year had been to add the capture of Arras to that of Douai, and this remained one objective. But his principal intention was to thrust south to Cambrai, and to do this he had to breach the *Ne Plus Ultra* Lines. On 4 May 1711 he began to probe the French positions along the marshy Sensée at Arleux, a zone he had raided and controlled for a time during the siege of Douai. Private Deane, of the 1st Guards, noted that the troops took tin boats and river equipment with them, but were beaten off by French fire. Constant bickering would take place around Arleux for the next three months, and as it forms part of the inner history of this campaign the reader should note carefully the reasons for the clashes on each occasion.

According to Deane, a new attempt on Arleux by Imperialist troops (seven squadrons and 500 foot) also failed on the night of 11 May; meanwhile, trouble occurred to the rear of Marlborough's army. On 9 May several supply boats on the River Scarpe, loaded with flour and hay, were attacked and sunk by the enemy at the junction with the Scheldt, polluting and blocking the rivers and endangering rations. Cadogan was sent at once to oversee clearance work, six battalions and as many as twenty squadrons were detached to guard the sector, and labour had to be hired from the council in Brussels; though the enemy maintained some artillery fire on the work, the clearance was completed without further loss within the week. Cadogan's excellent Dutch colleague d'Ivoy undertook the improvement of the river defences along the Scarpe and Marlborough himself gave careful instructions to d'Ivoy and to the governor of Douai, General Hompesch, to test water depths and co-ordinate escort parties before letting supply boats resume their passage. That is the measure of how significant the raid had been, how logistics dominated operations and how anxious the duke was about matters of transport and supply.

The trouble on the Scarpe was followed almost immediately by further worries much closer to Douai. Around 9 May 1711 the French dammed the Sensée in two places, extending Arleux's marsh defences – thereby lowering Douai's moat, interrupting its drinking water supplies and affecting the watermills upon which the army's bakers relied. Marlborough, when besieging Douai in 1710, had employed 1,000 horse to hold Arleux, stop the waters and reduce the water levels in the town's defences; now he promptly sent 300 foot and 400 horse to open the dams again.

Most historians treat Marlborough's tussles for Arleux as being an intended and integral part of an offensive master plan to cross the *Ne Plus Ultra* Lines. It may be so; but the historical record does not indicate this, even if hindsight does. The record suggests rather that his tactic of the previous year, the current threat to bread-making and drinking water and the worry that the French might attack the town all furnished Marlborough with sufficient supply and *defensive* reasons for taking Arleux on this occasion. There is no indication from any source that in May he tried to push beyond Arleux and attempt to force the French from the narrow and easily defended causeway. That does not mean that such an idea was absent – crossing the Lines was a constant preoccupation – merely that the *opportunity* was not perceived as yet.

By the time Prince Eugene at last met Marlborough in mid May, it was clear that the Imperial forces scheduled to serve in Flanders would be required by the new emperor to protect Germany from French interference there. Marlborough, with his eyes ranging over all the theatres of war, sought in vain to persuade the Habsburgs that with peace at last concluded in Hungary some troops might be sent from there to the Rhine, or a reinforcement made from Habsburg territory in Italy to assist the Duke of Savoy in an attack on Dauphiné. His arguments were in vain; what he saw clearly as 'the common good' made no impression upon the statesmen in Vienna. And so he was left to continue his campaign alone, in a much reduced state. One of his critics, Lord Raby, gave Tory ministers a private summary of the feeling in Brussels: 'the prospect of the whole is not the best to me; I expect no great matter without some such miracle as we used to have'. In these circumstances it is not surprising that on returning from his meeting with Eugene Marlborough underwent one of his nervous attacks with dizziness in the head and had to spend two days resting in his quarters. His complaints throughout the ten years of campaigning about his 'physical decay' are so frequent that some writers tend to treat them as hypochondria, but for a man over 60, isolated at home and with shrinking authority abroad, with so many recalcitrant problems for which solutions were either temporary or not forthcoming at all, the wonder is rather that he remained so active in mind and body, so courteous and so considerate.

But the price, in terms of stress, was exacted – and was duly paid.

Further enemy pinpricks came in late May. Far in Marlborough's rear the French in Ypres dashed east to the River Lys north of Courtrai and smashed sluices, thus temporarily interrupting boat passage. Allied troops from Lille and Menin hastened north and repair work began at once. Rumours also circulated of a planned raid on Brussels and the authorities and the garrison commander asked for reinforcements, which the duke provided by a careful juggling of garrisons from more secure places to the capital (much to those places' fearful concern). Yet, while calling for protection, the Council in Brussels remained generally obstructive in all matters of provision and payment and drove Marlborough almost to distraction. Their own contractor for supplies, who had advanced well over half a million florins on account, remained unpaid and was now without any further credit. Marlborough and the Dutch field deputies appealed on his behalf, but we find some weeks later that he remained almost entirely unpaid, that his outlay for Eugene's march from Belgium to the Rhine was not reimbursed, and that to enable him to survive Marlborough had to lend him English funds.

All these matters fill Marlborough's letter-books for this month, and he was careful to enlist the support of English ministers and ambassadors. He had always been punctilious in keeping the Secretaries of State informed of events on the continent: in the thirty days leading up to Ramillies in 1706, a period when he was at the height of his power, he had sent them no fewer than nine lengthy dispatches. By nature he was always ready to deploy sympathy and charm to ease his path and turn away annoyance. The new Secretary of State, St John, the Ambassador at The Hague, Lord Raby, and the English plenipotentiary on the Council at Brussels, Lord Orrery, had all three been his subordinates and all three were now his persistent critics. He was determined to conciliate them. In May 1711 he sent nine long reports to St John, seven letters to Raby and five to Orrery; in June the figures were ten, eight and one (but with six more to the Brussels Council itself); in July he sent eleven reports to St John. Marlborough extended confidences to them, seemed to draw them into his plans – and thus ensured that if matters went awry with The Hague and Brussels his unfriendly new colleagues would share some of the blame.

Although he sought to conciliate, the duke nevertheless made very plain the worrying military realities and the desperate shortage of troops in Flanders. As he pointed out at the month end in a hand-written postscript to one of his official letters, having detached eight battalions for the corps of neutrality in Germany, released five more for the Quebec expedition, and with the troops needed for the garrisons of his frontline towns of Aire, St Venant, Béthune and Douai (to say nothing of units along the river lines back to Ghent and Ostend), he was thirty battalions weaker than in 1710, while the enemy was stronger than the previous year. He added, 'we are in no condition to undertake a siege', since that would require a covering mobile force in addition to the besieging force; his chief hope was therefore 'to find a favourable opportunity of attacking the enemy'.

On 28 May Marlborough took a wing of his army on a sweep for forage along the Sensée almost down to Bouchain. His intention must have been to tempt the French out of their lines and over the causeway at Arleux and elsewhere, across to the Douai side of the Sensée, and there to bring them to battle with the marshes at their back. But as he told St John, though 'in sight of the enemy's army, [we were] without the least disturbance'. For Villars was hard at work strengthening his defences and had no intention of risking battle: let Marlborough consume all his supplies till hunger drove him away, or let him attack with inferior strength a most formidable and well-manned defence line, but in either case let him fritter away the campaigning season. Thus ended the first month of operations.

CHAPTER 19

Villars Frustrates Marlborough,
June and July 1711

MAY HAD YIELDED MARLBOROUGH very little success. The weather in the second half of the month had been poor and remained so well into June, and that meant sickness among the tented troops. Forage remained a constant concern, and on 4 June Marlborough foraged eastwards from his camp near Douai towards the French fortress of Valenciennes. The repair works on the Lys below Courtrai were completed and the duke gave the local commander, Robert Murray of the Scots-Dutch, careful instructions to protect the river-ways up to the outlying Allied posts at Aire and Béthune: the commanders of those posts were also instructed to send out escorts for the convoys Murray was sending them.

As the duke put it very plainly, 'our chief business at present is to subsist'. That had become a matter of despair for a regiment of hussars in the Habsburg service, as the Brussels Council overseeing Habsburg affairs in the Spanish Netherlands refused all requests for their pay and provision, and after endless correspondence and vain appeals Marlborough had to provide for these destitutes from English funds and stores – a worry that he should have been spared. A further irritant was a renewed threat from Berlin that the Prussians might march home because of a dispute with the Dutch (happily resolved in time), while the Saxons threatened likewise because they were less favourably ranked than the Prussians in the order of battle and thought this reflected on their sovereign's prestige. Marlborough's soothing letter to the Saxons was a perfect example of tact, simple and convincing in its reasoning, and of a winning courtesy.

Prince Eugene, with 30 squadrons and 18 battalions of Imperial and Palatine troops, began his march to the Rhine on 14 June. His departure and the demands for garrisons all along the waterways and in towns reduced the duke's field force to 145 squadrons and 94 battalions (say 22,000 cavalry and 47,000 infantry) as against Villars's 186 squadrons and 131 battalions (say 28,000 cavalry and 65,000 infantry) lodged behind the Lines.

On parting from the prince, Marlborough moved his own army westwards from its camp between Douai and Arleux to fresh feeding grounds in the plain of Lens, with his right wing at Lievin, a flat and featureless zone until the nineteenth century's coal-mines cast up great coal tips and tailings. He now lay a few miles north of Villars's earth and water lines along the River Scarpe and its tributary the Gy, praying that his presence would tempt the French to come out for battle. Though Villars promptly moved west, he kept firmly behind the Lines, with his right wing on the little hill of Monchy-le-Preux, his centre in Arras, and his left behind the Gy. To mislead Marlborough the marshal built eighteen little bridges across the waterways and announced that he would give Marlborough a battle, thus keeping the duke's attention firmly on this sector; meanwhile, Villars detached fifteen squadrons and fifteen battalions (about 9,000 troops) to the fortress of Givet 80 miles to the east, whence they could threaten the country from Charleroi to Brussels or menace the German states further east. Villars also sent more dragoons into Bouchain, replacing them with troops drawn from Ypres and St Omer. Marlborough learned that a vast magazine was being filled at Cambrai and that sixteen heavy artillery pieces and 350 ammunition wagons had arrived to give a total of 110 battering pieces there: such a massive 'park' was scarcely needed for the Lines, so that it suggested rather a plan to take Allied fortresses, of which Aire, Béthune and Douai were the most exposed.

The Dutch, anxious over the destinations for Villars's detachments, sought reassurance from Marlborough. Though he persuaded them that the French were reduced to the defensive in Artois, and that if the Givet force went to Germany then all risk would disappear on that side also, he was far less cheerful to Eugene: he would stay in position while provisions came and while water lasted, but he would soon have to decamp westward to new foraging grounds nearer Aire and Béthune. From mid June the weather became blazing hot, the dust intolerable, water in short supply; rain which began again on 29 June provided only slight relief. By 20 July, after five weeks in the plain of Lens, the army had exhausted local resources, and all the while the enemy sheltered behind the Lines. Marlborough marched west to Bruay, and the next day continued towards Aire, to a camp south of Lillers, with headquarters at St Hilaire Cottes. He was now a three days' march (34 miles) from Douai.

Marlborough could not concentrate exclusively on his problem with Villars; he had to defend his position both at The Hague and in London. His correspondence with Pensionary Heinsius reiterated his fundamental belief that without unanimity between Holland and England the war could not be won, but also that he needed Heinsius's protection from his domestic enemies. Heinsius had a deep distrust of Tory motives but knew that he must not be deemed to be in the duke's pocket. Lord Raby, the new ambassador to the Dutch, sought Heinsius's support for Tory policies, but although the Dutch statesman made a suitable response, the searching questions he also asked showed his continuing wariness over Tory intentions and their new initiatives. The old bond of trust and friendship between the pensionary and the duke still held.

Marlborough also maintained private contact with the Elector of Hanover, and with his fallen kinsman Godolphin. He secured the Elector's support for his military plans for the coming winter and beyond. He let Godolphin know that he was 'a blank paper' upon which his displaced Whig friends 'could write', and that he would obediently follow their instructions. In early July he was visited by his friend and agent Craggs, a member of Marlborough's Board of Ordnance, who carried with him confidential messages from the Whigs. Later in the month a prominent physician, Dr Garth, came to France for three days, carrying about him letters from Sarah, Godolphin and Craggs: Marlborough joked with his inner circle 'that by the colour and smell of them it would seem as if the doctor had made use of no other paper on any occasion during the whole voyage'. The contents may have remained secret, but that Marlborough was receiving such letters was soon reported to ministers.

At the same time Marlborough attempted to shore up his position by seeking some rapprochement with Harley, newly promoted Lord Treasurer and created Earl of Oxford. He employed Lieutenant General Lord Stair, a former ADC and close friend, as an intermediary with Oxford on a double project. Given the poor prospects for the present campaign, the duke now proposed that instead of the army breaking up as usual at the end of the autumn, it should build forward magazines and overwinter in garrisons along the front. This would totally exhaust French resources, virtually bankrupt them, and force them either to abandon northern France or sue for peace.

The English ministry seemed not unfavourable to the project; but the Dutch rejected it. While Oxford may have guessed that the Dutch would act thus, he used the scheme as a bargaining ploy in the separate peace conversations with the French – his emissary Matthew Prior was at this moment at Versailles, talking with Louis XIV himself. And here one sees Marlborough once more as 'the old gamester' (St John's description of him), for though the mutual enmity between him and Oxford was a dominant theme throughout Queen Anne's four last years (1710–14), the duke suggested a second scheme, a political alliance with Oxford, with the duke acceding to any policy that Oxford should develop for the future conduct of the queen's affairs. He made only one proviso: 'and for the conduct of the war to a successful conclusion'.

Stair left headquarters for London on 26 July and spent several days with ministers and even the queen, gaining approval for the first project and privately explaining to Oxford the duke's hopes for the second. The Lord Treasurer temporized week after week; only on 21 September was Stair able to hand Marlborough what the messenger realized years later was 'a bamboozling letter' from Lord Oxford. Oxford, a dilatory and devious man, instinctively cautious, indecisive, and yet with a shrewd grasp of political realities, was now at the height of his power and popularity. The wound he had received in the April assassination attempt may have shaken him, but it lifted him far above his ambitious and politically extreme young rival St John. This surge in his own prestige and the progress of the secret peace conversations with Versailles (which ran flat counter to Marlborough's tenets) rendered unnecessary any Oxford–Marlborough alliance. The episode thus had no outcome. But among 'what-ifs' that alliance has a certain curiosity: imagine Marlborough, ageing and tired, beset by fresh military problems, the man so often speaking of resting in his beloved garden at home, suddenly joining his and Godolphin's old enemy and abandoning the Whigs – who admittedly had never been his best friends. True, except over some moderate Anglican tenets, he had never held 'party' views. Certainly he was constant in his loyalty to the queen. Perhaps his hunger for wealth and the fear that the government might cease paying for half-built Blenheim Palace played their part. But what fury there would have been at home, with an incandescent arch-Whig of a wife, who hated Oxford's confidante, the triumphant bedchamberwoman

Mrs Masham. Would – *could* – Marlborough have withstood Sarah?

To return to the armies. As we have seen, so little had been achieved in four months that the duke was already thinking of 1712. And yet a series of minor incidents had occurred throughout May and June, with bickering increasing over the little post of Arleux, a short way beyond Douai.

Douai lay alongside the eastward-flowing Scarpe, and was defended by the most modern fortifications and waterways. From close to the town a canal ran south-east for about 9 miles to link the Scarpe with the River Sensée, which flowed parallel with the Scarpe and ended in the Escaut near Bouchain fortress. All these rivers were marshy, but particularly the Sensée, and marsh and morass are a more effective barrier than plain running water. About 6 miles from Douai and within a half-mile of the canal's east bank was the village of Cantin, with a château, and 3 miles further south, where the canal met the Sensée, lay Arleux. This village stood at the northern end of a narrow causeway which passed over the marsh and river to a tiny place on the south bank called Palluel. At that time it was the only causeway over the river for many miles in either direction. About 2 miles to the east lay two settlements facing each other across the river, Aubigny and Aubencheul, but their suffixes 'au Bac' (at the ferry) indicate that no causeway was there, making passage by punt or barge slow and constricted. (Modern engineering has obscured this: the maps show the Arleux road as merely *Départementale*, whereas Aubigny and Aubencheul are on the *Route Nationale* 45.) Villars controlled the causeway's southern exit at Palluel and also held Aubencheul-au-Bac. If Villars could hold Arleux, the causeway ceased to be 'no-man's-land' but became a valuable jumping-off point towards Douai, enabling him to cut off the canal water to it, possibly as a prelude to besieging and retaking the fortress from Marlborough.

By the end of June the French had returned to Arleux, repaired the dams and sluices and cut off the town's water supply, occupied

Cantin and fortified its château halfway between Douai and Arleux, and built a redoubt just north of the latter place. This force was in total some 300 strong, with six cannon. From headquarters at Lens the duke concerted matters with Hompesch at Douai, for a dawn assault on 6 July. The duke's chaplain, Dr Hare, wrote on the evening of the 6th, 'Douai being in some distress for water, 700 men marched from Douai in the [previous] evening and were supported by the whole picket of our army, and as this might occasion *a general engagement* [my emphasis], the army were all ordered to be in readiness to march'. Deane put the striking force at 1,500, with eight cannon. At daybreak on a misty 6 July this force captured the defences, smashed the dams and restored the flow of water, taking ninety prisoners in Cantin château and twenty-five in the little Arleux redoubt for a loss of two or three men. Hare added, 'This little success was the more extra-ordinary by the enemy's nearness to Arleux compared with the distance we are at, which is four or five to one'. Marlborough at once ordered defences at Arleux to be improved 'so that Douai shall have sufficient water', and to ensure that the workmen made all possible progress he sent twelve squadrons and ten battalions (about 6,000 troops) to cover them.

Villars's pride was stung. At daybreak on Sunday, 12 July, under cover of marsh fog, a French force of thirty squadrons of horse and dragoons (say 3,700 troops) surprised the sleeping troops in the Allied camp and overwhelmed four squadrons. As the French surged from the causeway, they summoned the English troops in the post at Arleux to surrender, with the alternative of no quarter if taken by assault. The post's commandant was Colonel Thomas Savary (or Savery), FRS, a soldier highly regarded by William III and Marlborough, a Devon man, a remarkable engineer, inventor of the paddle wheel and of pumps for draining mines – which perhaps explains his position here. He rejected the French call and the counter-attack soon proved him right to have done so. The 3rd (Selwyn's, Buffs) and 8th Foot

(Webb's) and some Dutch, buckling their cartridge boxes over their shirts and breeches as they leaped from sleep, drove the attackers back. Some of the captured horses and men got free, so that the final tally of prisoners taken by the French was about 200 men, though the duke lamented that the four squadrons would be of no further use that summer. After the French withdrawal, body counts gave Allied and French dead as about equal.[18]

Besides the duke's full report to the Secretary of State, dated 13 July, and his letters to his friends, there are other accounts of the French dawn attack from Sergeant Millner, from Private Deane and from Brigadier Hans Hamilton, an officer hostile to Marlborough, all of whom add some details and confirm the duke's account. Hamilton emphasized three points: the vital importance of water for Douai's defences, the risk facing Arleux due to the army's having to move to more distant pastures,[19] and the sad probability that except for such little clashes 'we' would not see much action.

The duke personally inspected the scene on 13 July (before penning his account for St John), altered the siting of the camp covering the Arleux works, and strengthened it by two more battalions drawn from the Douai garrison. He saw to it that the Arleux post was made much stronger, and the works which he ordered were considerable for so small a place – three ditches, three palisades and *chevaux de frise*. When they were completed on the 18th, the fort Savary commanded contained a garrison of 400 troops, with eight cannon and two mortars.

Meanwhile, the duke attended as usual to a multiplicity of little problems. He gave time to reassuring a French lady whose property was adjacent to the soldiers' camp at Cantin, promising that strict orders for its protection would be given. He gave great attention to getting 200 wagons of flour safely from Tournai to Douai, with precise instructions to local commanders on escorts and points of junction. He studied new disciplinary rules emanating from London and wrote a polite but firm protest at a change which would bring hardship on the widows and orphans of junior officers killed on active service: it is good to know that after a little delay, the change was reversed as he had requested.

Marlborough reached his new Pas-de-Calais camping place at Cottes on 21 July, only to hear of further French reinforcements (eight squadrons and eleven battalions, say 5,700 men) going east to Bouchain, possibly for a thrust at Belgium. He instantly sent additional forces to Brussels, and called on the governor of Tournai to dispatch two of his best battalions to Hompesch at Douai, while Murray at Courtrai was to send a battalion to strengthen the garrison at Lille. But Villars was not yet looking northward at Brabant. On the day that the duke ordered these moves, 23 July, Villars swooped on Arleux from both west (Arras) and east (Bouchain) with some 15,500 men.

The degree of surprise at Cottes can be judged from the dispatch Marlborough wrote to the supercilious Mr Secretary St John. It clearly was only an interim report:

Today at noon I had notice from Lieutenant-General Hompesch, governor of Douai, that the enemy having passed the Senset [sic] early in the morning with a detachment of 30 squadrons and 28 battalions, were come before Arleux, whereupon I ordered 40 squadrons, with all the grenadiers of the army, to march that way under the command of General Fagel, supposing these, if they arrive in time, may be sufficient, with the assistance of the governor of Douai, to prevent the enemy's design. I likewise sent Lieutenant-General Cadogan, with the regiment of hussars, who will be at Douai some hours before our detachment in order to take proper measures with M. Hompesch against they arrive, and have ordered the army to take bread and load their baggage, that they may be ready to march immediately if it should be found requisite. [Here followed a description of the positions of his and Villars's main camps, concluding the afternoon's report. After nightfall the report began again:] At seven o'clock this evening I had a second express from Lieutenant-General Hompesch, wherein he acquaints me that, at one o'clock, the enemy were firing with a battery of 7 pieces of cannon ... and that they had another battery which played from the other side of the water. We have a garrison in the fort of 400 men, commanded by Colonel Savary who has always had the character of a very good officer. I shall stop the post till midnight, and if I hear anything more by that time I shall give you an account of it by a postscript to this. I am, truly, Sir, etc.

Although Marlborough did not hear of it until 8 a.m. the next day, the fort had been overwhelmed at the fourth assault at 3 p.m. on the 23rd. Initially he thought that losses might not exceed thirty, but he later confirmed that all 400 men had been lost (French claims were for 500): in other words, it was a considerable setback by the scale of the time.

And a considerable setback was just what the duke could no longer afford. In writing to Hompesch he called it a *'fâcheuse'* affair and offered all help in anything the governor might deem useful. When Cadogan returned from Douai with a full report on the action, Marlborough learned that 'the enemy are now at work in strengthening the place', hardly a promising prospect if one wanted to snatch it back again, and of course this had implications for the water at Douai. Stair was about to leave on his mission to England and to him Marlborough handed two brief letters: one concerning overwintering and 1712; the other, to his old protégé turned master, St John, which concluded with 'hearty thanks for the many instances I have had of your friendship since my being on this side, and [I] assure [you] that, whatever becomes of me, I shall ever be sensible of them'. It is hard to see this as other than an apology for the setback and an attempt to turn away wrath.

Marlborough's private letters to Godolphin are very different from those to ministers: he lamented that the chances for a battle were slipping away, and he admitted that he was 'so out of humour' over Arleux that he could not at once bring himself to write any acknowledgement to Godolphin's letter received on the day of the setback. This ill humour was observed by Captain Parker of the 18th Royal Irish, who wrote of the duke declaring 'in a kind of passion' that he would avenge the 'affront' he had suffered. That bitterness was further stimulated by Villars's treatment of his captives, demonstrating how much Savary's earlier refusal to surrender had angered the marshal; he stripped his prisoners naked and proved obdurate about exchanging Savary for a French officer prisoner. Few letters in all Marlborough's correspondence breathe so much anger as that of 27 July, which recounted Villars's behaviour, and expressed a grim determination: 'I hope yet this campaign to return him some of his men as naked as they came into this world'. Perhaps this shock and anger provided the real stimulus for what was to come.

By the time Stair left for England on 26 July Marlborough had had time to take stock and reshape his plans. Nothing was put in writing, but Stair gave ministers a briefing about an attempt to pass the lines 'in one part or other'. Marlborough began calling in his troops on this day. He sent Lord Albemarle with twenty-four squadrons and twelve battalions eastwards some 9 miles to Béthune, and on the 27th he took a party of general officers and 2,000 horse forward to examine the *Ne Plus Ultra* Lines along the River Gy, west of Arras and 10 miles south of Béthune.

From Sunday, 26 July, in some way that can only be sensed, a change began to take place in Marlborough's thoughts, which from about Thursday the 30th affected those of Villars. They had studied each other for years, spent each day trying to penetrate one another's mind and thinking, estimating troop strengths, places of weakness, and the attitudes of Versailles, and of London, The Hague, Vienna – and, not least in this campaign, Brussels. A day or two before Marlborough began to concentrate in the west and make his showy inspection of the Gy defences, Villars had resumed his diversionary pinpricks by ordering thirty squadrons and seventeen battalions (but with no artillery or baggage wagons) under Comte d'Estaing into Brabant, close to Mons and thus towards Brussels. Villars had such enthusiasm for this foray that he half thought of taking command himself. The news reached Marlborough on 28 July, the day after his Gy inspection. He promptly sent warnings and some reinforcements to Brabant, fearing treachery among French supporters in Brussels, but he made no move to break camp. His powerful detached force at Béthune was 50 miles from Mons but received no orders to march east to cover it; instead it remained close to the Arras front.

Brabant remained safe. D'Estaing first stopped short of Mons, then returned to the main army. For though Villars had written to the court on 29 July that he enjoyed complete ascendancy over the enemy armies, almost immediately afterwards he began calling back every available man to bolster the defences along the Lines west of Arras; later he even tried to blame d'Estaing for departing on this distant mission to Brabant.

Marlborough's early biographer Lediard said that Villars overconfidently told his king that the duke had been 'brought to his Non Plus Ultra' and Villars certainly implied this so late as 29 July. Although the marshal's memoirs ignore the next and decisive period from late July to early August, one can nevertheless suggest his probable train of thought. Villars knew that Marlborough, that most skilful commander to whom Allied troops always gave total trust and support, was inherently offensively minded and ready to pay the butcher's bill in return for victory – the Schellenberg and Blenheim were instances of this. He was not frightened of storming strong earthworks and defensive lines, as witness the Schellenberg again, the Lines of Brabant in 1705 and more recently the Lines of La Bassée. Less than two years before, Marlborough and Eugene had attacked Villars in his woods and entrenchments at Malplaquet. On that day they had enjoyed a numerical advantage over Villars of about seven men to five, a tiny superiority for an attack on so strong a position, and yet they had launched it and persisted with it in the face of horrifying losses until they had smashed through. Now, unless all French outlying troops and d'Estaing's force could be gathered in, the numerical balance might be about equal. With domestic support waning and time running out, Marlborough might decide to risk everything on a ferocious attack to secure victory or, failing that, death in battle. To ensure Marlborough's defeat every man should be collected.

But whatever Villars may have thought, his actions show that by Thursday, 30 July the initiative had passed to Marlborough.

CHAPTER 20

The Tables Turned:
Marlborough Passes the Lines,
4–5 August 1711

BETWEEN WEDNESDAY, 29 JULY and Saturday, 1 August 1711, Marlborough secretly reached his great decision on exactly how he would breach the Lines and where: at Arleux. Claims that he had long foreseen and planned the place, that he had double and treble bluffed, are mistaken.

By letter and word of mouth Marlborough gave one reading of the situation and something of his intentions. On Wednesday 29th he wrote to Hompesch at Douai, remarking on the importance and difficulty of penetrating enemy plans, but hoping the enemy would lay siege to Douai 'since indications are that this would offer us the best chance of coming at them'; consequently, recruits stationed along the Scarpe should be ordered to join their regiments. He explained that he would have written sooner had Cadogan not been in regular contact with Hompesch, adding as a postscript: 'Please inform me the exact state of the waters, and whether the enemy has altogether stopped the canal and the river, or whether it still comes to you.'

On that same Wednesday orders were given for the army's baggage and artillery to move away under escort to Douai.

At headquarters on the evening of Thursday, 30 July, the duke's chaplain, Dr Hare, had written to his cousin in England that 'whatever the designs of the French be, we are endeavouring to make what advantage we can of such a number of troops being detached from them [a reference to d'Estaing in particular], and shall march on Saturday towards their lines in order to attack them, if it be found practicable'. Another Blenheim veteran, the shrewd Deputy Judge Advocate Watkins, wrote on 30 July of the very melancholy state of affairs, but went on:

> if we can do anything here to better our circumstances, you may chance to hear of it in a few days, *not* from the side of Arleux, that project is already defeated for want of M Hompesch being trusted with the intelligence money, but on the side of *Arras*. We are making roads to the lines the enemy have made that [Arras] way, between the sources of the Canches and the Ugy. We are gathering all the outliers we can take in, and shall march on Saturday in order to come at the enemy through all their fences, if it be possible. I find State and generals are all unanimous for this expedition; and if we come to action I cannot but believe the success, whatever it is, must end in a peace [my emphasis].

From Thursday onwards a force of 1,200 foot had been at work in front of the main camp levelling roads towards the *Ne Plus Ultra* Lines west of Arras. Secretary St John was officially informed that day that the duke meant to attack the Lines on Saturday 'if it be found practicable', and Godolphin was privately told the same. By Thursday evening Marlborough had heard of d'Estaing's hesitations and the next morning learned from the military governor of Brussels that there were no longer fears in that quarter; he replied on Friday that he intended to attack the enemy lines 'tomorrow', if at all possible. General Murray, having finished his repair work on the locks and fort below Courtrai, was under orders to hasten to the main army and join before it marched 'on Saturday morning'.

Albemarle had been sent 10 miles from Cottes to Beuvry, near Béthune, his force consisting of twelve squadrons and twenty-four battalions (10,000 men). On the Saturday he wrote from Beuvry to a correspondent in Holland that he had 'just now received orders from 28 [Marlborough] to rejoin the army which marches to-day to attack the enemy within their lines ... 28 tells [i.e. writes to] me he is resolved to do it, but I declare that I doubt the result, the enterprise appears to me very dangerous, the enemy, in spite of detachments is yet much superior to us, and it is true that the defection of our army has been terrible this campaign and still continues'.

Putting all these letters and orders together, one sees that Marlborough had been unusually open in discussing plans. Both his own troops and the French knew he had examined the lines along the Gy on Monday, 27 July. He had told his masters he would attack the lines 'if it be found practicable' and the intention and the words 'practicable' and 'possible' are freely repeated in other men's letters and must have come from his conversation at headquarters. By Thursday, the 30th, Watkins knew what the senior commanders in camp thought of the planned assault on the lines, which means that it must have been fully discussed before then. Rumours of a frontal assault were rife in the camp, said Captain Parker. Mess waiters, invisible and yet constantly coming and going, are a marvellous source for overheard remarks and sergeants know all about 'pumping' them; moreover, spies, were all around the billets of the armies on both sides. Much of what Marlborough's troops learned Villars's agents learned also, and if the effect on the Allied side was to cause a widespread anxiety and gloom among certain people, the effect on Villars was galvanic.

Unlike the marshal, Marlborough 'never boasted and never confessed' and it is no easier for us to read his mind than it was for his contemporaries, who, if they knew nothing of his correspondence, could at least study his expression and gestures. All one can do is to compare the private accounts and judge possibilities. Watkins implied that Hompesch was in some way inept with intelligence money, or perhaps clumsy and unable to extract value for money; and Watkins discounted Arleux as a way forward. And in a sense this is what Marlborough himself said: his remarks to Hompesch on 29 July about intelligence-gathering and a siege seemed calculated to make Hompesch concentrate his men– but against attack, to regard the arrival of Marlborough's troops as defensive support. The answers to the duke's questions about Arleux could be given only after careful reconnaissance, but the questions themselves could be read 'defensively'. Yet if one reads the letter another way what emerges is an 'offensive' scheme: study of the water levels and garrisons of the Sensée to judge whether it might be possible to cross and what resistance might be met; the forces in or near Douai placed to reinforce an Allied crossing; the trusted Cadogan brought into the planning and control of local operations because Hompesch had proved rather slow and even obtuse in that summer's events; and all this without compromising secrecy by revealing the offensive scheme now hatching.

The camp at Cottes was about 20 miles distant from the Gy, and on Saturday the army marched 12 miles towards the Lines, and then halted till Monday, 3 August, when it continued south another 5 miles to Villers Brûlin, close to the source of the Scarpe. The weather now turned windy and cold with a great deal of rain, but although his men must have been depressed the duke was noticeably cheerful. The next day (the 4th) he ordered the cavalry to cut fascines for filling moats and ditches and he went to within cannon-shot of the Lines 'with all the grenadiers of the army and 2000 horse, in order to attack them tomorrow', wrote Hare. Captain Parker, of the Royal Irish, says that he was in this force and close to the duke, saw the formidable strength of the Lines 'crowded with men and cannon, the ground before them levelled and cleared of everything that might be any kind of shelter', and saw the duke, whose 'countenance was now cleared up, and with an air of assurance ... point out to the General Officers the manner in

NE PLUS ULTRA' AND BOUCHAIN, 1711

which the army was to be drawn up, the places that were to be attacked, and how to be sustained'. The captain undoubtedly speaks for others besides himself in adding that some thought the latest affronts had 'turned the duke's brain and made him desperate', and yet ... such was Marlborough's ascendancy that, despite the 'dismal aspect', men still hoped that he 'had something in his head more than we could penetrate into'.

Small wonder if Villars had recalled all outlying troops from Ypres, St Omer and Hesdin on one side and from the Sensée on the other, including the six battalions from south of the causeway at Palluel. Arleux was razed so as to deny the Allies any facilities: Deane says that a sergeant and twenty-five men remained to watch the road. French sources state that immediately after Arleux's capture on 23 July Villars had intended to maintain this fortified position, but that his subordinates eventually persuaded him that it would tie down too many troops in garrison and could provoke Marlborough into a riposte of such intensity as to force a general action (a prospect abhorrent to Versailles).

Meanwhile, Marlborough had had six days' bread ration stealthily baked at Lille. On Monday, 3 August, Brigadier Richard Sutton with the field artillery and pontoons slipped away north hidden by Vimy Ridge and marched east to the banks of the Scarpe at Vitry, where bridges were needed. That evening the duke's secretary wrote to Hanover that preparations were complete for an attempt to pass the Lines 'before two days are at an end' and Marlborough on the 3rd likewise informed St John that he 'intended to march tomorrow in the evening, so that on Wednesday I hope we may find means of passing some part of their Lines'.

After Marlborough's showy inspection of the Lines on the Tuesday, Hare wrote, 'we are to march this evening, in appearance to attack him [Villars], but by the morning he will find he is duped, for we have a body of troops that assembled about four this afternoon at

Douai, who will before morning I hope have passed the Sensett, and our army, instead of marching towards the enemy, will make the best of their way with all possible diligence, to pass the Scarpe at Vitry, and join them'. Cadogan had ridden to join Hompesch at Douai with a detachment of hussars. They were joined by Murray and five battalions from the outlying posts on the eastern Scarpe, from Tournai and Lille, so that the combined force totalled seventeen squadrons and twenty-three battalions (almost 10,000 men). Albemarle, too, marched east towards Douai.

The speed with which this plan had been developed, the careful logistical preparations, the skill with which the deployments were made day by day without compromising secrecy, imply that only a tiny circle close to Marlborough knew what the plan was; but to those within the circle he must have been totally open and utterly clear so as to avoid any confusion or misunderstanding about objective, routes, order of night march, timings. The scheme depended on the narrowest of margins. His every word must have been explicit, with nothing superfluous.

Towards evening on the 4th the weather improved. As evening light faded the French saw a conspicuous force of Allied cavalry swing westwards to Sart-le-Bois (towards Frévent on the Canche): the commander of the French left wing feared an attack in the morning, but although this must have increased Villars's original concern for his western flank he did not strengthen it. However, the uncertainty kept him from making any move at all, either west or east.

By 9 p.m. it was dark, with no moon. And now, as uncertainty increased among the defenders waiting on Marlborough's initiative, so it lifted from the Allied side. Marlborough was not throwing away men in a frontal assault. Orders came through the Allied camp to strike tents and march silently eastwards without call of drum, leaving campfires burning to confuse the enemy. The main army, in four columns, faced a testing night: those of the right wing had a 40-mile march to accomplish under 50 pounds of kit and on poor roads. But there was to be no waiting 'for any that dropped behind'. Part of their road, from Neuville St Vaast to Thélus, is now covered by the modern autoroute just south of the great Canadian memorial on Vimy Ridge. According to modern astronomers this was 'one of those nights where the background illumination steadily increases as the moon rises higher and higher'; dark to start with, by midnight it was 'quite bright' and by 2 a.m. it was 'as though dawn were breaking', though that was still nearly two hours off. It was 'the finest night in the world to march in', said Hare. A little after 3 a.m. the leading troops were at Vitry and found Sutton's pontoons in place. Whatever the troops had thought during the day, once the meaning of the orders at dusk became clear to them, spirits rose. In six hours the leading files tramped upwards of 25 miles at a remorseless 4 mph, and still had over 6 miles to cover.

By 3 a.m. Cadogan and Hompesch had reached Arleux, found it deserted, pressed over the causeway to Palluel and sent word to Marlborough that the leading files of cavalry were south of the Sensée. Marlborough had ridden ahead of his army with fifty squadrons (over 6,000 cavalrymen). He must have had scouts patrolling his southern flank along the Scarpe, watching for any French moves, and now the French were seen. With Cadogan's message in his hand, the duke called for his infantry 'to step out'. For at 2 a.m. Villars, having half suspected a night attack on his front, at last discovered the truth and was in desperate pursuit, his vanguard marching in parallel to the duke's infantry, 'sometimes within half cannon-shot', but separated from them by the river. Only one thing mattered for Villars: to bring enough troops to Palluel to destroy Marlborough's vanguard before it was reinforced across the causeway.

The duke and the cavalry were across the lines by 10 a.m. and a furious Villars racing to Palluel with a hundred cavalry as an escort almost blundered into Marlborough's troops and had to swerve away.

To check the duke's progress Villars threw the troops into a fortified post nearby but they were soon captured. Marlborough's exhausted infantry staggered over the causeway during the remainder of the day and were placed in battle order. So many had fallen by the roadside on the march that they continued to arrive for some days; some even died of exhaustion. But the impassable had been passed.

On Thursday afternoon, 6 August, Marlborough wrote to St John outlining in a few sober sentences the plan and its execution. 'You will have seen by my former letters I have been for some time meditating the passage of the enemy's lines.' It was with that view that he had advanced to the Gy, drawing all Villars's troops west, 'while I was taking measures to pass on this [Arleux] side'. He explained how he had collected his forces for the endeavour and how it was executed. He also had some thoughts about his unfortunate opponent: 'The surprise will be the more mortifying, since you may remember the Maréchal some time ago assured the King he had taken such precautions for preserving all his lines, and was so confident of his superiority that he offered to send a third detachment to the Upper Rhine if it was thought proper.' Having remarked on his army's 'cheerfulness' (a word also used by Parker in describing the night march) in their great endeavour, he promised that 'nothing shall be left unattempted that may tend to improve this advantage' and he ended with a modest claim that 'this success must give a great reputation to Her Majesty's arms in all parts'.[20]

Brigadier Sutton hastened to Windsor with this dispatch of 6 August, arriving on the night of Saturday, the 8th (even before the duke's letter of 3 August which had forecast success). It caused amazement, as St John indicated to the duke on the 11th. For although Stair had told the court of plans for passing the lines somewhere, St John confessed that it was, however, hard to imagine, and too much to hope, that a plan which consisted of so many parts wherein so many different corps were to co-operate punctually together, should entirely succeed, and no one article fail of what Your Grace had projected. I most heartily congratulate with Your Grace on this great event, of which no more needs I think be said than that you have obtained, without losing a man, such an advantage as we should have bought with the expense of several thousand lives, and have reckoned ourselves gainers.

His conclusion was also magnanimous, 'God grant Your Grace a sequel of the same prosperity and success which you have begun, and make you the happy instrument of concluding, as you have been of pushing, the war'. Only one customary pendant to a Marlburian victory was lacking: there was no letter from Queen Anne herself.

CHAPTER 21

'The Best Conducted Siege We Have Made in This War':

Bouchain, August and September 1711

BY A MASTERPIECE OF MANOEUVRE Marlborough had reduced *'Ne Plus Ultra'* from proof of 'the inherent superiority of the defensive' to a lesson on that doctrine's dangers. He now had to improve upon his opening, and he did not delay. All through the afternoon and evening of Wednesday, 5 August his infantry crossed the causeway and formed front against a possible attack, camping at l'Abbaye du Verger, midway between Palluel and Aubencheul, and extending downriver. Villars's rash decision to throw a hundred dragoons into a château at Oisy, within musket shot of the camp, merely led to their capture: a measure of his desperation. With Marlborough's army approaching, Villars declared that he would attack the next morning, 6 August, an attack which the duke said he was 'ready to receive'.

Since the events of 6 August became the subject of controversy and highlight how Marlborough's weakened position at home encouraged his critics abroad, it is worth examining the evidence of Marlborough's correspondence, the remarks of those at headquarters, the condition of the two armies, and the nature of the terrain. Marlborough's prime objective now was Bouchain and he would call on his soldiers' remaining energies to press eastwards towards it, rather than expend effort on going south after Villars. If the latter attacked him, Marlborough at least could allow his own troops a few hours to rest in a defensive position while Villars further exhausted his own equally tired men by fresh manoeuvres. This is confirmed by the shrewd Judge Advocate Watkins, who wrote on this day that the most desirable outcome would be for the French to 'revenge the affront' by 'seeking' battle. Moreover, Marlborough's artillery was still not concentrated south of the Sensée because the horse and foot had been given priority of passage; by standing on the defensive he would give it time to join whereas if he marched southward against the French he would deprive himself of its support in an attack on a strong position in poor weather.

It had been wet until late on the 4th, and the dry interval was not of long duration, for the night of 6–7 August was one of 'continual rain'. Villars had moved some 5 miles south-east and taken up a superb position between the fortress of Cambrai on the Escaut and Marquion on the marshy Agache stream. The north-flowing watercourses covered both flanks; in the centre Bourlon wood dominated the country around, standing ominous and dense 100 or so feet above the northern approaches, which at that time were protected by hollow roads and marsh (a word which still features in place names below the wood), a defensive position stronger than Malplaquet. In these circumstances Marlborough's decision undoubtedly was wise.

Yet one of the Dutch field deputies, Goslinga, now told Marlborough that the army should improve on its success by attacking Villars. The duke's reaction seems to have been less patient than usual, for Goslinga admits it was 'curt', and Marlborough resorted to a council of war to smother the proposal. Despite Goslinga's urgings, virtually all the generals – Dutch, Hanoverian, Württemberger and Prussian – sided with the Duke in saying that an attack was impracticable. The incident is curious, for of all people a Dutch official must have remembered Malplaquet, where Dutch troops had died in thousands in a frontal attack; and nobody who looks at the frowning Bourlon position from the north can have any doubt as to its strength. The furious deputy persuaded his three civilian colleagues to complain to The Hague of Marlborough's pusillanimity, but Watkins later wrote that two of the deputies came to the duke to absolve themselves. He added that the Austrian civilian Count Sinzendorff at The Hague (an inveterate critic of Marlborough, and someone fully aware of Vienna's neglectful attitude to the common cause) was treating the duke 'like a dog' in saying to his face that he trusted Marlborough's judgement in declining to attack on the 6th, but needed a written explanation 'to satisfy others': certainly Marlborough declared himself 'mortified' by the count's remarks. As it happens, a Scotsman in Holland independently reported to Harley that Sinzendorff was declaring that though a general 'had won 20 battles' Marlborough deserved hanging 'for this one neglect' at Bourlon. Such agreeable comments soon reached the ears and spoiled the composure of the ever-sensitive duke, nor was their bitterness entirely removed by Heinsius's genuine congratulations and his remarks on the hollowness of Villars's boasts to Versailles.

While Goslinga fumed, Marlborough used the short dry interval of 6 August to move across Villars's front and to the further bank of the Escaut in pursuit of his main objective, Bouchain. By 10 a.m. bridges had been thrown across that river and all afternoon the troops crossed the water without interference. With night came continuous rain but by the morning of 7 August the army was camped southeast of the French fortress of Bouchain, which controlled the confluence of the Escaut and the Sensée. And at this point Marlborough disclosed his true intention, concluding his dispatch of 6 August: 'If the enemy decline a battle, which in that case it will be impossible for us to give [i.e. Marlborough would only accept a battle on his own terms and choice of ground], I design to besiege Bouchain.' The design surprised many of his generals, who saw the risk and difficulties of a siege in such swampy land, and his master gunner, Pendlebury, recorded that almost everyone except Cadogan was opposed to Marlborough opinion. In contrast to his method with Goslinga's proposal, the duke did not convene a council of war; he turned to Colonel Armstrong, his trusted principal engineer, who considered that the siege was practicable, and with Armstrong's opinion once given, the necessary orders followed.

The Escaut valley was a good route into France. On the river to the north of Bouchain the French still held Valenciennes and Condé; to its south they held Cambrai. But the first two could be half strangled by the fall of Bouchain and totally so if little Le Quesnoy (east of Bouchain) was also taken, while the capture of Cambrai (112 miles from Paris), the southernmost of the frontier fortresses, would permit an invading army to move from the Escaut to the upper valley of the Oise, which flows south to the Seine near Paris.[21] Thus Marlborough's vision. On the other hand, Villars had two advantages: he was much stronger and did not have to divide his forces (part of Marlborough's somewhat smaller army would be employed on the siege, thus reducing his mobile covering force); and secondly, with the lower Escaut at Valenciennes and Condé in French hands Marlborough could not use that river: his supplies had to sail up the Scarpe to Marchiennes and then be drawn 8 miles overland to Bouchain, and westward raids upon the Scarpe from Valenciennes or a thrust by Villars north across the Sensée could impede or paralyse the duke's operations. That is why Marlborough's decision was so bold and why, as a technical achievement, the siege and taking of Bouchain is a fitting successor to the masterpiece of passing 'Ne Plus Ultra'.

The strain of chief command in ten years of war was telling on Marlborough. The complex arrangements of the past week had been followed by a long-distance manoeuvre, the success of which turned entirely on the number of minutes he could steal before Villars began his pursuit. An all-night ride and a day spent waiting for his infantry and watching against an attack, followed by another studying the Bourlon position, dealing with Goslinga's importunities and writing or dictating several important letters and dispatches, left him by 7 August 'so fatigued that I had to stay in bed to recover a little', so that he left Cadogan and the other senior generals to agree on the next moves and then to visit him with their opinion.

He was soon active again. He had already cut off Bouchain from the east. He now put 300 men downstream at the fort of Denain, thus checking any southward attack from Valenciennes and covering the construction of more bridges over the river just north of Bouchain at Neuville. Troops were then filtered over the river to close the northern approaches while others marched from Douai to block the north-west. But Villars advanced from Bourlon to the Sensée with some forty battalions and cavalry, putting troops into Aubigny (just north of the river) and Wavrechin village among the marshes on the south-western flank of Bouchain. Villars's superior force thus threatened supplies, interrupted work on the lines of circumvallation which would protect the besiegers from outside interference, and restored contact with the besieged garrison by a 'cow path' through the marshes, a path protected and floored with fascines along its whole length and with a 'nest' halfway along.

Marlborough tackled all three difficulties. During this and subsequent weeks he paid special attention to convoy routes from Ghent to Tournai, to Marchiennes and on to Bouchain, to the size, provenance and dispositions of escorts, and to his principal needs: bread in particular. When Hompesch at Douai reported on the parlous state of his locks and the need to drain the Scarpe so as to repair them, the duke sympathized but insisted on the waters being maintained for the supply boats under all circumstances.

At the same time Marlborough wished to force Villars back, and for a time considered a frontal assault on the rapidly strengthening French forward positions on the western side of his camp. Captain Parker, one of those told off for the attack, decidedly did not like the prospects. His account of what followed stands among a half-dozen of the finest tributes any British soldier has ever paid to his commander. Quite suddenly, the duke,

> ever watchful, ever right, rode up quite unattended and alone, and posted himself a little on the right of my company of grenadiers, from whence he had a fair view of the greater part of the enemies [sic] works. It is quite impossible for me to express the joy which the sight of this man gave me at this very critical moment. I was now well satisfied that he would not push the attack unless he saw a strong probability of success; nor was this my notion alone: it was the sense of the whole army, both officer and soldier, British and foreigner. And indeed we had all the reason in the world for it; for he never led us on to any one action that we did not succeed in. He stayed only three or four minutes and then rode back. We were in pain for him while he stayed, lest the enemy might have discovered him and fired at him, in which case they could not well have missed him. He had not been longer from us than he stayed, when orders came to us to retire.

Despite continuing sickness and headaches Marlborough nevertheless persisted with his plans. First, he erected his own curved earthworks ('lunettes') for counter-battery use opposite Villars's guns. Secondly, he seized the 'cow path' across the marsh. By 18 August the lines of circumvallation were almost complete, the lunettes had been joined by linking walls, and the cow path and nest taken with only five or six British casualties, the 400-man crack force wading through the marsh waist deep while covered by eight battalions of infantry. The fortress was now cut off, most of the siege artillery and munitions had arrived, and the siege trenches were duly opened on the night of 23–24 August, with operations concentrating on three separate sectors.

Nor was this all. Marlborough had begged the Brussels Council for wagons and a small army of labourers, and despite some difficulties and delays he was soon able to undertake the digging and building of two parallel earth lines some 8 miles long and 2 miles apart to create a safe corridor between his port of Marchiennes on the Scarpe and his siege force. In total the earthworks for the siege and the corridor measured some 28 miles. They proved most effective, for Villars could not retake the 'cow path' and did no more than bombard the besiegers as they in turn bombarded the fortress. But on the other hand Villars continually strengthened Valenciennes so as to annoy the Scarpe convoys, and early in September he launched an unsuccessful attack from the Sensée against Douai. These raids obliged Marlborough to divert parts of his covering force, but the siege continued. On Saturday, 13 September, after a long period of rain and with sickness increasing on both sides, the garrison surrendered. Villars and his army, though so close, looked on helplessly. Of the original garrison of some nine battalions and 600 Swiss (roughly 5,000 men), 3,000 became prisoners of war; the cost to the Allies was about 4,000 casualties.

Early in September St John had written to Marlborough, 'I believe there is hardly one instance of an inferior army posting themselves as to be able to form a siege and keep the communication open with their own country, in sight of an enemy so much superior'. The implied compliment agreed with Chaplain Hare's assessment, written at headquarters on Friday, 19 September:

> The garrison beat the *chamade*[22] on Saturday noon, but to the great mortification of Monsieur Villars could obtain no better terms than to be prisoners of war, which after some difficulty they submitted to, and tomorrow they march out to be conducted to Holland. We shall be obliged to make some longer stay here to put the town into a condition of defence, which is at present a heap of rubble. This has been the best conducted siege we have

made in this war, and considering the great difficulties under which it has been made, nothing this war has been more glorious, particularly for my Lord Marlborough, who undertook it against the unanimous opinion of the Dutch, and I may say of most others, who had not the heart to think so difficult an enterprise could succeed.

Both men's praise coincided with Marlborough's opinion of the 1711 campaign: of the ten Blenheim Palace tapestries celebrating the greater victories (Ramillies was never woven, alas), one is of *Ne Plus Ultra* and two are of this siege.

A weary duke wrote to the queen on the 14th:

Madam, I send this by express humbly to acquaint Your Majesty that by the continued blessing of God Almighty upon your arms and those of your Allies, the garrison of Bouchain has been obliged to surrender prisoners of war. That the same good Providence may always protect the justice of your cause, and preserve your royal person for many years a blessing to your people, shall ever be the most fervent prayer of, Madam, Your Majesty's humble servant, MARLBOROUGH.

It was to be among the last letters this greatest of her servants ever wrote to the queen. Anne had written in gratitude and with concern for his safety after each of his great victories except Malplaquet and '*Ne Plus Ultra*'. On this occasion she did reply after a nine days' silence, though her letter is now lost.

CHAPTER 22

How It All Ended

THE REST IS SOON TOLD. The duke wanted to take Le Quesnoy to open a broad path into France before winter, then quarter his troops well forward as prelude to an early start in 1712, but the extensive repairs to Bouchain much delayed him. The Tory ministers had privately reached agreement with Versailles on the main Anglo-French desiderata for peace even while Marlborough was approaching Bouchain, and though they disagreed with his plans they used his operations to secure additional advantages in the secret talks. They informed the Dutch in an apparently frank but misleading way of the tenor of their discussions with France, and the Dutch, exhausted by the war, consequently declined the extra expense of overwintering on the frontier for a campaign which they now believed unlikely.

Oxford played with Marlborough, but as it became clear that the duke would never accept the Tory terms for peace but held to the old policy of the Grand Alliance, so the ministry determined to break him. Marlborough, though still England's senior diplomat, pointedly remarked to Sarah that he knew nothing of what was passing. To England's ambassador in Vienna he remarked of the peace talks, in words that Douglas Haig was to echo almost word for word in autumn 1918: 'You will hear from other hands of the measures that are taking for putting an end to this ruinous war. I do not enter into particulars because I have no share in the negotiations, but I can assure you no man living can be more desirous than I of a good and speedy peace ...'

The army broke up at the end of October and in mid November Marlborough reached London. No public reception was allowed him. All his letters to Oxford had been submissive and even humble, but Oxford was determined to destroy the last shreds of the queen's regard for him. Any of his letters which could be interpreted as criticizing peace negotiations were read to Anne. Oxford set up a Public Accounts Committee to investigate war expenditure, and Tory members were probing various items relating to Marlborough: believing himself in the right, he was at first fully co-operative.

The duke was granted a private interview with the queen, who noted 'his usual professions of duty and affection to me. He seemed dejected and very uneasy about this matter of the public accounts'. In mid December Parliament was informed of the preliminary articles of a peace treaty with France. The Whig opposition in the Lords reiterated the demand 'no peace without Spain' and rejected the government's proposals by one vote, Marlborough adding his voice to those of the Whigs. He refused to attend the Cabinet, which Oxford dominated, attendance at which his military offices and rank as a Privy Counsellor entitled him. In mid December the Public Accounts Committee published its findings that Marlborough had failed to account for £63,000 commission from bread contractors to the army, and accused him of taking £280,000 in commission on the pay of England's foreign auxiliaries. It rejected his defence of long precedent on the first count, and ignored his production of Queen Anne's warrant of 1702 authorizing him to continue King William III's practice over foreign auxiliaries' pay to create a fund for secret intelligence. To avoid examination of the accusations the government adjourned Parliament.

On 30 December (OS) the duke appeared at court but 'nobody

hardly took notice of him'. At this time, using a draft prepared by Oxford (still partly extant), the queen was writing to Marlborough over alleged financial irregularities complaining that she had not 'deserved the treatment I have met with', and dismissing him from all his posts. Like her dismissal letter to Godolphin, it fell below a majestic or even a gracious standard. He received it the next day. 'The Queen's letter was so offensive that the Duke flung it into the fire though he was not a man of passion', wrote Sarah. Marlborough's reply was on a higher plane:

> I am very sensible of the honour Your Majesty does me in dismissing me from your service by a letter of your own hand, though I find by it that my enemies have been able to prevail with Your Majesty to do it in the manner that is most injurious to me … But I am much more concerned at an expression in Your Majesty's letter which seems to complain of the treatment you had met with. I know not how to understand that word, nor what construction to make of it. I know I have always endeavoured to serve Your Majesty faithfully and zealously through a great many undeserved mortifications … I wish Your Majesty may never find the want of so faithful a servant as I have always endeavoured to approve myself to you.

THE FINAL YEARS OF THE DUKE'S curious career in English politics are best treated separately from the military and diplomatic conclusion of the long war.

Marlborough was condemned out of hand by a hostile Commons for misusing funds, though his explanations were cogent. In September his close friend Godolphin died, nursed to the end by Sarah. Unhappy and uneasy, in November 1712 John and Sarah went to live abroad. They were fêted on the continent, though the Tories and the French rightly worried over his intentions. As Anne's health failed,

Tory ministers became increasingly involved with 'James III's' exiled Jacobite court, and the Protestant and Hanoverian succession seemed at risk. Marlborough persistently advocated armed measures against a Jacobite coup. He loathed Oxford, yet was in touch with St John (now Viscount Bolingbroke), whose extreme Toryism was tending towards James.

Marlborough retained contact with Queen Anne and when one of his daughters died in March 1714 he wrote to her that he intended coming home. In June a diplomat in London recorded that Cadogan 'believes he knows from the Queen herself that My Lord Duke would be welcome'. By late July Bolingbroke had engineered the dismissal of Oxford, which came on the 27th, but his own ambitions were checked by Anne's personal dislike, and wider mistrust of his Jacobite leanings. She may have held off appointing a new ministry pending Marlborough's return, for while he was preparing his journey three Cabinet meetings were held but produced no reshuffle. On 29 July she suddenly collapsed. Shrewsbury and moderates in the Privy Council took key posts and eased the pro-Jacobites from centre stage. The Marlboroughs landed at Dover on 1 August, but Anne had died that morning and it was not a Marlborough ministry but the Shrewsbury moderates who proclaimed the Protestant and Hanoverian succession.

Although Marlborough's military posts were restored to him by the new king, he was no longer one of the inner council. The giddiness and headaches of earlier years culminated in successive strokes brought on by another daughter's death in 1716, and he lived the last years of his life a semi-invalid, a condition made worse by the savage disputes Sarah enjoyed waging with the remaining two daughters upon whom he doted. His death in June 1722, aged 72, came as a release. Buried in state in Westminster Abbey, at Sarah's death in 1744 his remains were brought to the chapel at Blenheim Palace to rest with hers.

IN 1712 MARLBOROUGH'S SUCCESSOR as captain general and c.-in-c. Flanders was the pro-Jacobite Duke of Ormonde, who was granted the same perquisites declared 'illegal' or 'unwarranted' in Marlborough's case. Under secret orders to withhold support from Allied operations against the French, Ormonde abandoned his Allies in mid campaign. Eugene was defeated by Villars, and many of Marlborough's recent conquests were lost.[23] An international peace conference was convened at Utrecht, and came to decisions very different from those projected in the years 1709–10; decisions which disgusted not only the Whigs of that time but also several generations of Whig historians.

Yet the provisions of the Treaty of Utrecht endured in the main for three-quarters of a century until the French Revolution swept away the whole system. 'Utrecht' confined Bourbon power and aspirations; established that France and Spain should never be united; gave Holland a measure of security; gave some satisfaction to Austria's insatiable territorial ambitions; helped the House of Savoy to a throne and future prominence in Italian affairs; and gave Great Britain that 'place in the sun' which she was to retain for over two centuries. There were injustices, but the benefits for Europe as a whole far outweighed them. 'Utrecht' endorsed in a modified form the schemes for 'Partition' that King William III had devised so many years before, hoping to avert a war for the Spanish succession.

In one sense the dozen years of that war, fought across many lands and oceans, had thus merely achieved at enormous cost what William had aimed to achieve without bloodshed. But long before his death William had seen that no peaceful solution was possible given the conflicting claims of so many powerful states. If he saw the desired ends better than any other statesman of his time, he also saw that war was necessary to attain them. His great pupil Marlborough, once trapped in the process of coalition war, its developing claims and competing demands, eventually failed to see the way to a balanced peace.

Here he fell short of his master, King William. To break the deadlock and win peace required a new policy, and perhaps devious methods. Certainly the new policy and the 'perfidious' diplomacy were not Marlborough's.

Marlborough's diplomatic skills had been used very much for 'coalition' purposes, to support 'the common cause'. Part of his greatness lay in his recognition – not always shown by leaders of alliances – that there were times when the Alliance required a larger view than that from one's native land, that Heinsius or (to think now of early 1704) Wratislaw should be supported against 'isolationists' or 'blue water enthusiasts' in England. It is true that his insecurity made him timid in pressing matters at home, that he forced on Godolphin the duty of making hard decisions and refusals to the Allies. That must qualify, but it does not extinguish, praise for his diplomatic achievement as a coalition leader in war.

Furthermore, neither King William nor any other British soldier then living possessed to the same degree Marlborough's extraordinary range of skills in war: his ability to endure and surmount endless frustrations from his Dutch and other colleagues, his understanding of the potentialities of seapower, his knowledge and ability in army administration, his tirelessness over his army's welfare in even the most trying conditions, his ability to win repeated and outstanding military success. William ruled the Dutch and though he, too, grasped seapower's potential, he had been a bad administrator and a clumsy general; the other Allied theatre commanders, save Eugene, all had serious limitations or difficult personalities.

Eugene is indeed of a different stature, and his partnership with Marlborough in their four campaigns was, in its harmony and absence of jealousy, almost unique in military history. As a fighting general, Eugene was more headstrong and single-minded than his English comrade whose moments of depression he seems never to have experienced himself. Eugene had been imbued with hatred for Louis XIV;

he had been formed by racial warfare in the Balkans where ruthless victory or massacre were the stakes; he was accustomed to starve and to force starving armies still to fight. Yet his record in the War of the Spanish Succession shows defeat as well as success, and whereas Marlborough defeated or outmanouevred every general sent against him, Eugene was worsted by Villars. Nor did Eugene really grasp how sea-power could enhance and render more flexible warfare on land as Marlborough did, and save for Viennese matters (and how narrow Vienna's outlook could be!) he seemed indifferent to the intricate diplomatic duties required of a coalition commander-in-chief.

At a time when forcing battle on one's opponent was extremely rare, Marlborough fought and won a succession of great battles and but for the frequent veto by his allies might have fought more. In an era when fortifications, manpower, and logistical constraints discouraged the offensive, he relished it. His vision of using joint operations against the French coast to bypass the French fortress barrier and so enable him to march on Paris was too bold for his colleagues and so he was obliged to reduce the barrier, fortress by fortress. Even at the slow pace of the times he had virtually done it by the end of 1711: though not totally completed, it was an astonishing achievement.

Marlborough so shook and weakened the great French monarch and nation in ten victorious campaigns that a just and lasting peace became possible. And not only that; for by those victorious campaigns the liberties and fundamental power of the England of Queen Anne were greater and more secure when her servant Marlborough laid down his command than when he entered upon it. The length and broad extent of his war service stands alone in English history. That is why Marlborough should be among the great commanders.

The Loss of Arleux,
23 July 1711

IN CHAPTER 19 I GAVE AN ACCOUNT of Marlborough's reactions to the loss of Arleux, suggesting that he was surprised and temporarily worsted by Villars. By contrast, most historians (save the maverick Belloc) have adopted the opinion of General Richard Kane (d. 1736) that Marlborough always intended to lose it as part of a master plan for crossing the Lines.

The information on the English side about the background and the events can be read in Marlborough's own reports and especially the letter written on 23 July, letters by Marlborough's chaplain (Hare) and Judge Advocate (Watkins), later memoirs by two officers (Kane and Parker) and a sergeant (Millner), all of whom had served in the 18th Royal Irish, and a journal of a private in the Guards (Deane). Of these, only the duke's letter discloses his own understanding of the events; the others may be accurate as to happenings that passed before their eyes but are not evidence on Marlborough's thoughts. Yet strangely Kane seems to be the preferred source.

In his *Campaigns of King William and Queen Anne, 1689–1712*, posthumously published in 1745, Kane stated (p. 89) that the duke always intended to lose Arleux, in order to have Villars demolish it himself. He [the duke] saw he could take it when he pleased and demolish it ... but he knew that as soon as he was marched from thence Villars would soon come and rebuild it, but should he pretend to fortify it, then he expected as soon as he was marched away Villars would come and retake it and demolish it.

This account of double and triple bluff is echoed by Captain Robert Parker (also of the 18th Foot) in his 'eyewitness' *Memoirs of the Most Remarkable Military Transactions, 1683–1718*, posthumously published Dublin 1746, London 1747, and reprinted by Chandler in 1968. His account tallies almost exactly with the above passage (see 1747 ed., p. 177; 1968 ed., p. 97) but with minor additions such as that Savary's Arleux garrison was 'slender', that the main army was moved 'upwards of 15 leagues' away, that Savary's message to the duke made clear that 'he could not hold out 3 days', but that – despite this warning – Cadogan did not march 'in such haste as the occasion seemed to require', and that even as Cadogan heard of the fall of Arleux the French were already demolishing it.

It has long been recognized (notably by Atkinson and Chandler) that so many passages in Kane and Parker are identically phrased that they cannot be considered independent: either one copied the other, or Kane and Parker each drew on some earlier version from within the Royal Irish. Thus the one should not be used to prove the truth of the other or be deemed corroborative evidence to the other. But there are further problems:

1 Kane left Ingolsby's 18th Royal Irish to become colonel of Maccartney's Foot in December 1710 and left Flanders for Canada early in 1711; his signature is on a document dated 'St Lawrence river, 8 September 1711'. His information on Arleux and the Lines is therefore hearsay. Yet in his memoirs he wrote apropos Marlborough's inspection of the Lines on

4 August 1711: 'I [sic] desired liberty to ride out with the Duke' and that his commanding officer Brigadier Durell 'readily concurred' (p. 92). This is plainly impossible.

2 While with hindsight the sequence of events may seem clear and logical, Kane's information concerning the struggles for the fort, its repair, the size of garrison and the strength and duration of Savary's defence, and subsequent projects, cannot be reconciled with Marlborough's *Dispatches* or contemporary reports by Hare and Watkins, who certainly were present on the Scarpe at the time, or with Deane's *Journal*, or with French reports.

3 Captain Parker does appear to have served in France throughout 1711, and when he personally saw something – the duke at the outposts near Bouchain, for instance – his account is extremely valuable. But the captain's notions of what the duke thought and planned are merely those of a regimental officer far outside the headquarters circle, and carry little weight. The duke disclosed his thoughts to very few people and certainly not to company commanders.

If we subject Kane's (and Parker's) account to analysis we find that:

a Far from Marlborough being able to 'take Arleux when he pleased', he tussled with the French for it during several weeks of the early summer – and this tussle was partly at least because of the water needs of Douai, a defensive concern.

b Nor, once he had at last taken Arleux, on 6 July, did Marlborough only 'pretend' to fortify it, for he told a Prussian general that 'we shall put it in a better state of defence so that Douai shall have sufficient water'.

c While these works were in hand the place was attacked

by the French, on 12 July. Instead of letting them capture it, the commandant of the post held out, and everything was done to repulse the attack.

d Far from admonishing the commandant and weakening his garrison, as one would for a serious 'error' and setback to the master plan in not letting the French 'win', the duke then further strengthened his forces at the place and improved the defences: three ditches, three palisades and *chevaux de frise*, eight cannon and two mortars.

e The 'slender' garrison of 400 men successfully withstood three assaults from a force that eventually totalled 15,000 men and two batteries of cannon, a size not far short of the English contingent at Blenheim.

f The attack began after dawn on the 23rd and Marlborough at Cottes, 37 miles away, received the first warning at noon. Hare says he called his generals to a rapid meeting and then sent Cadogan with a regiment of hussars on the 34-mile ride to Douai. Arleux fell 'about three in the afternoon' of the 23rd, three hours after the first message reached Marlborough; Parker's suggestion that Cadogan was secretly instructed to loiter and let the fort be taken, that he 'took not such haste as the occasion seemed to require', cannot stand against the distance and the lack of time. He could not have reached Arleux in much under six hours.

g By 1 p.m. the duke had ordered General Fagel with forty squadrons and 'all the grenadiers of the army' (i.e. the pick of the infantry) to march at once for Arleux 'supposing these, if they arrive in time, may be sufficient, with the assistance of the governor of Douai [Hompesch], to prevent the enemy's design' (his letter to St John of that day).

Clearly the nearby Douai garrison was expected to be proactive and not stand idle.

h The only puzzle is why Dutch Hompesch was so supine. Was he overawed by the vast size of the attacking force? Was he preoccupied with manning the town's defences rather than protecting Arleux? Was he 'a little past it' ? All we know is that thereafter Marlborough placed Cadogan beside him when action was required.

Nor do French accounts support Kane's theory. Their commander, Montesquiou, reported the day after Arleux's capture. He deployed, he says, twenty-seven battalions and twenty-six squadrons, twelve cannon from Cambrai, and the garrisons from along the river. It took him all night to pass his infantry along the Palluel causeway and over the *bac* at Aubencheul; meanwhile, most of the cavalry crossed the Sensée at Bouchain, 10 miles downstream. Advance guards went to the higher ground overlooking Arleux and the cavalry blocked the road from Douai. The attack opened about 6 a.m. and all the morning batteries pounded the fort from two sides, but even so, when at noon a storming party of grenadiers waded into the marshes it was soon in difficulties and had to be supported strongly by the massed infantry before the defenders were overwhelmed.

Large quantities of powder, munitions and equipment were captured and Montesquiou learned from the commandant that the duke had given him written orders to hold out at all costs for several days, by which time Marlborough would have come and forced a general engagement. The valuable stores and the instructions to Savary confirm that the duke had no intention of 'losing' Arleux in any circumstances.

Villars inspected the fort and initially determined to hold it as a fortified bridgehead north of the river. Only towards the month end was he persuaded to raze it, partly because of directives received from

Versailles some days after the capture. Again this undermines Kane's account.

Not only do these authentic facts challenge Kane's version in many details, but his double and treble bluff theory of an initial master plan which unfolded perfectly across several weeks is *in itself* altogether too complicated. I cannot believe it. Kane's text also implies, however inadvertently, that Marlborough considered Villars to be a puppet without independent will of his own. Not only does that diminish Marlborough's brilliant achievement a week later in seeing a sudden opportunity, seizing it, and outwitting an excellent commander by the most perfect timing and judgement; but by suggesting that the duke judged Villars's generalship so demeaningly and insultingly it would reduce Marlborough to the level of complacent and stupid generals. And that surely was not the case.

Acknowledgements

For permission to quote copyright material in the *Marlborough–Godolphin Correspondence* edited by Henry L. Snyder I thank Oxford University Press; that collection, together with General Sir George Murray's edition of *Marlborough's Letters and Dispatches* and B van 't Hoff's edition of the *Marlborough–Heinsius Correspondence*, form the basic structure for this book. I have, however, modernized Marlborough's orthography, which van 't Hoff called 'unusual, even for his time'.

I wish also to thank the Council of the Society for Army Historical Research for permission to use material from my article 'Marlborough and the Loss of Arleux', which they published in 1992: the article was a first version of the argument more fully developed here, but it does give some detailed source references. My friend of fifty years Roger Nelson kindly read an initial draft of Part One of this book and made invaluable comments for which I am most grateful. When I was struggling with the transactions for paying Marlborough's army overseas Professor Henry Roseveare gave me expert information, though I find that pruning my text to the publisher's limit has caused the subject virtually to disappear. Monsieur Vincent Doom, then of Douai's municipal archives, was a fount of information on the scene of the 1711 campaign. John Montgomery, librarian to RUSI (Royal United Services Institute for Defence Studies), was always most helpful, as were the splendid staff of the London Library.

Although this book is based on printed sources I have examined certain of the Marlborough papers now in the British Library, particularly Add MSS 61342 [Marlborough's maps and order of battle charts] and 61406 [army account books]. The format of this book precludes source references; hence I give a detailed list of sources consulted to help identify all the material I have used.

Sources consulted

BOOKS

Earl of Ailesbury, *Memoirs*, 2 vols (1890) – a Jacobite exile who remained friends with Marlborough; recollections in old age

R.C. Anderson (ed.), *Sir Thomas Allin's Journals, 1660–78*, 2 vols (Navy Records Soc, 1939–40) – vol. 2 records Churchill as a marine on Allin's flagship in the Mediterranean, 1670

Anon, *La Vie de Marlborough*, 3 vols (Paris, 1808)

C.T. Atkinson, *Marlborough and the Rise of the British Army* (1921) – a measured, reliable assessment by the great expert on regimental history; a good contrast to Churchill's lengthy oratorical approach

Correlli Barnett, *Marlborough* (1974) – excellent, thoughtful and well illustrated

S.B. Baxter, *William III* (1966)

Hilaire Belloc, *The Tactics and Strategy of the Great Duke of Marlborough* (1933) – useful on discussion of ground, etc.

Viscount Bolingbroke, *A Defence of the Treaty of Utrecht* (intro by Trevelyan, 1932) – comprises Letters 6 to 8 of his *Study and Use of History*, 1736

Bishop G. Burnet, *A History of His Own Time*, 6 vol. edition (1833), first published 1723–34

I.F. Burton, *The Captain-General: Marlborough's Career, 1702–11* (1968) – a short strategical study, taking issue with some of Sir Winston Churchill's opinions

David Chandler, *Marlborough as a Military Commander* (1976) – thorough and comprehensive; quotes Bolingbroke's inscription on the Column of Victory

David Chandler, *The Art of Warfare in the Age of Marlborough* (1976)

Earl of Chesterfield, *Letters to His Son*, 4 vols (9th ed., 1787) – describes at length Marlborough's 'manner' but fails to elucidate his other and greater qualities

J. Childs, *The Army of Charles II* (1976)

J. Childs, *The Army of James II and the Glorious Revolution* (1980)

J. Childs, *The British Army of William III, 1689–1702* (1987) – includes a chapter on the Brest expedition

J. Childs, *The Nine Years War and the British Army, 1688–1697* (1991)

[Sir] W.S. Churchill, *Marlborough, His Life and Times*, 4 vols (1933–8) – splendid, magniloquent, uncritical and partisan, but with excellent and plentiful operational maps

C. von Clausewitz, *On War* (English translation ed. Howard and Paret, Princeton, 1991)

[Sir] J.S. Corbett, *England in the Mediterranean, 1603–1713*, 2 vols (1904)

Archdeacon W. Coxe, *Memoirs of the Duke of Marlborough* (1818; ed. Wade, 3 vols, 1885) – still not totally superseded

A.R. d'Aiglun, *Vauban, sa Famille et ses Ecrits*, 2 vols (Paris, 1910) – vol. 2 prints correspondence about Brest, 1694

Charles Dalton, *English Army Lists and Commission Registers 1661–1714*, 6 vols (1892–1904) – vol. 5 contains the Blenheim Roll

J.M. de la Colonie, *Chronicles of an Old Campaigner, 1692–1717* (English translation ed. Horsley, 1904)

Private J.M. Deane, *Journal 1704–1711* (ed. Chandler, 1984)

D. Defoe (attrib.), *The Life and Adventures of Mrs Christian Davies, Old Mother Ross* (1928) – a sutleress with the army

W.C. Dickinson, *Sidney Godolphin, Lord High Treasurer* (1990)

Dictionary of National Biography, 22 vols (1907)

Major L. Edge, *Historical Records of the Royal Marines, 1664–1701* (1893) – details of the Churchill brothers' service as marines, also of Cork 1690

Encyclopaedia Britannica – the celebrated 11th edition of 1910–11 retains its value

J. Evelyn. *Diary*, 6 vols (1955)

J. Ferguson (ed.), *The Scots Brigade in the Service of the Netherlands, 1572–1782*, 3 vols (Scottish History Society, 1899) – vol. 2 deals with the War of the Spanish Succession.

Sir Charles Firth, *A Commentary on Macaulay's History* (1938) – the greatest seventeenth-century expert of his time reviews and corrects the supreme Whig historian

[Sir] C.H. Firth, *Cromwell's Army* (1902)

Hon [Sir] J.W. Fortescue, *A History of the British Army*, vol. i (2nd ed., 1910)

H.C. Foxcroft (ed.), *A Supplement to Burnet's 'History'* (1902) – Burnet's original drafts

GEC, *The Complete Peerage*, revised edition, 13 vols (1910–59)

G.S. Graham (ed.), *The Walker Expedition to Quebec, 1711* (Navy Records Soc, 1953) – St John's style in conjoint operations; Richard Kane in the St Lawrence and not in France

Edward Gregg, *Queen Anne* (1980) – a favourable portrait, with much source material, e.g. Harley's draft for the letter dismissing Marlborough in 1711

Frances Harris, *A Passion for Government: Sarah Duchess of Marlborough* (1991) – a scholarly political biography with much on Sarah's financial acumen

J.B. Hattendorf, *England in the War of the Spanish Succession* (New York, 1987) – unlike Trevelyan, essentially a study of grand strategy

[Sir] N. Henderson, *Prince Eugen of Savoy* (1966)

N. Hooke (ed.), *An Account of the Conduct of the Dowager Duchess of Marlborough* (1742) – Sarah's spirited version of her years at court, 1675–1710, with some of Anne's letters

R.D. Horn, *Marlborough, a Survey: Panegyrics and Satires, etc, 1688–1788* (1975)

D.W. Jones, *War and Economy in the Age of William III and Marlborough* (1988) – interesting in explaining the trade and monetary flows which hampered William but helped so much in Anne's reign

Brigadier General Richard Kane, *Campaigns of King William and Queen Anne, 1689–1712* (1745)

T. Lediard, *The Life of John, Duke of Marlborough*, 3 vols (1736) – still interesting; but see under 'Articles', Horn

N. Luttrell, *A Brief Historical Relation of State Affairs, 1679–1714*, 6 vols (1857) – miscellaneous details, and also newsletters about Brest expedition

J.A. Lynn, *The Wars of Louis XIV, 1667–1714* (1999) – extremely thorough, also draws upon Lynn's fine study of Louis's army (*Giant of the Grand Siècle*)

Lord Macaulay, *History of England from the Accession of James II*, 5 vols (1848–61, and ed. Firth, 6 vols 1913–15) – Marlborough is treated throughout with hostility and Chapter 20 handles the Brest affair with great prejudice

D. McKay, *Prince Eugene of Savoy* (1977)

Lt Gen Sir G. MacMunn, *Prince Eugene of Savoy* (1933) – breezy, but emphasizes Eugene's logistical problems and achievements; author was one of the best 'Q' officers in the First World War

Comte de Mérode-Westerloo, *Memoirs* (English translation ed. Chandler, 1968)

General Sir George Murray (ed.), *Marlborough's Letters and Dispatches* (5 vols, 1845) – a selection of the duke's official papers; invaluable

T.C. Nicholson and A.S. Turberville, *Charles Talbot, Duke of Shrewsbury* (1930)

Captain Robert Parker, *Memoirs of the Most Remarkable Military Transactions, 1683–1718* (1747; and also ed. Chandler, 1968)

R. Pearman, *The First Earl Cadogan, 1672–1726* (1988)

The Portledge Papers – newsletters about Brest, 1694

L. von Ranke, *History of England, Mainly in the 17th Century* (English translation, 1875) – vol. 6 Appendix contains letters of the Prussian envoy on the feud between William III and Marlborough

Admiral Sir Herbert Richmond, *The Navy as an Instrument of Policy, 1558–1727* (1953)

Major R.E. Scouller, *The Armies of Queen Anne* (1966) – organization and finance

Henry L. Snyder (ed), *The Marlborough–Godolphin Correspondence, 1701–11*, 3 vols (1975) – their full correspondence (and Sarah's to them), superbly annotated

D.M. Somerville, *The King of Hearts* [Shrewsbury] (1962)

Duc de Saint-Simon, *Mémoires*, 20 vols (ed. A. Cheruel, Paris, 1855) – sidelights from Versailles by a man whom Louis XIV disliked

Jonathan Swift, *The Journal to Stella, The Conduct of the Allies* and *Contributions to 'The Examiner'*, in vols 2, 5 and 9 of Swift's *Prose Works* (ed. T. Scott, 1897–1902)

Frank Taylor, *The Wars of Marlborough, 1702–1709*, 2 vols (1921), well written eulogy with excellent maps – unfinished at author's death in 1913

The Cambridge Modern History, vol. 5, *The Age of Louis XIV* (1908)

The New Cambridge Modern History, vol. 6, *The Rise of Great Britain and Russia* (1970)

M.A. Thomson [et al.], *Louis XIV and William III, Essays by and for Mark A. Thomson* (ed. Hatton and Bromley, 1968) – Thomson's superb essays on international policy and diplomacy in the period 1688 to 1714, and A.L. Ryan on Brest in William's war

G.G. Toudouse, *Camaret et Vauban* (Paris, 1967)

G.M. Trevelyan, *England under Queen Anne*, 3 vols (1930–34) – an agreeable companion to Churchill and still the fullest narrative history

F.C. Turner, *James II* (1948)

B. van 't Hoff (ed.), The *Marlborough–Heinsius Correspondence, 1701–11* (The Hague, 1951) – complements Murray and now Snyder

Vault et Pelet, *Mémoires militaires relatifs à la succession d'Espagne*, 11 vols (Paris, 1833–41) – the correspondence of the French high command (tomes 4 and 10 deal with 1704 and 1711 respectively)

Major P. Verney, *The Battle of Blenheim* (1976) – valuable

Maréchal de Villars, *Mémoires* (ed. Marquis de Vogüé in 6 vols) – tome 2 (1887) of this boastful account covers 1701–7 and tome 3 (1889) deals with 1707–13: both have appendices of additional correspondence

Voltaire, *Siècle de Louis XIV* (1751) – *inter alia* a mordant study on the cost of the wars to France

A. Wace, *The Marlborough Tapestries at Blenheim Palace* (1968)

[Field-Marshal] Viscount Wolseley, *The Life of Marlborough to the Accession of Queen Anne*, 2 vols (1894) – based on much research if with a limited viewpoint; still useful

PRINTED DOCUMENTS

The *Calendars of State Papers Domestic* (1660 to April 1704) and *Calendars of Treasury Books* contain a mass of miscellaneous information identifiable from the indexes of persons and subjects.

The *Journals of the House of Lords* and *Journals of the House of Commons* have useful material on subsidies to the Allies, and what they understood about recruitment, size and deployment of the forces (cf. Burton and Scouller's examinations).

The Historical Manuscripts Commission (early volumes were recorded as (e.g.) 4th Report, App 6):

Atholl (12R, App 8) – some Sarah and Godolphin

Bagot (10R, App 4) – Harley and Spanish affairs

Bath, i – Harley and Marlborough, 1711

Buccleugh, ii – Stepney's reports on Vienna's attitudes in the War of the Spanish Succession

Cowper, iii (12R, App 3) – Captain Pope's letters on the 1704 campaign

Egmont, ii – Marlborough's attitude to the war in Spain, 1707

Hare (14R, App 9) – Chaplain General Hare's letters, 1704 to 1711 and later

Marlborough (8R, Part 1) – very summary; extracts on the queen's warrant for deducting commission, and Sarah's report on how Marlborough reacted to dismissal, 1711

Moray (10R, App 1) – Henry Watkins letters, 1711

Portland – vol iii (14R, App 2) and viii on Brest, 1694; vols iv (1700–1711) and v (1711–14), Harley *passim*, Marlborough and Tallard after Blenheim, St John, Cranstoun (Ramillies and Oudenarde); Orrery, H. Watkins, Drummond, Hans Hamilton, Pendlebury (Bouchain), Stair, Albemarle letters, 1710–11; Matthew Prior's peace negotiations at Versailles, 1711; Ormonde letters,

1712; vol. ix Marlborough's fall and Ormonde; vol. x Harley's estimate of the Marlboroughs' official income (£63,000)

Roxburghe (14R, App 3) – Oudenarde, 1708 and the 1711 campaign

Rutland, ii (12R, App 5) – Schellenberg, Blenheim and 1708

Stuart, i – Marlborough's messages of support and gifts to the Old Pretender in 1715

ARTICLES

Abbreviations used: *Army Quarterly (AQ); Bulletin of the Institute of Historical Research (BIHR); English Historical Review (EHR); Historical Journal* (HJ); *Huntington Library Quarterly (HLQ); Journal of the RUSI (JRUSI); Journal of the Society for Army Historical Research (JSAHR); Scottish Historical Review (SHR); The Mariner's Mirror (MM); Transactions of the Royal Historical Society (TRHistS*, preceded by *series number*)

C.T. Atkinson and C.R.L. Fletcher, 'The Flanders Battleground', *AQ*, vol. 1 (1920–21), pp. 154–67 – draws parallels (mud, trenches, torrential summer rains) 1702–12 and 1914–18 and some contrasts

C.T. Atkinson, 'Marlborough's Order of Battle', *JSAHR*, vol. 15 (1936), pp. 107–13 – valuable orbat (Orders of Battle) details for virtually the whole war (that for 1708 CTA published in *The Fighting Forces*, vol. 1 (1924), pp. 489–97)

C.T. Atkinson, 'Marlborough's Sieges', *JSAHR*, vol. 13 (1934), pp. 195–205; and 'Marlborough's Sieges: Further Evidence', *JSAHR*, vol. 24 (1946), pp. 83–7

C.T. Atkinson, 'Material for Military History in the HMC Reports', *JSAHR*, vol. 12 (1942), pp. 17–34 – invaluable alphabetical lists of the Reports and itemized lists by wars and theatres from Tudors to Waterloo; my constant companion

C.T. Atkinson, 'Notes on the War of the Spanish Succession from PRO Sources', *JSAHR*, vol. 21 (1942), pp. 83–96 – establishments, recruiting, casualties, movements

C.T. Atkinson, 'One of Marlborough's Men, Corporal Matthew Bishop', *JSAHR*, vol. 23 (1945), pp. 157–69 – extracts from an interesting chapbook-cum-memoir

C.T. Atkinson, 'Queen Anne's Army', *JSAHR*, vol. 36 (1958), pp. 25–9, 48–60 – more data extracted from the *Calendars of Treasury Papers* on recruitment, establishments, casualties, hospitals, pensions and petitions, subsistence for POWs, etc.

C.T. Atkinson, 'Queen Anne's War in the West Indies, *JSAHR*, vol. 24 (1946) pp. 100–109, 183–97 – events and problems in a minor theatre

C.T. Atkinson, 'The Cost of Queen Anne's War', *JSAHR*, vol. 33 (1954), pp. 174–83 – mainly drawn from Treasury papers

C.T. Atkinson, 'The Peninsular Second Front in the Spanish Succession War', *JSAHR*, vol. 22 (1944), pp. 223–33 – the growing drain of what was intended as a secondary theatre

I.F. Burton, 'The Committee of Council at the War Office', *HJ*, vol. 4 (1961), pp. 78–84 – the scheme to remove Marlborough's control over army appointments; Burton may not allow sufficiently for Harley's deepest intentions

I.F. Burton, 'The Supply of Infantry for the War in the Peninsula', 1703–7, *BIHR*, vol. 28 (1955), pp. 35–62 – fundamental to understanding recruitment and the confusion between establishments and effectives, which so baffled Parliament

S.J. Cohen, 'Hester Santlow', *Bulletin of New York Public Library*, vol. 64 (1960), pp. 95–104 – a theatre and dance historian suggests (on vague and misunderstood evidence) that Hester was Marlborough's mistress

P.M. Cowburn, 'Christopher Gunman and the Loss of the *Gloucester*', *MM*, vol. 42 (1956), pp. 113–26 – adds to and corrects Churchill's and Turner's accounts of the Duke of York's shipwreck in 1682

H.H.E. Cra'aster (ed.), 'Letters of the 1st Lord Orkney during Marlborough's Campaigns', *EHR*, vol. 19 (1904), pp. 307–21 – invaluable (unaccountably not used by Fortescue in his 1899 *History*'s revised edition, 1910)

C. Dalton (ed.), Contemporary account of 'Blenheim', with plan (by d'Ivoy ?, 1704) and valuable orbat, *JRUSI*, vol. 42, part 2 (1898), pp. 1074–85

J. d'Auriac, 'Le Marquis de Chamlay', *Revue Historique*, vol. 70 (1899), pp. 301–317

Godfrey Davies, 'Letters from Queen Anne to Godolphin', *SHR*, vol. 19 (1921–2), pp. 190–95

Godfrey Davies, 'Macpherson and the Nairne Papers', *EHR*, vol. 35 (1920), pp. 367–76 – here Firth's closest pupil convincingly countered Parnell's arguments (in *EHR*, 1897) on whether Jacobite documents concerning Marlborough in 1692–4 were forged

Godfrey Davies, 'The Stuart Papers at the Scots College at Paris', *SHR*, vol. 19 (1921–2), pp. 326–8 – a pendant to the preceding; describes and quotes from eighteenth-century accounts of Jacobite papers

Godfrey Davies, 'Recruiting in the Reign of Queen Anne', *JSAHR*, vol. 28 (1950), pp. 146–59

Godfrey Davies, 'The Seamy Side of Marlborough's War', *HLQ*, vol. 15 (1951–2), pp. 22–41 – letters showing how the civilian paymaster general in London and Cadogan in Flanders used army intelligence and funds for personal enrichment

A.D. Francis, 'Marlborough's March to the Danube, 1704', *JSAHR*, vol. 50 (1972), pp. 78–100 – much useful detail on the origins of the scheme

Edward Gregg, 'Marlborough in Exile, 1712–14', *HJ*, vol. 15 (1972), pp. 593–618 – his idea possibly to invade England to preserve the Hanoverian succession, and Anne's and Bolingbroke's separate rapprochements towards him in early and mid 1714

F. Harris, 'The Authorship of the Manuscript Blenheim Journal', *BIHR*, vol. 55 (1982), pp. 203–6 – Coxe had attributed this journal to Chaplain General Hare and Murray quoted it extensively in *Letters and Dispatches*, vol. 1, but Harris convincingly argues that it was by the chaplain of Charles Churchill's 3rd Foot, the Revd Sandby

R.D. Horn, 'Marlborough's First Biographer', *HLQ*, vol. 20 (1956–7), pp. 145–62 – dates Dr Hare's first published work to 1705, earlier than Hare's *Conduct of the Duke of Marlborough in the Present War* (1712), from which Lediard borrowed unashamedly and without real acknowledgement. On p. 160 Horn gives evidence from this 1705 work and Marlborough's letters that the assaults on the Schellenberg slopes lasted for ninety minutes before Baden's attack went in

John Hussey, 'Marlborough and the Loss of Arleux, 1711: Accident or Design?', *JSAHR*, vol. 70 (1992), pp. 4–14

Major S.H.F. Johnston, 'The Letters of Samuel Noyes, Chaplain to the Royal Scots, 1703–4', *JSAHR*, vol. 37 (1959), pp. 33–40, 128–35 – valuable on the 1704 expedition (marches, casualties, ravaging Bavaria) and the autumn sieges

Major S.H.F. Johnston, 'The Scots Army in the Reign of Anne', *5s*, *TRHistS*, vol. 3 (1953), pp. 1–21

Colonel E.M. Lloyd, 'Marlborough and the Brest Expedition, 1694', *EHR*, vol. 9 (1894), pp. 130–32 – helpfully sorts out the dates of correspondence OS and NS in a non-contentious way

Colonel Hon A. Parnell, 'James Macpherson and the Nairne Papers', *EHR*, vol. 12 (1897), pp. 254–84 – the attempt to prove that Jacobite papers in Paris were original forgeries or were forged by Macpherson in the 1770s, that they were forged to implicate Marlborough and others in treacherous dealings, including the betrayal of the Brest expedition (see also Davies in *EHR* and *SHR*);

Ivan P. Phelan, 'Marlborough as Logistician', *JSAHR*, vols 67–68 (1989–90), pp. 253–7, 36–48, 103–19 – builds on Chandler and the Hungarian scholar Pérjès to demonstrate further the duke's supremacy in this matter

J.H. Plumb, 'The Organization of the Cabinet in the Reign of Queen Anne', *5s*, *TRHistS*, vol. 7 (1957), pp. 137–57 – the first full explanation

E. Roger (ed.), 'The Royal Regiment of Scots Dragoons', *SHR*, vol. 14 (1917), pp. 216–37 – letters of Lord John Hay of the Scots Greys, a few interesting details

Major R.E. Scouller, 'Marlborough's Administration in the Field', *AQ*, vols 95–96 (1967–8), pp. 197–208 and 102–13

H.L. Snyder, 'The Duke of Marlborough's Request of his Captain Generalcy for Life', *JSAHR*, vol. 45 (1967), pp. 67–83 – shows that the request was not made merely once, as previously thought, but was repeated again and again, to the queen's annoyance

H.L. Snyder, 'The Formulation of Foreign and Domestic Policy in the reign of Queen Anne', *HJ*, vol. 11 (1968), pp. 144–60 – illuminates how matters were discussed during Godolphin's time

H.L. Snyder, 'The Last Days of Queen Anne: Sir J. Evelyn's Account', *HLQ*, vol. 34 (1970–71), pp. 261–76 – revises Trevelyan with this new material

A.J. Veenendaal, 'The Opening Phase of Marlborough's Campaign of 1708', *History*, New Series vol. 35 (1950), pp. 34–49 – a significant modification from Dutch sources of Churchill's and Trevelyan's Anglocentric interpretation; also indicates Cadogan's corrupt practices.

Notes

1 George (1654–1710) transferred from the Marines to the Navy, and rose to be an admiral on the Lord High Admiral Prince George of Denmark's council – ill-tempered, he became a nuisance politically to John; Charles (1656–1714) began as a page, entered the Marines, switched to the land service and rose to full general – and inherited Sir Winston's property; Theobald (1662–85) took orders at Oxford, became chaplain to John's Royal Dragoons in 1683 and was being pushed for a fellowship at Eton when he suddenly died; Jasper (1663–82) died as an ensign of marines; Arabella (1649–1730) 'retired' to marry Colonel Godfrey, who became Keeper of the Jewel House, and their daughters were among Anne's maids of honour.

2 Arabella had four illegitimate children by James, one being the famous Duke of Berwick (1670–1734), later a marshal of France.

3 Like John a natural dynast, Sarah secured for her sister's husband, Colonel Griffith, the secretaryship to Prince George; she placed her poor Hill cousins in Princess Anne's household, Abigail as a bedchamberwoman, Alice as laundrywoman, Jack as a page to the prince.

4 All my dates for November 1688 are OS.

5 It says something about Marlborough's insecure personality that he maintained these contacts and protestations of repentance with the exiled court until 1715. It says everything about James II that he could be fooled by them.

6 In the circumstances of 1691 such a leakage may have suggested treacherous intent. But we should also remember Kitchener's refusal to disclose military plans to Cabinet in 1914–15 'because they told their wives'.

7 But if Marlborough's friends Russell and Godolphin could successfully run with the hare and hunt with the hounds while enjoying ministerial office, why should he not do likewise? William kept Godolphin at the Treasury until 1696 and (to adapt William's distrustful verdict on Marlborough) 'thought it was for the good of his service to entrust Russell with command of the fleet' until 1699.

8 Floyd, the Jacobite agent involved in the Brest affair, was also involved in Fenwick's plot and lived thereafter in exile. In August 1702 Marlborough interceded on his behalf and the English government (which must mean Godolphin *and* Anne) allowed Floyd to return to England. It is very curious.

9 Ramillies and the decision to commit at Oudenarde are further proof of this.

10 This was Chamlay's stated opinion.

11 In 1703 Colonel Lord John Hay applied to Marlborough for the command of the Scots Greys, whereby he might serve on campaign with the duke. Lord John noted: 'I never met with more civility from anybody in my life'.

The duke helped secure him the place when it became vacant, and both men were the gainers.

12 Clausewitz's calculation. In total that army numbered some 680,000 men, so that 95,000 wastage on the road would be only (!) 14 per cent and not 33 per cent. But the point he sought to make remains valid.

13 After covering some 150 miles in sixteen days, Captain Richard Pope (Schomberg's Horse, 7th Dragoon Guards) wrote on 4 June of the cavalry's excellent condition despite the length and speed of the march, 'we having been very well provided with forage'.

14 'Blenheim' has come to represent the name of this campaign and victory; however I consider 'Blindheim', the village's real name, more helpful and distinct when describing the place in the context of the battle for it and the other villages.

15 This modesty was also noted at home. During the winter of 1704–5 old John Evelyn waited on Godolphin, 'where was the victorious Duke of Marlborough, who came to me and took me by the hand with extraordinary familiarity and civility, as formerly he was used to do, without any alteration of his good nature. He had a most rich George in sardonyx set in diamonds of an estimable value: for the rest very plain. I had not seen him in two years, and believed he had forgotten me.'

16 Sarah's first cousin whom she had introduced to Anne's household as a bed-chamberwoman.

17 Of the dauphin's three sons, the eldest (Burgundy) died in 1712 and the youngest (Berri) in 1714. In the last months of Louis XIV's life only Burgundy's sickly baby son lay between the old king's French crown and the late dauphin's middle son, Anjou, now

Felipe V of Spain. A union of the 'Two Crowns' had never seemed nearer. But, in one of the great ironies of histories, the baby became Louis XV in 1715 and lived until 1774.

18 As a study in character, compare Marlborough's: report of 40 Allied killed and almost double that number wounded but with at least as many French casualties, with Villars's report of 150 French killed and wounded but 950 Allied dead and more wounded.

19 But what of the Douai garrison as support?

20 On 2 August the French Minister for War, Voysin, summarized Villars's latest reports as showing that he might lead the attack in Brabant if it promised well, and that Marlborough was now too overstretched for any prospect of his besieging Le Quesnoy 'or anywhere else', or even to effect anything of significance against the Lines and the French army. When Voysin next wrote (15 August) it was to express concern for the safety of Bouchain.

21 Dr Hare always maintained that Marlborough and Eugene had a plan for the 'easy' reduction of Cambrai. If this last fortress fell would French morale collapse? Could Marlborough really have hoped to reach Paris in 1712? Historical parallels are never exact, but after the French disaster at Waterloo Wellington took Cambrai and its citadel by a two-day siege; one week later (1 July 1815) his headquarters were pitched 10 miles from Notre Dame.

22 A signal by beat of drum to request a parley.

23 When Villars captured Bouchain from Eugene in October 1712, Ormonde wrote to the marshal with his personal congratulations.

Index

Abbaye du Verger, l' 212
Abbeville 164, 168
Admiralty, Board of 27, 66 *see also* Royal Navy
Agache stream 213
Ailesbury, Lord 71
Aire 189
Aire fortress 192
Albemarle, Lord 200, 205, 208
Allin's naval expedition 23
Almanza 164
Alsace 23, 55, 89
Amerdingen 115
Anglican bishops 28
Anglicans 24, 26, 30
Anhalt-Dessau, Prince of Prussia 144, 147
Anjou, Philip of 48, 49 *see also* Felipe V, King
    of Spain
Anne, Queen of England (formerly Princess
    of Denmark) 56, 57, 64, 75, 153–154, 165,
    169, 170, 219, 221, 222–223
    as Princess of Denmark ('Mrs Morley')
        25, 27, 28, 29, 30, 31, 35, 39, 49, 50
    and relationship with Sarah, Duchess of
        Marlborough 25, 36, 40, 84
    and the Dutch 89, 90, 91
Antwerp 78
Antwerp, Lines of 78
Arco, Field Marshal Count d' 113–114,
    116–117
Argyll, Lord 65
Arleux 182, 185, 189, 195, 196, 197, 200,
    203, 206, 209

attacks 186–187, 198, 207
    redoubt 196–197, 199
Armstrong, Colonel 215
Arras 167–168, 182, 185, 191, 204
artillery, British 66, 68–69, 70, 98, 100
artillery, French 69
Artois 192
Ath 'barrier fort' 40
Athlone, Lord 75, 76, 77
Atkinson, C.T. 97
Aubencheul-au-Bac 195
Aubigny-au-Bac 195, 216
Augsburg 121, 127, 128, 129, 130, 133, 135,
    136
Austria 48, 49
Austria, Emperor of 56
Austrian army 54
Austrian Imperial War Council 56, 108
Austrian troops 163–164
Austrians 84

Baltic war 51
Bavaria 79, 92, 103, 106, 108, 110, 121, 122,
    125–127, 135 *see also* Franco-Bavarian army
Bavarian campaign 59
Bavarian infantry 113
Bavarian negotiations 91
Beachy Head 34
Bedburg 94, 98, 104
Belgium (Spanish Netherlands) 48, 78, 158,
    159, 163, 165, 184 *see also* fortresses,
    barrier

Belloc, Hilaire 97, 151
Berg 115, 116
Berlin 157, 190
Berri (dauphin's son) 48
Béthune 168, 189, 200, 201
Béthune fortress 192
Beuvry 205
Black Forest 95, 105
Blenheim Palace 158, 194, 219, 223
Blenheim (Blindheim), Battle of 140–152,
    153–154, 201
    order of battle 67
    Rowe's attack 68
    casualties 152
'Blenheim Bounty Roll' 70, 97, 120
Blindheim (Blenheim) 140, 141–142, 143,
    144, 145–146, 147, 149, 151
Blood, Colonel 116, 117, 138, 148
Board of General Officers 66
Board of Ordnance 66, 193
Bolingbroke, Viscount see St John, Henry
Bonn 78
Bouchain 183, 191, 198, 212, 214–215, 216,
    220
    'cow path' 216, 217, 218
    earthworks ('lunettes') 217
    siege of 59, 217–219
Boufflers, Marshal 75, 76, 78, 166
Bourbons 47, 48, 50, 53, 54, 55, 79, 224
Bourlon wood 213, 214, 216
Boyne, Battle of the 33, 35
Brabant 201
Brabant, Lines of 78, 158, 202
Brazil, gold mines 55, 79
Brest 37–38
Brihuega 171
Brisach 79
Bruges 180
Brussels 162, 184, 187, 188, 198, 201, 204
Brussels Council 188, 190, 218
Burnet, Bishop 26–27, 35

Cabinet 56, 57, 58, 64, 223
Cadiz 77
Cadogan, Brigadier William 70, 87, 94, 115,
    145, 175–176, 186
    as Lieutenant General 198, 199, 203, 206,
        208, 209, 215, 216, 223
Calais 182
Camaret Bay 37
Cambrai 185, 191–192, 215
Canche, River 182, 183

Canterbury, Archbishop of 36
Cantin 195–196, 197
Cardonnel, Adam de 66, 70, 157
Carlos II, King of Spain 45, 47–48
Catalonian forces 162
Catholics/Catholicism in England 24, 27, 30,
    45, 47
Cavaliers 21
cavalry, British 68
cavalry, Danish 114
cavalry, French 148
Cevennes rising 84, 85
Chamlay 60
Chandler, David 97
Charleroi 'barrier fort' 40
Charles, Archduke of Austria 79, 84
Charles, Archduke of Spain ('Carlos III') 47,
    48, 162, 178–179
Charles I, King of England 21
Charles II, King of England 22, 23, 24, 25, 41
Chesterfield, Lord 107
Churchill, Arabella (Marlborough's sister)
    22
Churchill, General Charles (Marlborough's
    brother) 34, 98, 100, 110, 137, 146
Churchill, John see Marlborough, John
    Churchill, Duke of
Churchill, Sarah see Marlborough, Sarah
    Churchill, Duchess of
Churchill, Captain Winston (later Sir
    Winston) (Marlborough's father) 21, 22,
    23
Churchill, Sir Winston (1933) 39
Clausewitz 58, 59, 101
Cleveland, Duchess of 23
Coblenz 90, 94, 98
Cohorn, General 78
Commons, House of 128, 158, 222
Condé, General Prince Louis of 22, 60, 69,
    215
Corbett, Sir Julian 86
Cork, siege of 34, 35, 109
Cottes (St Hilaire Cottes) 192, 198, 206
Courtrai 198, 204
Craggs (agent) 193
Cromwellianism 24
cuirassiers, Imperial 147
Cutts, Lord 140, 144, 145, 146, 149

Danish cavalry 114
Danish infantry 144
Danish troops 100, 124, 184

Danube, River 83, 95, 97, 106, 140, 148, 149
    and the Schellenberg campaign 110, 111,
        113–114, 121, 124, 133, 136
Dartmouth, Lord 170
Dauphiné 177, 187
Davenant (servant) 70
Davies, Godfrey 39
Deane, Private 99, 102, 185, 186, 196, 197,
    207
Denain fort 216
Dillingen 137, 138
Dillingen-Lauingen position 109, 113, 124,
    136
Donauwörth 110, 112–114, 116, 118, 120,
    124, 128, 134, 137, 138
Douai 167, 168, 176, 182, 185, 186, 189
    fortress 192
    and Bouchain campaign 195, 196, 197,
        198–199, 203, 206, 208, 216, 218
'Dr Hare's Journal' 108
Dragoon Guards, 7th (Schomberg's Horse)
    122–123
dragoon regiments 68
Drake, Lady (Marlborough's grandmother)
    21, 32
Dunkirk 36, 54, 182
Dutch, the 31, 35, 36, 48, 52, 180, 184, 192,
    193, 220
Dutch army 54, 62
    auxiliaries 63
    infantry 119, 120
    'Scots Brigade' 63, 91
    siege train 133
    troops 103, 104
Dutch navy 54–55
Dutch Republic 52 see also Holland
Dykevelt 27

Ebermergen 115, 116
Elixheim 161
England, population 53–54
English Army 22, 40, 54, 62–63
    artillery 66, 68–69, 70, 98, 100
    cavalry 68
    Dragoon Guards, 7th (Schomberg's Horse)
        122–123
    dragoon regiments 68
    Ferguson's brigade 146
    field headquarters staff 70
    Foot, 3rd Regiment of 196–197
    Foot, 8th Regiment of 196–197
    Foot, 10th Regiment of 139

Foot, 15th Regiment of 139
Foot, 21st Regiment of 139
Foot, 23rd Regiment of 118, 139
Foot, 24th Regiment of 139
Guards 118
Guards, 1st 67, 139, 185
Hamilton's (third) brigade 148
Horse Guards, 1st troop 26
Horse Guards, 3rd troop 26, 32
infantry 67–68, 92, 100, 101–102, 119, 120
King's Guards 22
march from Maastricht to the Danube
    98–102
and Marlborough 64–65
remodelled 31
Rowe's brigade 145
Royal Dragoons 25, 26
Royal Fusiliers 33
Royal Irish 206
Royal Irish, 18th 68
Royal Scots 67, 118
Schomberg's Horse (7th Dragoon Guards)
    122–123
Scots Greys 118, 119
strength 97–98
supply train 69, 71, 124
English Civil War 21, 24
Escaut (Scheldt), River 180, 213, 214, 215
Estaing, Comte d' 201, 202, 204
Eugene, Prince of Savoy 48–49, 50, 99, 101,
    106, 161, 162, 164, 224, 225–226
    as War Council president 56, 83, 86
    first campaigns 77, 80
    and the Schellenberg campaign 107–108,
        121, 124–125, 128, 129, 130, 131, 132,
        134, 137–138
    and Battle of Blenheim 69, 143–144, 147,
        148–149, 151, 154
    and Ne Plus Ultra Lines campaign 176,
        178, 186, 191, 202
Evelyn, John 157
Exeter 29

Fagel, General 198
fascines 116, 117, 118, 119, 121
Felipe V, King of Spain (formerly Philip of
    Anjou) 48, 49, 163, 166, 179
Fenwick 39–40
Ferguson's English brigade 146
Feversham, Lieutenant General the Earl of
    26, 29
Fils, River 95, 97

Flanders 33, 35, 63–64, 78, 87, 92–93, 164, 166, 177, 189
Flanders campaign 69–70
Floyd (or Lloyd – agent) 37, 38
Foot, 3rd Regiment of 196–197
Foot, 8th Regiment of 196–197
Foot, 10th Regiment of 139
Foot, 15th Regiment of 139
Foot, 21st Regiment of 139
Foot, 23rd Regiment of 118, 139
Foot, 24th Regiment of 139
foraging 59–60, 69–70, 71, 190
Fortescue 34–35, 59, 97, 98
fortresses, barrier 40, 49, 60, 61, 226
France 24, 31, 33, 45, 53, 55, 165–166
Franco-Bavarian army 113, 114, 119, 120–121, 132, 135, 136 see also French Army
Frederick the Great 58
'Freeman, Mr John' see Marlborough, John, Duke of
'Freeman, Mrs Sarah' 36, 40 see also Marlborough, Sarah, Duchess of: and relationship with Princess Anne of Denmark
Freiburg 111
French Army 22, 45, 54, 55, 75, 105, 183, 196
  artillery 69
  cavalry 148
  Grande Armée 101
  infantry 69, 113
French fleet 33, 54, 55, 85
  Brest squadron 37
  Toulon squadron 164
Friedberg 129, 134

Galway, Lord 27–28, 162, 164
Garth, Dr 193
George, Elector of Hanover 123
George, Prince of Denmark ('Mr Morley') 25, 29, 35, 57–58, 64, 75, 90
Georgia 125
German auxiliaries 63–64
Germany 54, 78, 92, 107, 163, 183, 187, 189
Ghent 164, 180, 216
Gibraltar 63, 85–86, 164
Gieslingen pass 95, 97, 99, 100
Givet fortress 191, 192
Gloucester 25
Gloucester, Duke of 40
Godolphin, Sidney ('Mr Montgomery') 36, 39, 84, 87, 89, 91, 101, 107, 130, 171, 225
  Brest attack 37, 38

relationship with Queen Anne 40–41, 57, 58, 162, 165
  Toulon attack 85
  dismissed 169, 176, 222
  and Ne Plus Ultra Lines campaign 193, 200, 204
Goor, General 109, 115, 117, 120, 129
Goslinga (Dutch field deputy) 213, 214, 215, 216
Grand Alliance 48, 50, 52, 53–54, 79, 80, 178, 220, 225
Grand Alliance Treaty 51, 162, 179
Grande Armée 101
Granville 176
Great Northern War 176
Gross Heppach 99, 101
Guards, 1st 67, 139, 185
Guards, English 118
Guelders 79
Gustavus Adolphus 58, 112
Gy, River 180, 182, 183, 191, 200, 201, 205, 210

Habsburgs 45, 47, 48, 79, 155–156, 162, 163, 178, 187, 190
Hague, The 50, 51–52, 76, 77, 84, 88, 157, 175, 178, 214
Haig, Douglas 220–221
Hainault 184–185
Halifax (Marlborough's friend) 37
Hamilton, Brigadier Hans 197
Hamilton's (third) English brigade 148
Hanover 55, 157
Hanover, Elector of 170, 193
Hanoverian succession 223
Hanoverian units 104
Hare, Chaplain General Dr Francis 70, 108, 144, 145, 147, 150, 196, 209, 218–219
  and Ne Plus Ultra Lines campaign 203–204, 206, 207–208
Harley, Robert 163, 165, 169, 171, 175, 179, 193–194 see also Oxford, Earl of
Hedges, Secretary 87, 88
Heidelberg 23, 93–94
Heinsius, Anthonie 48, 50, 56, 76, 84, 88, 89, 90, 103, 192, 214, 225
Hesdin 207
Hesse 51
Hessian units 104
Hessians 59, 145–146
Hill, Abigail (Mrs Masham) 165, 169, 194–195
Hill, Jack 169, 177

Höchstädt 83, 136, 137–138, 141, 143, 148
Holland 31, 41, 45, 48, 56, 163, 184 see also
    'Dutch' entries
    war with 22–23
    population 54
    threat of invasion 55
    defence of 75–77
    financial problems 80
    fears for southern borders 87
Holstein 51
Holstein-Beck, Prince of 145, 147–148
Holy Roman Empire 178–179
Hompesch, Lieutenant General 148, 149,
    186, 196, 198, 199, 203, 204, 206, 216, 209
Hop (Dutch Treasurer) 89
Hudson's Bay Company 25, 36, 88
Huguenots 24, 26, 27
Hume, David 35
Hungarian rebels 155
Hungary 48, 49, 187
Huy 158

infantry
    Bavarian 113
    Danish 144
    Dutch 119, 120
    English 67–68, 92, 100, 101–102, 119, 120
    French 69, 113
    Prussian 144
Ingolstadt 129, 132, 134, 154
Ireland 33, 34, 63
Irish 'wild geese' 59, 68
Italy 77, 163
Ivoy, d' 186

Jacobite expedition 164
Jacobite uprisings 33, 34
Jacobites 37, 38–39, 223
James II, King of England (formerly Duke of
    York) 22, 24, 25, 27, 28–29, 30, 33, 35, 36,
    37, 40
'James III, King of England' 40, 92, 223
Jennings, Sarah see Marlborough, Sarah
    Churchill, Duchess of
Joseph, Emperor 161, 178
Jura mountains, Swabian 95, 100, 111

Kaibach, River 112, 117
Kane, Colonel Richard 177
Kehl 83, 111
Kinsale 33, 34, 35
Kitchener, Lord 79

La Bassée, Lines of 168, 202
Ladenburg 99
Landau 95, 105
    fortress 79
    siege of 156
Lanier 35
Lauffen 99
Le Quesnoy 215, 220
Lech, River 121, 124, 136
Lediard 201
Lens, plain of 168, 180, 191, 192
Leopold, Emperor 47, 48, 49, 50, 161
Lerida, siege of 125
Lewis, Margrave of Baden 48, 55, 76, 86–87,
    89, 92, 95, 103, 104, 106, 107–108, 154, 156
    and the Schellenberg campaign 108,
        109–110, 116, 118, 119, 120, 122, 129,
        133–134
Liège 76, 158
Lievin 191
Lille 198, 207, 208
Lille, siege of 165
Lille-Douai region 185
Limburg 79
Lisbon 80, 85
Lloyd (or Floyd – agent) 37, 38
London 30, 146, 175, 177, 194, 221
Lord Lieutenants 27
Lords, House of 158, 221
Louis XIV, King of France 27, 32, 45, 58, 92,
    104, 163, 165, 183
    relationship with Marlborough 23, 25
    Brest attack 37, 38
    recognises King William 40
    begins aggressive war abroad 45, 47, 48, 53
    and War of Spanish Succession 49–50, 52,
        60, 61
    and Felipe V, King of Spain 166
Louvois 60
Low Countries 59, 176 see also Belgium;
    Holland
Lutzingen 140, 143, 146, 147
Luxembourg (commander) 69
Luxembourg 'barrier fort' 40
Lys, River 180, 181, 188, 190

Maastricht 91, 93, 98, 177
Maastricht 'barrier fort' 40
Mackay 35
Madrid 162, 164, 171
Mainz 99
Malaga, Battle of 157

Malplaquet, Battle of 61, 68, 166, 167, 202, 213–214
maps, British 94
Marchiennes 216, 218
Maritime Powers 56, 79, 80, 179
Marlborough, John Churchill, Duke of ('Mr Freeman')
  birth 21
  childhood 22
  commission in King's Guards 22
  serves as marine and earns captaincy 23
  marries Sarah Jennings 23–24
  rewarded with baronies 25
  as governor of Hudson's Bay Company 25
  promoted Major General, Horse Guards 26
  characterization by Bishop Burnet 26–27
  writes to William of Orange 27–28
  promoted lieutenant general 29
  defects to William of Orange 29, 30, 35
  promoted colonel, Horse Guards, and raised to Earl of Marlborough 32
  relationship with William of Orange 32, 36, 37, 41, 224–225
  given colonelcy of Royal Fusiliers 33
  in Ireland 34
  dismissed from Privy Council and loses posts and colonelcies 36
  and Brest attack 37, 38, 39
  restored to Privy Council and to Army rank 40
  appointed army commander and ambassador 50–51
  appointed captain general of home land forces 64
  awarded Garter 75
  awarded dukedom 77
  death of son 77
  taken prisoner 77
  plans Blenheim campaign 93–94
  health 130–131, 187–188, 223
  becomes Prince of Mindelheim 155
  dismissed over financial irregularities 221–222
  military posts restored 223
  death 223
Marlborough, Sarah Churchill, Duchess of ('Mrs Freeman') 57, 87–88, 171, 220, 222
  marries John Churchill 23–24
  and relationship with Princess Anne of Denmark (later Queen Anne) 25, 28, 29, 36, 40, 84, 162, 165, 170
  death of son 77, 78, 84

letters to/from husband 90, 93, 153
  death 223
Marsin, Marshal 60, 83, 105, 106, 142, 143, 148, 152, 162
  and the Schellenberg campaign 111, 113, 123, 127, 132, 133, 135
Mary, Princess 28
Mary, Queen of Orange (later Queen Mary III of England) 30–31, 34, 36, 39
Masham, Mrs (Abigail Hill) 165, 169, 194–195
Max Emmanuel, Elector of Bavaria 55, 77, 86, 88, 90, 91, 104, 105, 106, 142, 143
  and the Schellenberg campaign 109, 110–111, 113, 121, 123, 125, 126, 127, 132, 135–136
Mediterranean Sea 37, 55
mercenaries 59
Meuse forts 76
Milan 48, 50, 55
Millner, Sergeant 197
Mindelheim 155
Minorca 86, 165
Monchy-le-Preux 191
Monmouth, Duke of, and rebellion 23, 25–26, 27
Mons 201
Mons 'barrier fort' 40
'Montgomery, Mr' 40–41 see also Godolphin, Sidney, First Lord of the Treasury
'Morley, Mrs Anne' 36, 40 see also Anne, Queen of England: as Princess of Denmark
Moselle, River 87, 89, 94, 98, 104
Mundelsheim 99
Münster 134, 137, 138
Murray, General Robert 190, 198, 204, 208
musket-fire 67–68
Mutiny Act (1689) 62

Namur 'barrier fort' 40
Naples 163–164
Napoleonic Wars 101
Nassau-Saarbruck (commander) 75, 76
Ne Plus Ultra Lines 59, 167, 182–183, 185–187, 191, 192, 200–204, 206–207, 212, 215
Nebel, River 138, 139, 140, 141, 142, 144–145, 146, 147
Neckar, River 95, 97, 99, 105
Neuburg 124, 134, 137
Neuville 216
Newfoundland 85

Nieuport 'barrier fort' 49
Nijmegen (Nymegen) 75–76
Nine Years' War 33–40, 47
Nördlingen 115, 139, 142
Noyes, Chaplain 125–126, 156
Nymegen 75–76

Oberglauheim 140, 141, 142–143, 144,
    146–148, 151
Oise, River 215
Oisy château 212
Opdam, General 78
order of battle 66–67
Ordnance, Board of 66, 193
Ordnance, Master Generalship of the 35
Orkney, Major General Lord 144, 149, 150,
    151
Ormonde, Duke of 65, 77, 224
Orrery, Lord 65, 169–170, 188
Ostend 78, 162, 180
Oudenarde, Battle of 67, 164
Oudenarde 'barrier fort' 49
Overkirk, General 133
Oxford, Earl of 194, 214, 220, 221, 222, 223
    see also Harley, Robert

Palatinate 51, 126
Palleul 195, 207, 209
Palmes, Colonel 146
Parke, Colonel 153
Parker, Captain 102, 126, 200, 205, 206–207,
    210, 216–217
Parliament 21, 22, 25, 27, 30, 51, 53, 56–57,
    62, 65, 71, 158, 221 see also Commons,
    House of; Lords, House of
Parnell, Colonel 39
Partition Treaties (1698, 1700) 47, 51
Pas de Calais 168
Pedro II, King of Portugal 79
Pendlebury (master gunner) 215
Pérjès, Professor 69
Phelan, Ivan 69, 97
Philip of Anjou 48, 49 see also Felipe V, King
    of Spain
Philippsburg 90, 95, 98, 104, 105, 156
Piedmont 162
Poland, King of 178, 184
Pope, Captain Richard 122–123, 150
'Popish Plot' 24, 25
Portsmouth 38
Portugal 55, 79, 92, 164
Prior, Matthew 193

Privy Council 27, 36, 37, 40, 223
Protestants/Protestantism in England 24,
    25, 30
Prussia 55, 156
Prussian forces 100, 177, 190
Prussian infantry 144
Prussians 88, 101, 121, 184–185
Public Accounts Committee 221

Quebec 177, 189

Raby, Lord 187, 188, 192
Rain 124, 125, 137
Ramillies, Battle of 68, 162, 163, 188
Restoration 24
Rhine, River 76–77, 89, 94–95, 98, 104, 105,
    191
Richmond, Admiral Sir Herbert 86
Rivers, Lord 65
roads 97
Romans 97
Rooke, Admiral 77, 85–86, 157
Ross, Mother 149
Rottweil 105
Rowe 68, 139
Rowe's English brigade 145
Royal Irish 206
Royal Irish, 18th 68
Royal Navy 29, 54–55, 63, 93 see also
    Admiralty, Board of
Allin's naval expedition 23
Royal Scots 67, 118
Russell, Admiral 36, 37, 38, 39–40
Ryswick treaty (1697) 40

Sabia 110
Sacheverell 168
Sackville, Major General 38, 39
St Hilaire Cottes 192, 198, 206
St John, Henry (later Viscount Bolingbroke)
    65, 169, 171, 179, 188, 189, 204, 223
    Quebec expedition 177
    letter from Duke of Marlborough 198–199
    Ne Plus Ultra Lines campaign 207,
    210–211, 218
St Lawrence river 177
St Malo 54
St Omer 182, 207
St Paul's School 22
Saint-Simon, Duc de 154–155
St Venant 168, 189
Salisbury 29

Sambre, River 183
Sart-le-Bois 208
Savary (or Savery), Colonel Thomas, FRS 196, 197, 199, 200
Savoy 80, 85
Savoy, Duke of 48, 122, 155, 161, 177, 179, 187 *see also* Victor Amadeus, Duke of Savoy
Savoy-Piedmont 55, 156
Saxon forces 178, 184, 191
Scarpe, River 180, 182, 186, 191, 195, 203, 207, 208, 209, 215, 216, 218
Scheldt (Escaut), River 180, 213, 214, 215
Schellenberg, the 68, 108–109, 112–121, 130, 136, 137, 201–202
Schellenberg fort 112–113, 116–117, 118
Schomberg, Marshal 32–33, 35
son of 35
Schomberg's Horse (7th Dragoon Guards) 122–123
Schrobenhausen 134
Schwenningen 136
Scotland 84
'Scots Brigade' 63, 91
Scots Greys 118, 119
Secretary of War 65–66
Sedgemoor, Battle of 26
Sensée, River 180, 182–183, 185, 186, 189, 195, 206, 207, 209, 215, 216, 218
servants 70
Sherman, General William 125
Shrewsbury, Duke of 36, 37, 39–40, 41, 107, 223
sieges 60–61
Sinzendorff, Count 50, 214
Sophia, Electress of Hanover 157
Spain 53, 164, 170–171
Spanish army 54
Spanish fleet 77
Spanish Netherlands *see* Belgium
Spanish succession 45, 47–48
Spire 79
Stair, Lieutenant General Lord 193, 194, 199, 210
Stollhofen 55, 106, 111
Stollhofen, Lines of 104, 163
Strasbourg 95, 128
Stuart dynasty 24
Suchet 125
Sunderland (minister) 168–169
supply train, English 69, 71, 124
Sutton, Brigadier Richard 207, 209, 210

Swabia 87, 88
Swabian Jura mountains 95, 100, 111
Sweden 163
Sweet (servant) 70
Swift, Rev Dr 150
Swiss guards 59

Tallard, Marshal 60, 79, 89, 101, 104–105, 106, 111, 155, 158
and the Schellenberg campaign 121, 123, 124, 126, 127–128, 130, 131, 132, 133, 134, 135
and Battle of Blenheim 142, 143, 146, 147, 148, 150–151
Talmarsh, General 35, 38
Tangier 22, 23
Tapfheim 139
Thirty Years' War 54, 125
Tonbridge, Lord 153
Torbay 29
Tories 30, 57, 123, 163, 169, 171, 192, 222, 223
Toulon 85, 86, 163, 164
Tournai 198, 208, 216
Trarbach, siege of 156–157
Treasury 27, 66, 71, 89
Trier 156
Trier, Elector of 98
Turenne, General 22, 23, 60, 69, 94
Turin 163
Turkey 47
Turks 48

Ulm, Free City of 77, 83, 97, 135
Union of Parliaments (1707) 62
Unterglauheim 141, 145
Utrecht, Treaty of 224

Valenciennes 190, 215, 216, 218
Vauban (engineer) 37, 60
Versailles 53, 60, 104, 111, 155, 167, 175, 182, 193, 194, 220
Victor Amadeus, Duke of Savoy 80, 85 *see also* Savoy, Duke of
Vienna 48, 49, 56, 80, 83, 86, 106, 107, 220, 226
siege of 47
and the Schellenberg campaign 122, 126, 129
and *Ne Plus Ultra* Lines campaign 176, 178, 179, 187, 214
Vigo 77

Villars, Marshal 60, 77, 79, 83, 113, 143, 161, 163, 166, 167, 168, 224
and *Ne Plus Ultra* Lines campaign 182, 189, 195, 196, 200–202, 205, 207, 208, 209–210, 212–213
and Battle of Bouchain 183, 191, 198, 212, 215, 216
Villeroy, Marshal 60, 78, 87, 104, 111, 121, 124, 130, 133, 156, 158, 162
Villers Brûlin 206
Villingen 101, 105, 106
Villingen, siege of 128
Vimy Ridge 207, 209
Vitry 207, 208, 209

Walcourt 33
Waldeck 33, 34
Walker, Admiral 177
Walpole, Robert 65, 176
War of Spanish Succession 50, 55, 226
War Office 176
Warde 183
Watkins, Deputy Judge Advocate 204, 205–206, 213, 214
Wavrechin 216
weapons, flintlock musket 67
Webb, General 65
Wellington, Duke of 101, 183
West Indies 63
West Indies garrison 92
Whigs 30, 57, 123, 162, 163, 165, 168, 169, 171, 194, 221, 224
Wiesloch 99

Wilckes, General 139, 140
William, King of Orange (later King William III of England) 27, 33, 40, 47, 56, 109, 163, 196
lands in Torbay 29
claim to English throne 30–31
relations with Duke of Marlborough 32, 36, 37, 224–225
and Ireland 33, 34
and Brest attack 39
health declines 41, 50
Partition Treaty 47
and Spanish succession 47, 48
appoints Duke of Marlborough army commander and ambassador 50–51
death 52, 56
Windsor 210–211
Wittelsbach, Prince of 47
Woodstock 158
Wörnitz, River 112, 113, 115, 116
Wratislaw, Count 83–84, 86, 87, 89, 92, 103, 104, 106–107, 225
and the Schellenberg campaign 109–110, 123, 126, 127, 129, 134
Württemberg 95, 114, 130
Württemberg, Duke of 109, 137

York, Duchess of 24
York, James, Duke of 22, 24 *see also* James II, King of England
Ypres 182, 188, 207

Zenta, Battle of 49